The American Revisionists

The American Revisionists

THE LESSONS OF INTERVENTION
IN WORLD WAR I

WARREN I. COHEN

THE UNIVERSITY OF CHICAGO PRESS

CHICAGO AND LONDON

Library of Congress Catalog Card Number: 66-20594

THE UNIVERSITY OF CHICAGO PRESS, CHICAGO & LONDON
The University of Toronto Press, Toronto 5, Canada

For Murray Cohen
who couldn't wait

Preface

As a label for a man and his work, "revisionist" is probably no more meaningful than "liberal." In the sense that the revisionist revises an existing interpretation of an event in history the label is correct but of little value to the student who realizes that every generation of historians tends to give new interpretations to the past. To the American diplomatic historian, however, "revisionist" is the label given to a number of men who, after one or both world wars, took upon themselves the task of persuading the American people to change their view of the origins of those wars and of the reasons for American intervention in them. These are the men, the "revisionists" with whom I am concerned, and it is upon their writing between world wars that I have focused. Within these limits I have narrowed the focus a bit more by concentrating upon the revisionist interpretations of American intervention in World War I—although in tracing the emergence of these I have found it necessary to include the war-guilt question, the *Kriegsschuldfrage*.

I make no pretense of discussing every man who has ever been called a revisionist or who has made some contribution to revisionism. I began with the intention of concentrating on the work of C. Hartley Grattan, Walter Millis, and Charles Callan Tansill, the three men who have written "revisionist" histories of American intervention in World War I. After a year's work I concluded that revisionism should not be treated solely as a historiographical school, but as part of a controversy fired and maintained by men who sought to shape American attitudes toward war and foreign policy. Once I took this view of revisionism, Harry

Elmer Barnes and Charles Austin Beard also became major figures in my study. Thus, the study as it now stands is focused upon the writings of these five individuals, with some attention paid to other writings which seem to have been influential or otherwise important. I realize that my selection of writings may be deemed "arbitrary" and that some other student of revisionism might have chosen differently. As a result of my research, however, I am convinced that Barnes, Beard, Grattan, Millis, and Tansill were the most important figures in the revisionist controversy.

By way of warning I should note that I believe the label "revisionist" will be less meaningful to the reader of this study than it may have been previously. My research has made it obvious to me that the revisionists agree little more among themselves than they did with the "orthodox" historian or "epic-monger" whose interpretations they sought to refute. That this should be the prevailing impression left by my work is due, perhaps, to the fact that my approach is somewhat different from that of other diplomatic historians who have treated revisionism. First of all, I do not consider revisionism to have been an evil phenomenon that must be prevented from recurring. On the contrary, I consider my subject amorally, not only as a part of the diplomatic history of the United States between world wars, but also as an important part of the intellectual history of that period. I am, therefore, more interested in what were the revisionists' attitudes toward a variety of issues than I am in demonstrating the degree to which their attitudes and their interpretations were either accurate or inaccurate. This generation's search for the truth about American intervention in World War I has been masterfully accomplished by Arthur Link and Ernest May.[1] I have tried to limit my concern to the "truths" accepted by an earlier generation and the uses to which these truths were put.

It is worth noting, as Harry Baehr has,[2] that since World War

1. Link, *Wilson the Diplomatist* (Baltimore: John Hopkins University Press, 1957); May, *The World War and American Isolation* (Cambridge, Mass.: Harvard University Press, 1959).

2. "A Cycle of Revisionism between Two Wars," in Sheehan (ed.), *Essays in American Historiography* (New York: Columbia University Press, 1961), pp. 271–86.

II public attitudes on the interwar revisionist controversy have been reversed. The battle won in the 1920's and 1930's by men like Harry Elmer Barnes, Charles Beard, C. Hartley Grattan, Walter Millis, and Charles Tansill has since been lost. And, as Baehr noted, not new evidence but attitudes toward World War II and American intervention in World War II have reversed the tide. The prominence of Barnes, Beard, and Tansill on the side of those whose "truths" regarding FDR's policies have thus far been rejected has served further to bring their pre–Pearl Harbor work into disrepute.

Although convinced, as I believe most of my generation to be, of the necessity of American intervention in both world wars, I am equally convinced that if I had graduated from Columbia College in 1925 instead of 1955, the revisionist cause would have had one more adherent. It is not a question of the logic of the revisionist argument but, as Carl Becker suggested in a different context, largely a matter of the prevailing climate of opinion, of the receptivity of a generation to a given idea or conceptual scheme. Several of the men with whom I am concerned, perhaps all except Tansill, were reform-minded intellectuals who used revisionism as one weapon in their revolt against what they considered the reactionary, illiberal character of the dominant political and social values of the 1920's—a revolt in which I suspect I would have taken part. In the 1930's, all except Tansill were vitally concerned with consummating the promise of the New Deal. Barnes, Beard, and Grattan never permitted their obvious hatred of totalitarianism to override their recollections of the aftermath of World War I in democratic America. Millis became an ardent interventionist in World War II only after he was convinced that while war could do nothing to preserve democracy, intervention was the only hope of preserving an independent United States. I must agree with Millis, but this position does not spare me from sharing empathically the agonies of Barnes, Beard, and Grattan. They wrote as both social democrats[3] and

3. My use of "social democrat" and "social democracy," each in lower case, is intended in the same sense that Richard Hofstadter uses the term "social-democratic" when arguing that the New Deal was a "New Departure" from the reform tradition in the United States. See his *Age of Reform* (New York:

nationalists, and I would place myself in the same categories. I believe, as they did, that the preservation of the idea of social democracy is dependent upon the preservation of the United States—and I fear, as they did, that social democracy may die in the United States if it has to be fostered abroad by force rather than by precept. It is for these reasons, I suspect, that I am able to treat the revisionists more sympathetically than has Samuel Flagg Bemis, who claims that they assisted the rise of Hitler and the loss of the "first peace," and who cited as evidence of his own greater objectivity and wisdom the fact that he had never voted for Franklin Delano Roosevelt on any of the four occasions afforded him.[4]

Vintage, 1960), pp. 302 ff. and especially p. 308. The intended implication is that these men were vitally concerned with social legislation and that they had gone beyond the earlier reform quest for equality of opportunity and had sought governmental acceptance of responsibility for the economic well-being of every citizen, or in terms of slogans, the "welfare state."

4. "First Gun of a Revisionist Historiography for the Second World War," *Journal of Modern History,* XIX (March, 1947), 55–59.

Acknowledgments

Over the years I have accumulated many debts. This is my first opportunity to acknowledge those of the intellectual variety. I would like to begin by thanking Robert Burke and Thomas Pressly for their guidance when I first drafted this volume as my doctoral dissertation. Professor Pressly also introduced me to Robert Osgood's *Ideals and Self-interest in America's Foreign Relations*—from whence comes my approach to the subject of revisionism.

My greatest intellectual debt is to W. Stull Holt, whose teachings offered more than I could fully absorb and to whom I attribute most of what is of value in my work. Most important, his example, not only as a scholar but as a man, provided standards which I shall always strive to meet.

Harry Elmer Barnes and C. Hartley Grattan gave me countless hours of their time in discussions and correspondence. Their extraordinary generosity is particularly admirable given our disagreement on so many of the issues involved. Walter Millis was kind enough to read an early draft of the manuscript and to give me a few hours out of his busy life. I spent one day with the late Charles Tansill, who was more than cordial.

Gene Gressly and his staff at the Coe Library of the University of Wyoming were most generous with their services. I am grateful to the members of the history department at that university for their hospitality during my visit.

My friends Wolfred Bauer, Philip Nordquist, and Robert Skotheim helped me to formulate many of my ideas, and my stu-

dents at the University of California, Riverside, helped me to re-
fine them. Charles Cumberland, Lawrence Gelfand, Charles Hirsch-
field, and Paul Varg read the manuscript in various stages of
preparation and made numerous helpful suggestions. Of course, I
alone stand responsible for any shortcomings the book may have.

My wife and children were the blessings I counted while waiting
for the Press to accept the manuscript. No man has a right to
ask more of his family. Vernon Lidtke became part of the family
in his constant concern for my success.

And, finally, I would like this book to be a tribute to my father.
I regret that I am capable of nothing more worthy of him.

Note on Sources

This book is a study of a particular set of ideas about foreign policy, and the primary sources for it were the words of the men who formulated or expressed these ideas. The public record, the published books, articles, reviews, and records of speeches of Barnes, Beard, Grattan, Millis, and Tansill were, obviously, the basic materials for this study of revisionism. No single volume sufficed to reveal the structure of their thought; rather, the evolution of their ideas became apparent as various threads were followed through the record.

Both to supplement and to check the public statements of the revisionists I also used certain manuscript sources, to wit: the Harry Elmer Barnes Papers, University of Wyoming, Laramie, Wyoming; the C. Hartley Grattan Papers, then in Grattan's possession, Katonah, New York; the Franklin D. Roosevelt Papers, Roosevelt Library, Hyde Park; the George Sylvester Vierick Papers, University of Iowa, Iowa City. All of these collections, and especially the Barnes Papers, were of considerable interest. But none of them provided as valuable an insight into the minds of the men concerned as did close analysis of their published works. Moreover, in seeking manuscripts I was denied access to some and doubt whether any of those I saw were complete. Living men and the relatives and friends of the dead do not always have the same motivation for collecting and selecting such materials as do the scholars who seek to use them. Regrettably, any faith in a new "scientific history" based on the conscientious use of manuscripts is a vanity which must founder on the vanities of those who produce the manuscripts.

Additionally, over a period of years I corresponded with Barnes, Grattan, Millis, and Tansill. My correspondence with the first two adds up to several hundred pages. Finally, I spent a day with Barnes, Grattan, and Tansill, and an hour with Millis, after each had seen the first draft of this book. Each session had its own fascination, and I shall always pity medievalists, who lack the opportunity for such confrontation.

Three secondary sources were of transcendent importance. The first of these, Eric Goldman's *Rendezvous with Destiny* (New York, 1952), provided brilliant insights into the thought patterns of reformers and raised enough questions to stimulate a generation of historical research. The second, Robert Osgood's *Ideals and Self-interest in America's Foreign Relations* (Chicago, 1953), is an equally thoughtful and useful study of ideas about American foreign policy. More specifically, Richard Leopold's essay, "The Problem of American Intervention, 1917: An Historical Retrospect," in *World Politics*, Volume II (April, 1950), provided both a foundation and the point of departure for this volume. Beyond these, I shall refrain from using this opportunity to list the books I have read. The concerned reader will find full bibliographic references in the footnotes.

Contents

CHAPTER ONE

Introduction: Seeds of Revisionism 1914-1919

The shock with which most Americans reacted to the outbreak of World War I is legend. A generation which wanted to believe in the inevitability of progress could not conceive of such madness. Alongside the initial horror were countless expressions of gratitude for the thousands of miles of ocean which isolated the United States from the war and for what was considered the foresight of generation after generation of American statesmen who were alleged to have kept the United States separated from Old World balance-of-power politics.

Whether or not the United States could have remained neutral in that conflict or whether or not the United States should have remained neutral in that conflict are questions this study will not attempt to answer. In 1917, a troubled President did in fact call his country to war, and his call was phrased in terms which enabled many men who had supported his domestic reform program to overcome their aversion to war and to lend their support to his foreign policy. When the war ended and when the terms of the Treaty of Versailles began to filter back to the United States, many of these men concluded that the ends for which they had been willing to fight had not been achieved. Some joined in the assault upon Wilson and his treaty and helped to bury both. Most became members of the disillusioned legion that for twenty years provided a willing and receptive audience for arguments that attempted to demonstrate that the United States

1

should not have intervened in the World War; arguments advanced in the hope that future generations of Americans would profit from that generation's experience upon the next occasion of European madness.

As though publication of the Treaty of Versailles was not torture enough for the anguished, the end of the war was followed by a number of European books critical of the Entente role in the origins of the war. Even before the Germans had the opportunity to raise the *Kriegsschuldfrage,* books by French and British authors spread indictments of the policies of Raymond Poincaré and Sir Edward Grey in the events immediately preceding the war.

Then, in unprecedented fashion, the opening of the Russian archives was followed by the opening of the archives of the defeated Central Powers. Numerous historians sat down to years of laborious research. The publicists and historians of lesser patience took a quick look and began writing. Almost all concluded what every intelligent American had known all along: that the Germans had not been one hundred per cent "evil," nor France and her allies one hundred per cent "good." But the "revisionist" interpretation often went further, to the extent of shifting primary responsibility for the origins of the war from the Central to the Allied Powers—and, ultimately, condemning American intervention.[1]

The object of this study is not to support or refute this "revisionist" interpretation but to describe the controversy that it caused and to examine the suppositions of some of those men who came to believe that American intervention in World War I was a mistake. Of primary concern will be those features of the interpretation which were relevant to the idea that intervention had been a mistake and which were used subsequently as weapons of the "alienated intellectuals" in their battle against the establishment during the 1920's and again in the 1930's as lessons designed to influence American foreign policy.

1. For a "composite-revisionist" interpretation, see Dana Fleming, "Our Entry into the World War in 1917: The Revised Version," *Journal of Politics,* II (February, 1940), 75–86.

2

After the initial shock resulting from the outbreak of World
War I, the apparent unanimity of American opinion was shattered.
As the months passed, following the assassination at Sarajevo, the
drums began to beat and increasing numbers of Americans came
to favor intervention on behalf of the Allies. There were, too,
vocal groups of German-Americans who demanded action on behalf of the Central Powers. But the basic foreign policy issue
was whether or not the United States *should* intervene in the
European war.

Early in the war it became apparent that if the United States
did intervene, it would lend its support to the Allies. The efforts
of "hyphenate" groups, particularly German- and Irish-Americans,
who were hostile to the Allied cause were, therefore, directed primarily toward keeping the United States out of the war. Initially,
the "hyphenate" opponents of war received support from the majority of reform-oriented intellectuals who hoped to avoid intervention on humanitarian grounds and out of fear of what war might
do to the reform movement. By the winter of 1916–17, however,
within the ranks of the reform-minded intellectuals[2]—supporters
of the New Nationalism, of the New Freedom—a split over
foreign policy became apparent.

In the pages, and more often in the offices, of the *New Republic,*
most influential of the publications supporting reform, the split
was visible in microcosm. With Walter Lippmann among the editors, Randolph Bourne and Harold Stearns among the regular
contributors, and Charles Beard and John Dewey among the
frequent, if irregular, contributors, the *New Republic* covered
much of the spectrum of reform attitudes toward the war. These
men were not insignificant intellectuals speaking into the wind.
Dewey and Beard were, by 1917, men with national reputations,
giants astride the dominant intellectual currents of the years immediately preceding the war. Lippmann had not yet acquired the
pontifical aura that was to surround him in later years, but his
reputation was growing rapidly. While the journal may not have

2. Throughout this study the terms "reform-minded" or "reform-oriented"
are used in preference to the less precise "liberal" or "progressive."

deserved the reputation it had as an influence on President Wilson, its influence within reform circles very likely extended beyond its more than 15,000 subscribers.

To the editors of the *New Republic,* particularly to Lippmann, emphasis on domestic reform did not preclude efforts in behalf of a more vigorous foreign policy. As with their approach to domestic problems, which stressed conscious social control, their approach to the World War called for activism, for positive control rather than the more passive neutralism of the past. Lippmann grew impatient with Wilson's diplomacy, particularly after the sinking of the *Lusitania*—which provided a rationalization for pro-British sentiment and enabled the editors to choose between what had once seemed equally deplorable imperialistic alliances. Lippmann became annoyed by what he considered Wilson's failure to warn the American people of the extent of their involvement in the war, of the extent of their stake in the Allied cause. By the election of 1916, however, Lippmann and the other *New Republic* editors, Herbert Croly and Walter Weyl, had fallen in behind Wilson, subordinating their own preference for power politics to Wilson's strategy of appealing to world public opinion, subordinating their own image of the desirable world order to Wilson's vision of democratic internationalism, a league of all nations, strong and weak.[3]

With the Lippmann position, generally endorsed by Croly and Weyl, prevailing in the pages of the *New Republic,* the dissident contributors continued the office debate in other media. Beard's impatience with Wilson's words and "sermons" did not subside. Unlike the *New Republic* editors, he openly advocated intervention and was scornful of Wilson's peace overtures and soul searching. When the *New York Times* sent a reporter up to Morningside Drive to see what Beard and some of his colleagues at Columbia thought of Wilson's December, 1916, peace proposal, Beard

3. For more extensive discussions of Lippmann's position, see Charles Forcey, *The Crossroads of Liberalism* (New York: Oxford University Press, 1961), chap. 7; David W. Noble, *The Paradox of Progressive Thought* (Minneapolis: University of Minnesota Press, 1958), chap. 2; and Robert E. Osgood, *Ideals and Self-interest in America's Foreign Relations* (Chicago: University of Chicago Press, 1953), pp. 115–21.

was quoted as saying: "The document is very general—not much of a basis for negotiation. Unless the President is acting upon the basis of some information which he has received from one or the other contesting party, he is just preaching a sermon—just a sermon."[4] In February, 1917, during the controversy over the arming of American merchant ships, Beard declared: "Personally I favor more drastic action than the President has taken up to date. I have thought for some months that this country should definitely align itself with the Allies and help eliminate Prussianism from the earth."[5] Shortly after the war, Beard replied angrily to charges that he was allied with pacifists, anti-interventionists, or those who obstructed the war effort. "I am not and never have been a pacifist. I never belonged to Mr. Wilson's sweet neutrality band. I did not vote for him in 1916 because I believed his pacifist policies wrong. I voted for Charles E. Hughes. I was never 'too proud to fight.' "[6]

At the other end of the reform intellectuals' spectrum were Bourne and Stearns. Both were leaders among the "radicals" of the literary set. Although Stearns was not widely known until after he edited *Civilization in the United States* several years later,[7] Bourne, the gnarled hunchback, had, by 1917, become a legendary figure haunting Greenwich Village. While Lippmann and Croly had difficulty restraining their pro-Entente leanings, Stearns and Bourne alone among the *New Republic* regulars were genuinely neutral, fearing a victory by either side in the European war. As cultural nationalists they were less concerned with what Beard saw as a possibility of being plunged into "the black night of military barbarism" in the event of a German victory and more concerned about the dangers of a return to the status of England's cultural colony. Participants in a rebellion which sought to free American literature from British influence, they could no more be comforted by an Anglo-American alliance than by a German-American alliance. And they were among the few reform intellectuals who dreaded war even more than Woodrow Wilson did.

4. *New York Times*, January 23, 1917, p. 2.

5. *Ibid.*, February 27, 1917, p. 2.   6. *Ibid.*, January 26, 1919, p. 8.

7. New York: Harcourt, Brace, 1922.

Although by the end of the war all of these men but Lippmann had become critical of Wilson and his foreign policy, it is important to note that none of them belonged to the group of intellectuals, personified by John Dewey, who supported Wilson's call for intervention primarily because they saw in his words a call for a holy war, men who could resort to force only when it became "creative" force. Stearns and Bourne never supported Wilson; Beard was ready for war when Wilson was begging Americans to be neutral in thought; Lippmann came over to Wilson's side only reluctantly, but with a reluctance based more on his distinct view of world politics than on scruples about the use of force. Lippmann alone remained undisillusioned because he was able to fall back on his early reasons for intervention—the stake of the United States in the defense of the existing Atlantic community—and his conviction that the defeat of Germany was essential to American security—reasons which escaped Dewey and the others who fought to make the world safe for democracy.

But to all the reform-minded intellectuals, Wilson's talk of "peace without victory," of a "war to make the world safe for democracy," of a war not in response to America's self-interest, but rather in the interest of civilization, had an undeniable appeal. As Henry May[8] and others have demonstrated, the dominant intellectual currents in prewar America contained as a basic element the belief in the inevitability of progress. The outbreak of the war in Europe was a tremendous blow to this faith, but Wilson's intellectualizations of the interests of the United States in the war offered an escape. If the war could be remade, transformed from an instrument of international greed into an instrument for spreading democracy throughout the world, a war to end all wars, then it could be used for the reaffirmation of faith in progress. The war was to be used as a catalyst to assist the "liberals" or "progressives" or "reformers" of the world to unite to rid the earth of the scourges of autocracy and militarism.[9]

Shortly before Congress declared war, Dewey wrote an article

8. *The End of American Innocence* (New York: Alfred A. Knopf, 1959).

9. Noble, *Progressive Thought*, pp. 47–48, demonstrates this process as it occurred among the editors of the *New Republic*.

indicative of the attitude of the intellectual of tender conscience.[10] With reluctance he declared that "the gallant fight for democracy and civilization being fought on the soil of France is not our fight." This realization he found painful, but recent years had disclosed that "for better or for worse we are committed to another democracy and another civilization." This he called "the fact of a New World." In these few lines, Dewey's sympathy for the Allied cause was apparent—and equally apparent was his belief that the United States did not have a stake in the existing war in Europe. Certainly there was little to prepare his readers for the fact that between the writing of the article and its publication, the author had come to favor intervention. In the context of any debate over foreign policy since 1917, Dewey's statement would be considered rather an obvious argument in favor of non-intervention in European affairs. Indeed, these were the very arguments brought forth in the late 1930's to contend that intervention in World War I had been a mistake and that intervention in World War II would be a repetition of that mistake.

As Dewey continued, it was obvious that he realized that intervention was imminent and that there were conditions under which intervention would have his wholehearted support. The act of intervening would not conclude the "deeper hesitation." Let no one think that because the United States fought with "unreserved energy" Americans had joined the conflict with full "heart and soul": "Not until the almost impossible happens, not until the Allies are fighting on our terms for our democracy and civilization will that happen."[11]

In the months following American intervention, Dewey's articles in the *New Republic* continued in this vein. He addressed himself primarily to intellectuals of pacific bent. While attempting to justify his position in support of war, he sought to rally them behind intervention. The United States was not warring on the same terms as had nations since antiquity. Appeals to fear and hatred, wailing about rights and honor had not stirred the American people. The people had risen to fight only when Wilson "addressed himself to the American desire for stable peace and

10. "In a Time of National Hesitation," *Seven Arts*, II (May, 1917), 5–6.
11. *Ibid.*, p. 6.

an established amity of peoples through comity of democratic nations."[12] Dewey became impatient with the pacifists. He could never lose his balance to the point of endorsing the suppression of their Greenwich Village rallies, but he argued: "To go on protesting against war in general and this war in particular, to direct effort to stopping the war rather than to determining the terms upon which it shall be stopped, is to repeat the earlier tactics after their ineffectualness has been revealed."[13] Apparently he still wanted to consider himself a pacifist, but saw the role of pacifically minded intellectuals as quite different once war was a fact. Now the real challenge was in taking control of the war and using it as an instrument for attaining American ideals. He seemed to feel that he was begging a question that worried others besides pacifists: could American ideals be spread by force? It was "absurdly sentimental," he contended, "to say that force can never be so exercised as to affect men's minds," and he made it clear that he believed defeat *could* aid "in a reform of German lust for spiritual and political monopoly."[14]

There remained, however, a number of intellectuals, neither Anglophobes nor Germanophiles, who were unmoved by Dewey's agonized decision to support the war. Scott Nearing, onetime University of Pennsylvania professor who had been fired for his militant socialism, was one of these. With a backward glance at the years of the New Nationalism and the New Freedom, he saw that big business had been on the run before the progressive tide. The Morgans and the Schwabs had seen only one hope for reversing the tide and had leaped at the opportunity for war. Thus he could declare that American intervention in the World War "was the greatest victory that the American plutocracy has won over the American democracy since the declaration of war with Spain in 1898."[15]

12. "What America Will Fight For," *New Republic*, XII (August 18, 1917), 69.

13. "The Future of Pacifism," *New Republic*, XI (July 28, 1917), 359.

14. "Fiat Justitia, Ruat Collum," *New Republic*, XII (September 29, 1917), 238.

15. *The Great Madness* (New York: Rand School of Social Science, 1917), p. 5.

Nearing was not, of course, in the *New Republic* circle, or revising anything. The position outlined in his little book was the position of the doctrinaire socialists. While other socialists in the United States and throughout the world had found the call to arms irresistible and the appeal of nationalism greater than the appeal of doctrine, Nearing was one of those who stood by doctrine. His was an a priori position which might or might not have been relevant to the facts of the specfic situation. Nearing was not in possession of the evidence, nor did he claim to be; he simply *knew* the truth, as would any well-versed socialist, Marxist or otherwise. However, in the 1920's and 1930's, when men who had supported intervention were appalled by the war's aftermath and embarrassed by the positions they had taken in 1917, Nearing's theories seemed most attractive. Particularly during the 1930's, after the depression had wiped away much of the luster the captains of industry and financiers had acquired in the 1920's, the American "plutocrat" made a most delightful scapegoat. Nearing should have been pleased and probably was astonished to see his argument triumph and receive its ultimate laurels in the neutrality legislation of the 1930's.

It was Randolph Bourne, however, who, in a series of articles in *Seven Arts,* led the attack on Dewey and upon the position of the reform intellectuals who supported intervention. In June, 1917, he underscored the realignment that had taken place over foreign policy, an occurrence repeated in the debates over intervention in World War II and again in post-World War II America over policies in the "Cold War." In each of these periods, as foreign policy became the major issue, the reform impetus was smashed. Those reformers who favored a more active or aggressive foreign policy found themselves separated from large numbers of men with whom they had previously found intellectual rapport, particularly in the areas of social and economic reform, and allied with many of the most reactionary elements in American society. Bourne demanded that it "never be forgotten that in every community it was the least liberal and least democratic elements among whom the preparedness and later the war sentiment was found." In short, he declared, the intellectuals had identified themselves with the least democratic elements in American life. "Only in a world where irony was dead," he wrote, "could an intellectual class enter war at the head of such illiberal cohorts in the avowed cause of world-liberalism and world-democracy."[16]

Bourne was particularly upset by what he saw as a parallel to the action of the German professors who had closed ranks in support of German militarism. The German intellectuals supported war as an effort to preserve German culture from barbarization. Now the American intellectual fought to save the world from subjugation. He wondered "whence our confidence that history will not unravel huge economic and imperialist forces upon which our rationalizations float like bubbles?" He wrote of the Jew who "often marvels that his race alone should have been chosen as the true people of the cosmic God" and asked if the American intellectual was not "equally fatuous" for declaring that "our war of all wars is stainless and thrillingly achieving for good."[17]

Thus Bourne set the course for the mainstream of revisionist historiography. When the war fever subsided, when publication of the secret treaties led to the disillusionment of the more militant reform intellectuals, they were ready to accept Bourne's thesis, and evidence to support it was readily found. Lest they overlook the task he had set for them, he wrote: "There is work to be done to prevent this war of ours from passing into popular mythology as a holy crusade."[18] Twelve years later, these words appeared on the title page of C. Hartley Grattan's *Why We Fought*,[19] the first revisionist history of the intervention of the United States in World War I.

3

There were, of course, others, perhaps less articulate than Bourne, men rarely accused of being intellectuals, who also expressed opposition to American intervention in the war. Most significant of these were the fifty-six congressmen who voted "No" on the war resolution. Since the outbreak of the war in Europe,

---

16. "War and the Intellectuals," *Seven Arts,* Vol. II (June, 1917); reprinted in Bourne, *Untimely Letters* (New York: B. W. Huebsch, 1919), p. 26.

17. *Untimely Letters,* p. 32.

18. *Ibid.,* p. 45.   19. New York: The Vanguard Press, 1929.

numerous congressmen had indicated concern over the drift of American policy. To many, the shipment of arms and munitions to the belligerents, however "legal," seemed to be voluntary complicity in mass murder. And, when it became increasingly apparent that only one side in the war was profiting from this trade, the policy of permitting it seemed decidedly unneutral. Later, the policy of permitting credits to be extended to the Allies also evoked criticism in Congress.

When in April of 1917 Wilson appeared before Congress to request a declaration of war, there were congressmen who remained unconvinced that American intervention was necessary, who did not believe that the Wilson administration had done all that could have been done to keep the United States out of war. Rising in the Senate to oppose the war resolution, George W. Norris, Republican from Nebraska, voiced the arguments that dominated the statements of the congressional opponents of war:

> While such action was legal and countenanced by international law, there is no doubt in my mind but the enormous amount of money loaned to the allies in this country has been instrumental in bringing about a public sentiment in favor of our country taking a course that would make every bond worth a hundred cents on the dollar and making the payment of every debt certain and sure. Through this instrumentality and also through the instrumentality of others who have not only made millions out of the war in the manufacture of munitions, etc., and who would expect to make millions more if our country can be drawn into the catastrophe, a large number of the great newspapers and news agencies of the country have been controlled and enlisted in the greatest propaganda that the world has ever known, to manufacture sentiment in favor of war. It is now demanded that the American citizens shall be used as insurance policies to guarantee the safe delivery of munitions of war to belligerent nations. The enormous profits of munitions manufacturers, stockbrokers, and bond dealers must be still further increased by our entrance into the war. . . .[20]

On and on, Norris railed at Wall Street, crusading with familiar Populist rhetoric against the "interests," becoming blatantly Bry-

20. United States, *Congressional Record,* 65th Congress, 1st Session, 1917, LV, Part 1, p. 213.

anesque: "We are going into war upon the command of gold. We are going to run the risk of sacrificing millions of our countrymen's lives in order that other countrymen may coin their lifeblood into money. . . . I feel that we are about to put the dollar sign upon the American flag."[21]

Although two of Norris' colleagues immediately suggested that he was guilty of treason, and similar allegations were cast as other congressmen hammered away at Wall Street and the munitions manufacturers—at the Morgans, Rockefellers, and DuPonts—Norris' charges were hardly unfamiliar to those present; nor were the charges to be exorcised by the cries of treason. In parts of the South, of the Middle West, wherever the Populist mentality prevailed, these Wall Street names had long been anathema. The charges might have changed since 1896, but the Morgans, Rockefellers, and DuPonts were men to be considered guilty until proved otherwise. The "interests" had long led the nation in directions which failed to serve the people—why should 1917 be different?

And the complaints about the insidious role of the munitions manufacturers—these had echoed in the halls of Congress many times since 1914, particularly when some aspect of preparedness was being aired. Prominent Americans had sought to nationalize the munitions industry, to do something about taking the profits out of war. Arthur Capper, Republican Governor of Kansas, had led one such movement, supported by Oswald Garrison Villard of the New York *Evening Post* and the *Nation*.[22] As for loans to the Allies, Bryan himself had once insisted on banning credits and few of his many admirers could appreciate the reasons for the subsequent lifting of that ban—unless it had been lifted to enhance Wall Street's profits.

In explaining their votes on the floor of the Senate or House, or before their constituents, the overwhelming majority of opponents of the war resolution played the same tune: this was a war sought by the "interests." Again and again it was insisted that the people opposed intervention; that a referendum on war would show the people opposed; that a referendum in this or that town had shown

21. *Ibid.*, p. 214.

22. Homer E. Socolofsky, *Arthur Capper* (Lawrence: University of Kansas Press, 1962), p. 94.

the people opposed.[23] As ever, the reformer saw the people as peace-loving and found in traditional foes the source of the war impetus. This time his contentions found warm advocates among men to whom reform was not a primary concern—men like those of the German-American Alliance, who feared for the homeland, and of the Clan-na-Gael, who longed for Ireland's freedom.[24] But the nation had gone to war, and the unreconciled soon had to deal with the Sedition Act or worse—mob violence. Those prosecuted under the Sedition Act or attacked by superpatriots were generally guilty of mouthing the old song, referring to war "for the big bugs in Wall Street . . . the money interests in the East." Socialist Victor Berger of Milwaukee had insisted that "if democracy were the object of the war, it would have a different set of enthusiasts," and a Non-Partisan League organizer in North Dakota was caught declaring that "if the United States had loaned money to Germany, we would be fighting on their side."[25]

Sending seeds to their constituents was a time-honored means by which congressmen sought to retain good will at home. In 1917 a

23. Paul S. Holbo, "They Voted against War" (unpublished Ph.D. dissertation, University of Chicago, 1961).

24. *Ibid.* Holbo concluded that at least 33 of the 56 congressmen who voted "No" had "progressive ideas." Fifteen were influenced by the ethnic composition of their constituencies and two of these were pro-German themselves. Holbo also cites a report in the *Boston Herald*, April 2, 1917, of a Clan-na-Gael meeting protesting intervention as "a blow at Ireland's hopes for freedom" and "a war for the right to deliver munitions to the Allies."

25. H. C. Peterson and Gilbert C. Fite, *Opponents of War: 1917–1918* (Madison: University of Wisconsin Press, 1957), pp. 36–65. Peterson and Fite contend that: "Probably at no time in American history up to that time did the capitalistic system come under such attack as during the second decade of the twentieth century. Some people opposed the war because they believed it was a capitalistic plot" (p. 43). A contemporary writer, Philo M. Buck, Jr., referred to the "economic pacifism" of the Middle West, reporting that Middle Westerners, particularly in Kansas and Nebraska, thought intervention absurd and could not "conceive how any sane and patriotic American could think otherwise, and they began to look for sinister motives; and at once to their minds came their old-time devil, Wall Street. It must be 'high finance' and its little demons the munitions makers who were inciting the President to take up arms. . . ." "Pacifism in the Middle West," *Nation*, CIV (May 17, 1917), 595–97.

number of them sent the seeds of postwar revisionism to their constituents—and the seeds took root in places where Populist ideas prevailed, in places where there were large concentrations of German-Americans or other ethnic groups hostile to the war. And so, when the war ended in disillusionment for some of its supporters, these erstwhile crusaders could harvest fields of simple explanations of how and why they had been deceived.

4

Bourne continued the attack through the summer and early fall of 1917, until *Seven Arts* was suppressed by the government. Having made his point on the act of going to war, he shifted his focus to war strategy. Vainly he tried to remind the reform intellectuals of their own arguments in favor of intervention: that they had admitted that the United States had no cause for grievance; that intervention had been adopted without selfish purpose; that "the American liberals trusted the President to use American participation as an instrument in liberalizing the war-aims of all the Allied governments."[26] He argued that American "liberals" had interpreted intervention as primarily defensive, "an enterprise to prevent Germany's threatened victory on the sea." American strategy had been designed to appeal to the democratic forces within Germany, a reliance upon "self-motivated regeneration" by the Germans, a belief that democracy could only be imposed from within. But now Wilson was talking of conquest: conquer or submit. Democracy was to be imposed upon Germany by force. Convinced that the blessings of democracy could not be so bestowed, Bourne warned: "We have encouraged the reactionary elements in every allied country to hold out for extreme demands. We have discouraged the German democratic forces."[27]

When Dewey then wrote that it was "absurdly sentimental" to deny that force could be used to alter the German mind, Bourne turned his wrath on Dewey, pragmatism, and the "pragmatist intellectual." He would have no part of Dewey's explanations, no

26. "The Collapse of American Strategy," *Seven Arts*, Vol. II (August, 1917); in *Untimely Letters*, p. 74.

27. *Ibid.*, p. 88.

part of Dewey's effort to use intervention as an instrument for the spreading of progress. For Bourne, a view of war as a "grim and terrible cleanser" was infinitely preferable to "this optimism-haunted mood that continues unweariedly to suggest that all can yet be made to work for good in a mad and half-destroyed world."[28] Painfully, Bourne recalled Dewey's part in the efforts to develop American greatness through internal measures, his dedication to educational reform, his moment of hesitation when American civilization had seemed more important than the forced redemption of the world. He marveled at the "relative ease with which the pragmatist intellectuals, with Professor Dewey at their head, have moved out their philosophy, bag and baggage, from education to war."[29] If they really expected a "gallant war, conducted with jealous regard for democratic values at home and a captivating vision of international democracy," they had made little effort toward these ends. Rather, he suspected, they did not believe they could prevent intervention and had concluded it was best to take it up in a manner which would give them some control over the ends for which it would be used. To Bourne, this was the ultimate absurdity: to think that being unable to stay out of war, you can, once in it, mold its course. He claimed that the United States was at war because the American government "practices a philosophy of adjustment, and an instrumentalism for minor ends, instead of creating new values and setting at once a large standard to which the nations might repair." He argued that the "promise of American life" had not yet been achieved, "perhaps not even seen," and until it was, "there is nothing for us but stern and intensive cultivation of our garden."[30]

No matter whether Bourne was right or wrong about intervention, he was striking at points on which the reform intellectuals were most sensitive. If in 1917 they tried to write him off as a crabbed pacifist, it was probably not without qualms. And as the power of the industrialists and financiers increased, as war fever in

28. "Twilight of Idols," *Seven Arts*, Vol. II (October, 1917) ; in *Untimely Letters*, p. 119.

29. *Untimely Letters*, p. 121.

30. *Ibid.*, p. 133; "A War Diary," *Seven Arts*, Vol. II (September, 1917) ; in *Untimely Letters*, p. 110.

the United States led to arbitrary coercion and suppression, doubts could only with difficulty be repressed. Wait until we win this war, many must have thought. Wait and see what a progressive's peace treaty looks like; wait and see the new world order based on American ideals and resulting in perpetual peace. For such as these the end was inevitable and disillusionment unavoidable—Bourne was right.

Meanwhile, Carl Becker and numerous other historians were heeding the call of the flag and reporting to Washington to work for George Creel. Becker was with the Department of History at Minnesota when war was declared. A meeting was called by the department to determine what should be its contribution to the war effort. In 1920 Becker reminisced: "We were only professors, but the world was still young, and we wanted to do something to beat the Hun and make the world safe for democracy."[31] Someone at the meeting suggested that Becker write a glorious history of "La Belle France" and of France's contribution to democracy. He survived the pressure to write this sort of "history," and for a year brooded about being too old to fight; finally his hatred of German militarism overrode his judgment and he produced *German Attempts to Divide Belgium* for the Creel Committee. This pamphlet may not have been as bad as he later recalled, but years afterward, Becker was still rebuking himself for this departure from his preferred position of detachment.

Whatever may be said of Charles Beard, he was never one to torture himself—particularly with memories of past inconsistencies. In October, 1917, the month in which Bourne's attack on Dewey was published, Beard resigned from his position on the faculty of Columbia University. He resigned because he was indignant over the use of war hysteria by the trustees as an excuse for getting rid of and coercing members of the faculty whose views were repugnant to them. Beard believed that the American people could be mobilized for war without mass hysteria. When the next occasion for war arose he was to be less sanguine. But though he was concerned about the pressures for conformity generated by the war, he shared few of the other concerns of men like Bourne. "Peace without victory" was a slogan he had never endorsed. Short-

31. "La Belle France," *New Republic,* XXIII (July 14, 1920), 207.

ly before his resignation he had called for a "smashing victory which will carry the soldiers of the Allies to the streets of Berlin."[32] Even in his letter of resignation, he retained this attitude toward the war.

> As you are aware, I have, from the beginning, believed that a victory for the German Imperial Government would plunge all of us into the black night of military barbarism. I was among the first to urge a declaration of war by the United States, and I believe that we should now press forward with all our might to a just conclusion. . . .[33]

A year later, Beard wrote a short article appealing to subscribers to the fourth Liberty Loan. With a year and a half of war in which to reconsider his support of intervention, a year and a half in which to weigh in the balance the evils of domestic suppression and the virtues of the war, there was no indication of doubt in Beard's mind.

> America and her allies are now pitted against the most merciless military despotism the world has ever seen. . . . Equipped by forty years of preparation for armed conquest, fortified by forty years' conspiracy against the democratic nations of the earth, supported by all the engines of destruction that science can devise, the German military machine threatens all mankind. It has made a religion of brutality. . . . A German victory means the utter destruction of those ideals of peace and international goodwill which have been America's great reliance, ideals which make life worth living in America or anywhere else.[34]

It is important to note that Beard's war was not being fought for the same reasons as the war with which Dewey, Wilson, and Bourne were concerned. Beard was not writing about a European war in which the United States had no interest, about a Germany with whom the American people had no grievance. Germany had conspired against *all* the democratic nations. A German victory

32. Letter to the Editor, *New Republic*, XI (June 2, 1917), 136.

33. *New York Times*, October 9, 1917, p. 1.

34. "A Call upon Every Citizen," *Harper's*, CXXXVII (October 18, 1918), 655.

was a threat to the American way of life. Beard had called for intervention and had supported intervention to preserve American ideals, and not, as President Wilson and Dewey had, for the purpose of extending these ideals to the Allies or the powers to be conquered. Thus the nature of Beard's disillusionment was to be both quantitatively and qualitatively different from that of the men whose intellectual position had approximated Dewey's.

Harold Stearns had not reacted as violently as Bourne had to the decision to intervene. Always less intense than Bourne, more the dilettante in his interests and activities, he simply ignored the foreign policy controversy as long as he could. He had been in England with Lippmann the day the British declared war, and he recalled in 1935 that he had not imagined that the United States, too, would intervene. He had been proud to be an American because he was convinced that the United States would never be "dragged into any such mass-murder." In 1935 he could write: "The trumped-up notion that we were in any danger as a nation, submarines or no submarines, struck me as slightly ridiculous. Just as today the notion of an invasion by the Japanese strikes one in exactly the same fashion."[35] Even after Wilson's war message, he thought that Congress, "which at that time, let historians say now what they wish, was essentially not keen to 'get in,'" might not declare war. But war came, and Stearns parted company with the *New Republic* editors and for almost a year restricted his literary output to subjects unrelated to issues of foreign policy. In March, 1918, he reviewed the events since the decision to intervene in an article entitled "A Year of Mistakes." He claimed that Wilson's major error in 1917 was one of emphasis rather than intention, "a mistake arising from lack of self-assertion of his diplomacy and delay in winning our co-belligerents to an acceptance of that diplomacy."[36]

The lesson Stearns drew was that we needed more Wilsonian diplomacy, not less. More like the "pragmatist intellectuals" than he either realized or cared to admit, Stearns had accepted the fact

---

35. *The Street I Know* (New York: Lee Furman, Inc., 1935), pp. 141–42.

36. *Dial,* LXIV (March 28, 1918), 294.

of war and could not resist the urge to direct the course of intervention. But like Bourne, he could not accept Dewey's concept of "creative force." He was convinced that the war could not be won by force of arms alone—that if it was not "a war of ideas," then it was "a war without meaning and purpose." But, he asked, if it was "a war between two conflicting attitudes of viewing the world, what is our ultimate goal?" Convinced as he was of the necessity of capturing the "hearts and minds of the German people," he insisted that "though we hoist our standards in Berlin and march triumphantly through Potsdam, we shall have lost the war unless we have achieved that moral capture."[37] Stearns thus took a position between Bourne's pacifism and Dewey's acquiescence in the use of force for pacific purposes. The clock could not be turned back: America had intervened; yet the United States could not achieve its ends through conquest. The only hope was Wilsonian diplomacy, but "the very ghosts of our dead will mock us for our failure if no cleaner and more decent system of international relations is created as a result of this war."[38] Apparently even Stearns's approval of Wilson's policies was pragmatic. He could not stop the war, so he gave the interventionists their head. But if they failed to produce, not only the "ghosts of the dead," but Harold Stearns, would mock them.

By following the thread out of the offices of the *New Republic* and glancing at Becker—the detached scholar sympathetic to reform—some insights into the war-stirred ferment in reform circles are suggested. The basis for the reformers' subsequent disillusionment with "Wilsonian Diplomacy" is also suggested. Beard early and aggressively advocated war. Dewey and many like him rationalized tortuously down the path to intervention, finally bringing themselves to support intervention for ends toward which no previous war had ever been fought. Bourne and Stearns, the latter less intensely, held out, unable to believe that any good could come from an alliance with those groups which they considered the most reactionary in the country. Bourne's gibes forced the interventionists of tender conscience to cling all the more tenaciously to the

37. *Ibid.*, p. 295.   38. *Ibid.*

Wilsonian vision of a new international order which would make the world safe for democracy and lead to perpetual peace. Even the more militant reformers—men like Beard—were not immune to Bourne's arguments. Beard based his intellectual position on his belief in the peculiar evils of Prussian militarism. When European archivists began releasing carefully selected documents to willing scholars and some of the myths of the early war years were exposed, Charles Beard, among others, forgot his early concern for the German threat to American civilization and began to wonder if the Bournes had not been right after all.

These were the waters from which the main stream of revisionist historiography flowed, from which came the revisionism of Harry Elmer Barnes, Charles Beard, C. Hartley Grattan, and Walter Millis.

But these men were not the only "revisionists," nor did disillusioned reformers provide the only segment of the American public receptive to revisionism. There were also the "radical" opponents of the war, like Scott Nearing or Max Eastman and John Reed of the *Masses*. Out of the tradition of "radical" opposition to the war came the work of John Kenneth Turner. There was also a large minority of pro-German or anti-British individuals who, suppressed during the war, were only too eager to accept arguments that justified their wartime sympathies and made them seem better Americans than those who had given wholehearted support to intervention. The durability of their grievance against the Wilson administration has been demonstrated by Samuel Lubell in his *The Future of American Politics*.[39]

5

With Bourne dying before the war ended, it was only natural that the first postwar volume critical of American intervention should be written by Harold Stearns. Immediately after the armistice, Stearns put pen to paper and in a few months produced *Liberalism in America*.[40] His major concern was the role of the "lib-

---

39. New York: Harper, 1951, pp. 129–46.

40. New York: Boni and Liveright, Inc., 1919.

eral" or reform intellectual in the movement toward intervention. Intervention was, to be sure, a mistake. He had believed this all through the war, and it served as the basic assumption of his study of what was wrong with the reform intellectual: what had enabled such a man to advocate and support the war? Unlike Bourne, Stearns was not a pacifist. He could, he said, justify the use of force for defensive purposes, for defensive wars. He could conceive of "plenty" of wars in which he would have been one of the first to volunteer his services. But he believed that the "true liberal" was skeptical of coercion, of the aggressive use of force. He simply did not believe that results achieved by force could be permanent—thus his repugnance to Wilson's war for democracy. He viewed American intervention not as a defensive measure to protect democracy in the United States, but as a means by which the United States would aggressively foster democracy abroad. But the cornerstone of liberalism, he insisted, was the "belief in the power and desirability of effecting changes by peaceable and rational persuasion."[41] By merging his disbelief in the existence of a threat to the United States, a disbelief nurtured by the words of Woodrow Wilson as well as those of John Dewey, with his conviction that ideas cannot be changed by force, Stearns was convinced that America was fighting for ideals and ideals alone and that such a fight was absurd: "We are tempted to agree with Anatole France's epigram that a war for ideals is infinitely worse than a war for material gain because in the first instance one cannot count the cost."[42]

The question of war guilt was not a part of Stearns's argument. There is no evidence of *Kriegsschuldfrage* revisionism in *Liberalism in America*. Although he was not particularly impressed by Allied professions of innocence, he did not question the claim that German militarism had been responsible for the war.[43] He made no effort to shift the onus or even to stress divided responsibility for the war. The *Kriegsschuldfrage* was irrelevant for Stearns. He was far more concerned with the effects of the crusade against militarism in the world in general, in which he found militarism more

41. *Liberalism in America,* p. 43.

42. *Ibid.,* p. 10.   43. *Ibid.,* see p. 24.

rampant than ever before, and in the United States, where he believed many of the worst features of German militarism had been adopted in the effort to smash it in Germany. There was no suggestion that America had intervened on the wrong side.

Nor did Stearns view the United States as being uniquely self-sufficient, in a position to isolate itself from the rest of the world. Talk of America's isolation or "self-complacency" he found incredibly naïve, indicative of a failure to appreciate the extent of economic "interlacing" of the world that had occurred since America emerged as a world power in 1898.[44]

The influence of Charles Beard and of Beard's economic interpretation of history was evident in *Liberalism in America*. The capsule history of the United States included in the volume was explicitly based on Beard's work, particularly Beard's interpretation of the Constitution and of Jeffersonian democracy.[45] Stearns went so far as to claim that

> if it were written into the Constitution that on the declaration of war, inasmuch as the majority of male citizens had to sacrifice or risk their lives on the field of battle, then it was fair and was hereby made compulsory that anyone with a fortune over $500,000 should immediately have the balance conscripted into the public treasury to pay for the cost of the war—if that were written into the Constitution, and it would be an eminently sensible thing to do, who can doubt that the provocations to war and the chances of it would be diminished much more strikingly than by any League of Nations ever devised?[46]

But Stearns disassociated himself from the socialist interpretation of the war, noting that neither the "plutocrats" nor the militarists had begun with an a priori desire to involve the United States in the war. He suggested, as Beard was to suggest sixteen years later in *The Devil Theory of War*, that most Americans in the peaceful pursuit of their interests instinctively, yet unwittingly, moved from neutrality to ardent espousal of the Entente cause.[47]

Primarily concerned with the basis for the support given to the intervention campaign by intellectuals, especially "liberal" intel-

44. *Ibid.*, p. 81.

45. *Ibid.*, especially pp. 35 ff.

46. *Ibid.*, p. 111 n.

47. *Ibid.*, p. 84.

lectuals, Stearns found this group climbing aboard the bandwagon "first, for economic reasons, since as a class they were either subsidized by or lived parasitically upon the ruling financial and social class."[48] But his explanation of why the United States went to war and of why the intellectuals supported intervention stressed psychological as well as economic factors.

In attempting a psychological approach to the study of war and the willingness of peoples to go to war, Stearns noted aspects of the American decision to intervene that were to be ignored by all of the revisionists save Walter Millis. His isolation of the phenomenon of war from specific questions of national interest and morality demonstrated an approach to the nature of war which would loom large both in the interwar peace movements and in revisionist historiography. He contended that modern wars involving the competing nationalisms of highly industrialized states had an "irresistible psychological attraction"—an attraction not diminished but increased "by the knowledge of the terrible consequences which must result from war's declaration." For this reason he suggested that pacifists were naïve in dwelling upon war's horrors—"it is these very horrors which constitute one of war's major attractions."[49] With considerable and explicit reliance upon Freud's *Reflections on War and Death* and *Totem and Taboo,* Stearns insisted that war satisfied a "fundamental and thwarted" human need—that "war compels us to live dangerously . . . war restores what civilization can hide: heroism which springs from our deep inability to believe in our own death, pleasure in the killing of the hated one in the enemy (the hatred which is the component of all love) and power to rise above 'the shock of the death of our friends.' "[50] The possibilities of this approach were to be exploited further by Millis. Stearns would only deduce that the American advocates of intervention were jealous of the European experience.[51]

Shifting from an analysis of war in the abstract to consideration of American attitudes toward war, Stearns found his countrymen tending to overromanticize the battles of the past. He was convinced that in the years ahead he would hear children "lisping in

48. *Ibid.*

49. *Ibid.*, pp. 155–56.

50. *Ibid.*, p. 158.

51. *Ibid.*, pp. 88–89.

the grammar schools" that the World War had been a "war to make the world safe for democracy"—"at the very time Congress is appropriating money for some punitive, imperialistic expedition against a weak—and rich—neighbor."[52] Looking further into the past, Stearns pointed to the Civil War as a "classic illustration" of what he considered one of the most fundamental and dangerous of American defects: "our willingness to resort to violence for purely abstract moral ends. (It is immaterial here whether economic ends are coincidentally encompassed; the popular driving force certainly is not conscious consideration of economic ends.)"[53] In another context his meaning was less veiled as he wrote of the "perverted moralism" which led to efforts "to impose our standards of righteousness by force and coercion."[54]

For all Stearns's discussion of why the United States intervened, he never provided an answer. But he would not have conceded that pointing to this failure was a relevant criticism of his treatment of the question. He simply did not know the answer and could not believe that anyone else did. It was a puzzle to his "everyday American citizen," and the easy answer provided by the intellectuals left him cold. They had "erected myths about international democracy or a league of nations or defense of the Atlantic world, or persuaded themselves that it was a moral issue between ruthless force and civilization."[55] The intellectuals had carried the revolt against "formalism" too far: they suffered from spiritual ennui. They "accepted the shibboleths of the war with an alacrity which otherwise would have been surprising, because they intensely wanted something to believe in, something worth fighting, and if need be, dying for."[56]

Underlying his inability to find the reasons for American intervention was Stearns's refusal to accept any arguments based on a threat to the security or interests of the United States. Stearns never asked himself what German domination of Europe or German control of the seas would have meant for the future of America. This, too, was irrelevant because a German victory was im-

52. *Ibid.*, p. 52.

53. *Ibid.*

54. *Ibid.*, pp. 98–99.

55. *Ibid.*, p. 90.

56. *Ibid.*, pp. 175–76.

possible. Years later he wrote: "And I thought then, when I was 23, as I think now when I am 43, that I shall never live to see victorious German troops marching down the boulevards of Paris."[57] Perhaps it is not totally irrelevant to note that Stearns was still alive, not yet fifty, when the day he could not envision arrived. In his analysis of Wilson, which in his reflections of 1935 he felt had stood the test of time, he insisted that Wilson's particular theories were unimportant, that it was most valuable to study Wilson as representative of the "problem of the idealist in politics." Wilson should have avoided intervention "not . . . out of a sentimental pacifism and moral love of peace in itself but because the practical exigencies of the situation made such a policy imperative. In a word, had he been a statesman instead of an idealist, he would have pocketed his natural sympathies for the Entente."[58] As Robert Osgood has justly noted,[59] Stearns's critique of Wilsonian idealism as a basis for intervention did not conclude with a plea for the "realism" advocated later by devotees of the so-called Morgenthau School, but neither was *Liberalism in America* a plea for the avoidance of "all reliance upon force." It was not intended as a guide to American policy planners, but as a warning to reform intellectuals, a warning that all they stood for was compromised by war, that ends for which the "liberal" strove could not be attained through war. Stearns was insisting that it had been irrational for the reform intellectuals to favor intervention. How could they have failed to realize the effect war would have on the domestic reform movement? How could they have overcome their dread of war with naïve visions of utilizing war to spread American ideals? Now Stearns called for a return to rationalism, for an uncovering of the "truth" about the war. Here was an invitation to twenty years of revisionist historiography.

6

The war ended. The Treaty of Versailles was rejected by the United States Senate. The reform currents of the prewar years had

57. *The Street I Know*, p. 124.

58. *Liberalism in America*, p. 133.   59. *Ideals and Self-interest*, p. 315.

been diverted without visible gains on the international scene. The words of Randolph Bourne and Harold Stearns took on the aura of brilliant prophecy to those who had expected more than the defeat of Germany to result from American intervention.

Americans thought they had a choice as to their country's role in world affairs. From 1918 to December 7, 1941, the debate raged on: would America again throw her weight into the world balance? Regardless of relevance, attitudes toward intervention in 1917 were crucial in shaping attitudes toward foreign policy in the years that followed.

CHAPTER TWO

The Emergence of Revisionism in America, 1919–1923

Before the war was over, the Bolsheviks gained control of the Russian government, opened up the state archives and hung the Tsar's dirty linen out for the world to see. Americans, not yet inured to this sort of thing, looked aghast at the so-called secret treaties in which the Entente powers spelled out the elaborate division of spoils contemplated upon the defeat of the Central Powers. Apparently there were in the United States a number of individuals who were surprised to find that the Tsar's government had not contracted to fight to make the world safe for democracy or to create a new world order in which peace would be perpetual. At the war's end, the archives of defeated Germany and Austria were "opened" and collections of documents spilled out into the eager hands of scholars and publicists.

Professor Selig Adler has suggested that the most important reason for the burst of revisionist writings after 1920 was this unprecedented availability of sources.[1] Never before had access to diplomatic correspondence been possible so soon after a major conflict. To be sure, the fact that the various issues of the war, par-

1. "The War Guilt Question and American Disillusionment, 1918–1928," *Journal of Modern History,* XXIII (March, 1951), 2. Despite a slight difference in emphasis here, I am much indebted to Professor Adler's article which should be the point of departure for every student of the *Kriegsschuldfrage* in the United States.

ticularly the matter of responsibility for starting the war, were still alive guaranteed a market for books dealing with the origins of the war; and the availability of source materials did indeed provide substance for the inevitable rehashings. But neither the "aliveness" of the issues nor the availability of the sources can be used to explain why many of these books were "revisionist." Far more significant was the fact that justly or otherwise, many people, Europeans and Americans, believed that the peace settlement was based on an error, on the false assumption of Germany's "unique" responsibility for the war as stated in Article 231 of the Treaty of Versailles. They believed sincerely that if this error were perpetuated the peace would fail. Lest these sentiments seem too sublime to a generation able to recall the brutality of Hitler's Germany, it should be noted that there are still respected foreign affairs specialists who believe that the rise of Hitler and the origins of World War II can be traced to the treatment accorded Germany at Versailles.[2]

The war-guilt question, which was to be a major controversy in Europe during the 1920's, had a special significance for Americans. Many believed that the United States had intervened in a war in which American security had not been threatened, in which American interests had not been at stake. In the process of mobilizing the population for total war, an image of the all-evil Hun had been provided by the Creel Committee and other independent groups, an image which left no gray areas, no room for a bumbling yet ambitious Germany which had sought to stay the hand of Mars in the closing hours of peace. Similarly, an image of the Allied Powers as innocent defenders of western civilization against the barbarism of the Hun had been placed before a populace grumbling about conscription and taxes.

There were, to be sure, many Americans familiar enough with world politics and the specifics of the European war to see beyond the simple picture of heroes and villains. But there were many others who saw American intervention as an act of chivalry, Coeur de Lion on a white charger, thwarting the efforts of the Hun to ravish

2. See, for example, George F. Kennan, *Russia and the West* (Boston: Little, Brown and Co., 1961), pp. 163–64.

French and English women as he had the women of Belgium. When these knights came in contact with books written by Englishmen or by Frenchmen, blaming the war on the policies of their own governments, exposing a few of the atrocity stories as the myths they were, the whole affair came to seem shabby—unworthy of American effort.

Few Americans had been aware of divisions within England and France over the war issue; few had realized that these countries also had their Bournes, their Norrises and La Follettes. When the protests of E. D. Morel, Francis Neilson, and Earl Loreburn reached the United States, Americans might have wondered. Here were respected, loyal Englishmen condemning the Entente Powers for their role in the outbreak of the war—as Professor Adler has suggested, a case of man biting dog. Those Americans who read French could find treatments of similar tendency pouring out of Parisian publishing houses.[3]

Pelted by documents, war memoirs, and "histories" of the war, almost all disputing the American's war-conceived images, it was likely that Americans would realize that responsibilty for the war, to the extent that the question of responsibility was meaningful, was divided. None of the involved powers was "guiltless," none absolutely villainous. But here and there someone kept remembering talk back in the early days of 1917, talk about the United States going to war for reasons unlike those for which any country had fought before. The United States fought, some may have recalled, not out of self-interest, not in answer to a threat, but to defend the forces of light and goodness against the forces of darkness and evil. If this was not the case, why had the United States intervened? For others there were undoubtedly fewer questions: if the Allied Powers did not represent the "good guys" and the Central Powers the "bad guys," then, obviously, the reverse might be true. And if this was the case, the United States had no business intervening, least of all on the side of the Allies.

The controversy over the war-guilt question had, then, a real

3. Professor Adler suggests that the British revisionists were most influential in the United States for the simple reason that no language barrier obstructed their ideas.

significance for American attitudes toward intervention in 1917. Once the moral case for intervention was broken down, Wilson's failure to lead his people to an understanding of the stake of the United States in the Entente cause left many Americans without answers to the question of why they had fought. In a sense, the debate over war guilt was a necessary prelude to the later debate over American intervention.

2

In 1917 the editorial position of the *Nation* had differed little on the war issue from its closest competitor, the *New Republic*. Like the pages of the *New Republic,* those of the *Nation* had been filled with doubts about the moral superiority of the Allied cause; but when Wilson called for war, the *Nation* was with him: "Americans may take deep satisfaction in the fact that they enter the war only after the display of the greatest patience by the Government, only after grievous and repeated wrongs, and upon the highest possible grounds." The editors even ventured to hazard the prophecy that "no present or future historian can charge that Woodrow Wilson was bent on embroiling this nation in foreign wars." To be sure, the *Nation* could not approximate the great exuberance of a Teddy Roosevelt over intervention, but there had been a growing concern over Germany's "cool brutality" or "criminal insanity," a growing conviction that the German government had left Wilson no alternative. This bothered Professor Preserved Smith of Cornell so much that he cancelled his subscription, calling the *Nation* "not only pro-English, but English." Smith insisted that the London *Nation* was fairer to the Germans.[4]

During the weeks and months that followed American intervention, the *Nation* continued to support Wilson, endorsing Senator John Sharp Williams' reply to La Follette's complaints about British affronts to American neutrality—in which Williams called La Follette's attention to the difference between a torpedo and a prize court—ridiculing claims that British propaganda was responsible for the actions of the United States. But when the new year

4. *Nation,* CIV (February 8, 1917), 147, 150; (March 1, 1917), 228, 238; (April 5, 1917), 388.

was ushered in, the *Nation*'s position waivered and then shifted sharply. For most, the change was easily understood. In January, 1918, Oswald Garrison Villard became the nominal editor of the *Nation,* and in the fall, Villard took over completely, "with the complete satisfaction of molding my historic journal according to my exact wishes and beliefs."[5] Not least among Villard's beliefs was the belief that the United States had erred in going to war.

Whatever Villard's early beliefs about Wilson, Wilson's role in leading the United States to war forced Villard to conclude that Wilson could not be trusted—that he lacked principle. Certainly if Wilson succeeded in bringing about the millennium when peace came, he could be forgiven, but Villard had little faith in the fine talk he heard about open diplomacy. In June, 1918, the *Nation* expressed fears that the peace terms would be dictated behind closed doors. After all, Villard had already seen and published the "secret treaties."

And so when the war ended, Villard packed his bags and headed for the Peace Conference to keep an eye on Wilson. He stopped off in London in December to tell some of his acquaintances about the "seamy side of our own war activity," about "those events which have given American liberals profound concern for our spiritual and moral welfare." He found that the British were pained when he told them that Wilson "permits the use of undemocratic methods at home, and that in Haiti, San Domingo, and elsewhere he has anything but lived up to his principles and platform."[6]

Almost certain that Wilson would yield before Old World pressures, that Wilson would compromise, Villard began complaining about secrecy almost as soon as he reached Paris. What was Wilson doing behind those closed doors? Why wasn't Germany represented? The world would not settle for a new Holy Alliance—at least Villard and the British Labor Party would not.[7]

As the weeks passed, Villard continued to be unhappy about "closed diplomacy," about his inability to see Wilson. He reported

5. Oswald Garrison Villard, *Fighting Years* (New York: Harcourt, Brace and Co., 1939), p. 349.

6. *Nation,* CVIII (January 4, 1919), 15.

7. *Ibid.* (January 11, 1919), 51; (January 25, 1919), 123.

that there were "open mutterings that this American Wilson is the greatest dictator the world has ever seen." When a draft of the League of Nations Covenant circulated in February, 1919, Lewis Gannett, who worked closely with Villard on the *Nation,* was less than thrilled; he noted that "many of Wilson's foremost European supporters are bitterly disappointed and declare it [the Covenant] offers a greater opportunity for a new unholy alliance than for a liberal league of nations." Shortly before the final draft of the Covenant was presented to the Peace Conference, the *Nation* reprinted a statement by the Englishman, J. A. Hobson, condemning the "sham league." Then came the "Bullitt letter" to Wilson, reprinted and endorsed. Young William C. Bullitt had resigned from the American peace commission in disgust over Wilson's failure to prevent intervention in the Russian civil war and unhappy about the provisions in the Treaty of Versailles pertaining to Shantung, Danzig, and the Saar: "I am one of the millions who trusted implicitly in your leadership and believed you would take nothing less than 'a permanent peace based on unselfish, unbiased justice.' But the Government has consented now to deliver the suffering peoples of the world to new oppressions, subjections and dismemberments—a new century of war."[8]

The story of how the editors of the *Nation* and the *New Republic* joined their archenemies, opponents of reform like Lodge and Penrose, in opposition to the Treaty of Versailles is familiar enough. Many, probably most, reform-oriented intellectuals had lagged behind Villard in opposition to Wilson—had accepted the necessity for intervention. But when it became apparent that Wilson had not fulfilled their utopian hopes, many more turned on the President. And if Wilson was not fulfilling their visions, then it was not terribly difficult to "discover" that he was, after all, a tool of the "interests." When A. A. Berle, Jr., accused Wilson of treason to the American cause at Paris, of a deliberate scrapping of principle, wasn't it Thomas W. Lamont, one of Morgan's men, who rose to Wilson's defense? What was behind Elihu Root's activities on behalf of the League? Villard knew: "The same international banking influences which are supporting the President

8. *Ibid.* (February 15, 1919), 252; (February 22, 1919), 279–80; (April 19, 1919), 626–28; (May 31, 1919), 859.

and the Democratic Party on the League of Nations issue, have again demonstrated their control of the Republican Party"—and what was good for the international bankers was obviously not good for the readers of the *Nation*.[9] In the course of the battle over the Treaty of Versailles, many more erstwhile supporters of Wilson became susceptible to the Norris-Villard contentions regarding the role of the "interests" in bringing about America's entry into the war. Coming on the heels of the days of Creel and the Sedition Act, the debate over the postwar settlement cleared the path for what was to become the "revisionist" interpretation of intervention.

Disillusionment over the peace led not only to hostility to Wilson but to a growing irritation with the Allies as well. Widespread awareness of the "secret treaties" revived old complaints about the war having been merely a contest between rival imperialisms. The absence of Germany from the Peace Conference aroused widespread sympathy among reformers appalled by the dictated peace—and absolved Germany from the condemnation meted out to those who dared to create so illiberal a peace. Many reformers were, like Bullitt, upset by the attitude of the Allies toward the Russian Revolution, angered by intervention in the civil war, But the issue that irked most Americans, reformers or not, was the apparently cavalier attitude the Allies took toward their war debts. Hints that the United States drop Allied war debts fell on deaf ears at the Peace Conference. The Keynes Plan for European economic and financial recovery, involving cancellation of war debts, was rejected because "President Wilson and his advisers were convinced that the proposals . . . were in great measure devised by Great Britain and the continental Allies in order to extricate themselves, at the expense of the United States, from the consequences of an unreasonable reparations settlement. . . ."[10] The insistence that the Allies pay their debts, the one issue upon which the American people seemed united in the years that followed, was not as a rule responded to very graciously in Europe. Traveler after traveler returned to the United States

9. *Ibid.*, CIX (August 9, 1919), 170–71; (September 13, 1919), 375.

10. Seth P. Tillman, *Anglo-American Relations at the Paris Peace Conference of 1919* (Princeton: Princeton University Press, 1961), p. 275.

incensed by talk he had heard in London or in Paris of "Uncle Shylock." Certainly the Allies seemed to show less gratitude than the frauleins who greeted American occupation forces.

Villard and the *Nation* took all this in stride. Peace was made with Preserved Smith, who liked the *Nation* of 1920 much better than the 1917 version. Smith became a reviewer for the journal, dealing with literature on the war, complaining about wartime hysteria in the United States, striking out at books that painted the Germans as "bad." By the spring of 1920, the *Nation*'s bogey had become "French militarism."[11]

3

Something about the summer of 1920 must have been conducive to disillusionment among American historians. Perhaps it was the prospect of being faced with a choice between Cox and Harding in November, perhaps not. But Carl Becker sat in his study at Ithaca, New York, and brooded about the interlude with George Creel, brooded about progress, about the war, about Wilson and the Treaty of Versailles. Then, as historians and sometimes mere mortals are wont to do, he wrote a letter or two of complaint to a more sanguine and complacent friend and colleague, Professor William E. Dodd. The war was "the most futile, the most desolating and repulsive exhibition of human power and cruelty without compensating advantage that has ever been on earth. This is the result of some thousands of years of what men like to speak of as 'political, economic, intellectual, and moral Progress.' If this is progress, what in Heaven's name would retardation be!"[12] Having concluded that the war was useless. "without compensating advantage," Becker, like countless others, was ready to accept the revisionist contention that the United States had erred in intervening.

But Becker's conclusion was somewhat different from that of most revisionists. He rejected the Enlightenment view of a world divided into good men and bad, intelligent and ignorant, a world

11. *Nation,* CX (March 6, 1920), 302; (May 15, 1920), 650.

12. Becker to Dodd, June 17, 1920, quoted in Burleigh Wilkins, *Carl Becker* (Cambridge, Mass.: MIT and Harvard, 1961), p. 132.

in which all would be well when the bad men were named and circumvented, the ignorant enlightened and directed. Unlike the revisionists, Becker did not believe that men would learn from an attempt to find the villains, an attempt to draw lessons from the experience of the war. There was little value in an appeal to reason because "for good men and bad, ignorant and enlightened (even as enlightened as Mr. Wilson), reason and aspiration and emotion— what we call principles, faith, ideals—are without their knowing it at the service of complex and subtle instinctive reactions and impulses." Mostly, Becker was disgusted with himself, irritated because he had been "naive enough to suppose, during the war, that Wilson could ever accomplish those ideal objects which are so well formulated in his state papers."[13] Becker did, however, see a moral in the story: *he* had no business becoming involved in political issues. Despite considerable sympathy for the revisionist side of the subsequent controversy over the war and America's part in it, Becker refrained from entering the lists.

In July of that summer, Sidney Bradshaw Fay's first of a series of articles on the origins of the war was published in the *American Historical Review*.[14] Working primarily from the "Kautsky Documents" and the "Austrian Red Book,"[15] Fay quickly demonstrated the inequity of the war-guilt clause of the peace settlement. To be sure, the Germans had foolishly given the Austrians a free hand with Serbia and a promise of support, but "Bethmann and the Kaiser . . . were not criminals plotting the World War; they were simpletons putting 'a noose about their necks' and handing the other end of the rope to a stupid and clumsy adventurer [Berchtold] who now felt free to go as far as he liked."[16] The legend of the crown council of July 5, when the Germans and

13. *Ibid.*, pp. 133–34.

14. "New Light on the Origins of the World War, I. Berlin and Vienna, to July 29," *American Historical Review*, XXV, 616–39.

15. *Die deutschen Dokumente zum Kriegsausbruck: Vollständige Sammlung der von Karl Kautsky zusammen-gestellten Amtlichen Aktenstucke* (Charlottenburg, 1919); *Diplomatische Aktenstucke zur Vorgeschichte des Krieges, 1914: Erganzungen und Nachtrage zum Oest-Urgar. Rotbuch* (Vienna, 1919).

16. Fay, "New Light, I," p. 628.

Austrians allegedly assembled to plot the war, also fell victim to Fay's scholarship. Not only had the Kaiser not decreed war, but, according to Fay, he left on his planned vacation cruise on July 6, not expecting any "serious warlike complications." In conclusion, Fay found that a declaration of Austrian guilt would be closer to the truth than the war-guilt clause.[17]

As a general rule it would seem safe to postulate that an essay written in the *American Historical Review* will have no influence outside the historical profession. Fay's article did not violate this rule directly, but the impact of the article on a number of historians resulted in a spilling over of Fay's findings into other, more popular media.

Probably the most significant conversion wrought by "New Light, I" was that of young Harry Elmer Barnes, soon to be Fay's colleague at Smith College. Barnes, while a graduate student, had been an ardent advocate of intervention long before Woodrow Wilson had been able to bring himself to ask for war. Later, he contributed pamphlets to the wartime literature distributed by the National Security League and the American Defense Society. But in those days, as now, and as perhaps it should be, few people were impressed by the opinions of graduate students. By 1920, however, Barnes was a full professor at Clark University. That summer he traveled out to the Pacific Northwest to teach summer school, and while there, a colleague brought Fay's article to his attention. Years later, Barnes would recall that the article undermined his faith in what his elders told him in much the same manner as had his earlier discovery of the non-existence of Santa Claus.[18] Whether the recollection be apocryphal or not, Barnes, who had hitherto been uninterested in diplomatic history, became increasingly concerned with the revisionist controversy, and by the late 1920's he had emerged as the driving force behind American revisionism.

Fay's second article appeared in the *American Historical Review* in October, 1920.[19] He found that from July 29 to July 31,

17. *Ibid.*, pp. 629–30, 638.

18. Barnes to author, April 1, 1962.

19. "New Light on the Origins of the World War, II. Berlin and Vienna, July 29 to 31," *American Historical Review*, XXVI, 37–53.

1914, Germany had tried desperately to persuade Austria to accept a peaceful solution to the latter's quarrel with Serbia. He found that the new documents placed Austria in a much more unfavorable light than before and that the evidence cleared the German government of charges that it had deliberately plotted or wanted the war: "there is no doubt that the Chancellor Bethmann-Hollweg, as the official representative of German foreign policy, aimed at peace and better relations with Germany's neighbors in the period just before the war." Fay was convinced that Germany had not willed the war and found it easy to understand "how the Germans have become convinced that the war was forced upon them."[20] Fay was not, however, willing to absolve Germany of all responsibility. Germany was still guilty of negligence in giving Austria a blank check on July 5, 1914. And, "in a still wider sense, also, Germany is responsible, because one may say that militarism was one of the great causes of the war. . . . And for the growth of militarism in Europe, no country was so much responsible as Germany."[21]

Two months later, Charles Beard reviewed Carlton Hayes's *A Brief History of the Great War* for the *New Republic*. Beard had obviously been affected by the German and Austrian documents and was not quite sure what to believe. The influence of Fay's work was stated explicitly: "Anyhow, the war began. That is a fact which will not be downed even by the painstaking and illuminating researches of Professor Sidney B. Fay."[22]

Fay's final article in the "New Light" series appeared in January, 1921.[23] Concerning himself with the role of "Russia and the Other Powers" in the origins of the war, he admitted that there was little substantial evidence available. He concluded that it appeared that Russian militarists upstaged the Tsar constantly, managing to mobilize against the Tsar's wishes and, essentially, contrary to his orders. When the Tsar refused to decree mobilization, the Minister of War, acting within his authority, ordered a "practice" mobilization. But while the Russian and Austrian

20. *Ibid.*, pp. 51–52.   21. *Ibid.*, p. 53.

22. *New Republic,* XXV (December 22, 1920), 114.

23. "New Light on the Origins of the World War, III. Russia and the Other Powers," *American Historical Review,* XXVI, 225–54.

mobilizations came almost simultaneously, neither influenced by the other, the German mobilization "was directly caused by that of Russia. In fact it came rather surprisingly late."[24]

As Fay's last article appeared, a conference to discuss reparations, still guided by the assumption of Germany's "unique" responsibility for the war, was held in Paris. A month later a similar conference was staged in London. The Allies were not unaware of the difficulty Germany had in making payments, but they felt they had their own cause for grumbling in the American insistence on repayment of their war debts. Editorially, the *Nation* granted that the American people and Congress were opposed to cancellation, but the journal insisted that the debts could never be payed. But this was not reason to be angry with bankrupt European nations—the real culprits were the American statesmen who had sanctioned the loans: "the American people was deceived about these 'loans' just as it was hoodwinked about a hundred other matters during the war." Still the *Nation* was not prepared for outright cancellation—"that would be another futile gesture of generosity as was our unconditional entry into the war." No, the debts should be used as a lever—to force a just peace settlement—or still later, after the French occupied Dusseldorf, Duisberg, and Ruhrort in March, to curb French militarism.[25]

Then the *Nation* began a campaign to revise the Versailles verdict on war guilt. Cognizance was taken of an apology by Robert Bridges, the English poet, for a poem in which he had contended that the Germans treated prisoners of war badly as a matter of policy. Bridges claimed he had been misled by the British press. With obvious satisfaction the editor commented: "Thus the fierce and bloody legends crumble in every land. But we must be on guard against those whose business and profit lie in rebuilding them."[26] A few months later, in a lecture delivered at the Institute of Politics in Virginia, Lord Bryce suggested that the war had taught no lessons. The *Nation's* retort was sharp:

24. *Ibid.*, pp. 250–51.

25. *Nation*, CXII (February 23, 1921), 282; CXIV (February 15, 1922), 181.

26. *Ibid.*, CXII (March 2, 1921), 327.

How can lessons be learned from the war, when the great object of national policy during and since the war has been to give it a purely one-sided and shallow explanation and interpretation, the truth of which the scholars who should have been the first, have in reality been the last to challenge? Who has contributed more to the myth of a guilty nation plotting the war against a peaceful Europe than the so-called historians who occupy distinguished chairs in our universities?[27]

No, the *Nation* would not attack the politicians again, but "the psychology of scholars who threw themselves unquestioningly and unembarrassed into the arms of a professional propaganda and made themselves its willing tools is more difficult to justify or palliate." Few if any of these historians would admit that French militarism was the great threat of the day. They had a vested interest in preventing further research—in blocking the truth.

It was in this vein that Harry Elmer Barnes made his initial appearance in print as a revisionist—one of the mildest sort, to be sure. In a generally favorable review of E. Raymond Turner's *Europe since 1870,* Barnes was critical of Turner's treatment of the origins of the war.[28] He was surprised, particularly in view of Fay's work, to find that Turner had retained the "wartime dualism and diabolism in treating the part played by Germany in this period since 1870." Benignly, Barnes hoped that the second edition would have a revised section on the World War. Unfortunately, the present pages on the war reflected the "excitement and heightened emotions of a period of active warfare and not the constructive moderation and the calm reflection and reconsideration which must come to dominate the postwar period if the 'fruits of victory' are to be other than universal misery and preparation for another conflict."[29] Clearly Barnes was not concerned merely with historical accuracy for its own sake. Underlying his entrance into the controversy was his conviction that a sound evaluation of the events of 1914 was essential for a stable

27. *Ibid.,* CXIII (September 14, 1921), 283.

28. *New Republic,* XXIX (January 18, 1922), 228, 230.

29. *Ibid.,* p. 230.

peace in the 1920's. His hope that Turner would revise his discussion of the war was based on his belief that "the persistence of this primitive 'scapegoat' psychology in our interpretations of contemporary European history is the most fatal obstacle to any sane appraisal and solution of the world situation today."[30]

Similar themes appeared in an article Barnes wrote for the *Nation* a few months later. He condemned ultra-nationalistic distortions in the writing of diplomatic history as conducive to the creation of "the state of mind which invited the crisis of 1914." The World War, he argued, was an illustration of the danger of relying upon popular historical notions—the implication being that there might not have been a war, or at least America might not have been involved, if historical treatments of Germany had been more objective. The influence of Fay was evident: Germany was guilty of carelessness and bungling, but not of wilful aggression; immediate guilt was attributable to Austria and Russia. Most important, history could be used as an instrument for the furtherance of international good will; to date, it was being used as an instrument for the spreading of nationalistic exclusiveness and international hatred.[31]

These were days when the American Legion and other organizations of patrioteers were peddling their brand of "Americanism." One manifestation of this activity was the rash of textbook investigations prompted by the absurd insistence that books available to school children portray the American past and its heroes without any of the darker tones—as a panoply of shining knights prevailing against insurmountable odds, without assistance, under God. The rebellious intellectuals parried wth equivalent nonsense, wallowing in the real or imagined sordidness of the American past. One means of striking at the version of "Americanism" that had sprouted during the war and exploded during the days of the Palmer Raids was to strike at the source, to deprecate the entry of the United States into the war—to "reveal" the sordidness of the Allied cause, of the circumstances of American intervention.

30. *Ibid.*

31. "History and International Good-Will," *Nation,* CXIV (March 1, 1922), 251–54.

For Villard and the *Nation* the task could only be a joyous one. Where had American liberalism gone, asked Herbert Croly, and the *Nation* responded: "The death knell of American liberalism was sounded the minute its false leader put it into the war."[32] What was needed were historians bold enough to tell the truth about the war—historians whose concern was for truth and not the inculcation of patriotism—and in Harry Elmer Barnes, Villard found a kindred spirit.

Whether or not one shared Barnes's faith in the ability of the historian to shape a people's image of other peoples, he was striving for a necessary corrective to wartime attitudes toward Germany— attitudes which he, like Beard, had once shared and had sought to foster. Beard, likewise affected by Fay's articles, also showed signs of regretting his wartime statements about Germany. In the week following the appearance of the Barnes article, the *Nation* carried Beard's review of H. G. Wells's *Washington and the Riddle of Peace*. Quickly disposing of what he believed to be the Wells thesis—that concessions made by England and the United States at the Washington Conference were indications of mutual affection—he began a sermon which was almost as applicable to the Charles Beard of 1917 as it was to any of his readers:

> Those persons who set out to love one country and those who set out to hate another are equally unfitted for correct and informed thinking in matters international. Moreover, they are usually found shifting their affections with the currents of affairs. They are hot lovers one day and hot haters the next, and in deadly peril of becoming a nuisance all the time. It is the man who gets religion the hardest who backslides the hardest. Especially is this loving and hating business dangerous to the intelligent pursuit of our own national interests.[33]

Included in the sermon was a warning about shifting affections— a warning which Beard would himself heed throughout the debate over war guilt, but which numerous others would ignore.

In June of 1922, Beard traveled up to Hanover, New Hampshire, to give a series of lectures on contemporary Europe at Dart-

32. *Nation,* CXI (November 3, 1920), 489.

33. *Ibid.,* CXIV (March 8, 1922), 289–90.

mouth College.[34] He was obviously not pleased with what he saw in Europe and not at all certain that the United States could play a useful role in European affairs. He gave little evidence of the influence of the budding war-guilt controversy on his changing attitude toward America's role in world affairs. Like Becker's, his "revisionism" on the war-guilt question stopped short of exchanging villains and heroes. Whether the Austrians or the Germans were primarily responsible for the war really mattered little; responsibility still seemed to rest with the Central Powers. The major theme of Beard's lectures was that American intervention had not produced a better world, particularly if the focus was on Europe. Like Becker he was disillusioned with the results of the war—the utter futility of it. What ultimately made Beard change his mind about the wisdom of intervention was the peace and its aftermath rather than any new light on the origins of the war.

Beard's disgust with the Entente Powers, their secret diplomacy, and their secret treaties was blatant, but "no one is more responsible than William II for encouraging Austria to light the European fire."[35] In sum, he saw little hope for Europe, little hope that Europe would reform and end the habit of indulging in internecine wars: "A new constitution of nations, a grand European league, appears to be the only alternative to new combinations, new wars more ghastly and deadly than ever."[36] But this implicit attack on European nationalism was immediately followed by a disclaimer, a denial of the advisability of the United States taking action to become a part of the federation Europe required. It was quite another thing, Beard said, for the United States, "enjoying the comparative security of this hemisphere," to attempt to take part in a co-operative system to solve the problems of all the other nations of the world. He saw nothing on the European scene which suggested that the United States might be successful in such an endeavor, "even if America had the courage and the will."[37] From this point it was an easy transition, easier for others perhaps than for Beard, to the conviction that intervention in Europe's war had been a mistake. Beard did not

34. Published as *Cross Currents in Europe Today* (Boston: Marshall Jones Co., 1922).

35. *Ibid.*, p. 76. 36. *Ibid.*, p. 139. 37. *Ibid.*

in 1922, nor in the years that followed, seek to blame any individual for that mistake; nor did he seek an explanation in hypotheses of conspiracies.

Becker reviewed the published lectures for the *Nation* and wrote that Beard's book should be read by everyone who desired to know about the origins and results of the war.[38] Thus Becker, Barnes, and Beard indicated their early dissatisfaction with the war, and each endorsed the "mild revisionism" of Professor Fay. But while these historians complained rather gently about world affairs and gave some indication of questioning their earlier attitudes toward America's participation in the war, of questioning their initial information as to the origins of the war, two men less addicted to scholarly research began to rock the boat.

4

Judge Frederick Bausman was true to the title he had acquired as a result of brief tenure as a Justice of the Supreme Court of the State of Washington. When he had read about the origins of the war and weighed the available evidence, he proceeded to pass judgment: The verdict was guilty—for France and Russia.

When he published his first book, *Let France Explain*,[39] Bausman was sixty-one years old and a man of considerable significance in his home state. He had come to the Northwest in 1886, after completing his formal education at the University of Pittsburgh and at Harvard; and shortly thereafter he became secretary to the Territorial Governor, Eugene Semple. He had been a member of the commission that had codified the laws of Washington, and by 1915 he was a power in Democratic politics. When, in 1915, he accepted an appointment to the State Supreme Court, many who knew him reacted with surprise. They found it easy to see why the Governor had selected him: beyond the fact of political expedience, both bar and bench acclaimed the choice the best possible. But as the Seattle *Town Crier* said of Bausman, "his is a nervous, energetic personality which few would have thought likely to be attracted by the routine grind of the bench

38. "The Shaking World," *Nation*, CXV (November 22, 1922), 552–53.

39. London: George Allen and Unwin, Ltd., 1922.

or the placidity of life in Olympia."⁴⁰ His resignation from the court in 1916 probably surprised no one. Then came American intervention in the war. His attitude toward intervention at that time is not a matter of public record.

Shortly after the war, however, he wrote a series of articles on various aspects of the war and of American foreign policy for the Hearst press. Then in 1922 he wrote *Let France Explain,* the first book to be written by an American in which responsibility for the origins of the war was attributed to the Allies rather than to the Central Powers. Unable to find a publisher in the United States—"no American house was brave enough"⁴¹—he finally was able to publish the book in England.

Bausman's views on American intervention were, perhaps, most interesting of all. He was, with a German name, understandably bitter about the domestic intolerance and the suppression of civil liberties in the United States during the war. He felt that the United States, unimperiled, had enforced conscription for overseas service, asking nothing in return.

> When I think of the noble host we sent abroad, when I think of their boyish hope, their sanguine ardor to aid mankind, when I think of the good-will we hoped to bring about, the lasting peace between nations that had hacked each other in so many wars, I know that no army ever embarked in pursuit of a purer glory. No, there never went to battle legions with so little desire to bring back anything for themselves or their native land. It was not America we were saving; not one in a thousand believed we were ourselves in danger. It was England that we would aid, France that should not die.
>
> Not since the crusades had a soldiery gone forth with a purpose so high. . . .⁴²

Wistfully he wrote of the romantic feeling that the United States could, with one great effort, "put an end to war for ever." But his countrymen were innocent, naive; they knew nothing of European

40. "In the public eye and ear," *Town Crier,* October 30, 1915, p. 16.

41. Bausman, review of *The Genesis of the World War* by Harry Elmer Barnes, *Nation,* CXXIII (September 1, 1926), 198.

42. *Let France Explain,* pp. 63–64.

politics. They should have realized the absurdity of viewing the war as one of democracy against autocracy.

Rankled by what he believed to be the lack of gratitude on the part of America's recent allies, their belittling of America's war effort and of the idealistic ends to which that effort was directed, their attempts to get out from under the war debts, Bausman had started off on the war-guilt question.[43] In particular, the works of E. D. Morel and Francis Neilson, leading British revisionists, provided the case upon which he passed judgment.[44] Concluding that the Allies had deceived the United States regarding the origins of the war, that the Allied powers were at least as "guilty" as the Central Powers—France and Russia probably guiltier—Bausman was left without a cause for the selfless crusade. His views in 1922 simply underscored the idea that the United States had not had an interest, a stake, in the World War. If there was one thread that ran through the material of all of the American revisionists, it was this assumption that the outcome of the war in Europe mattered little as far as American interests were concerned.

Although convinced that it had been a mistake for the United States to intervene on behalf of such deceivers and ingrates, Bausman did not blame Wilson; nor did he seek to blame Wall Street or any other domestic group. In *Let France Explain* he was content to condemn the iniquitous Europeans. Though his condemnation of the Allies, and England in particular, would soon become more violent, even ludicrously violent, the circle of the guilty would also come to include those insidious internal forces that worked toward intervention, forces to be savagely revealed by John Kenneth Turner.

5

John Kenneth Turner was a journalist and free-lance writer whose primary achievement prior to World War I was a muckraking exposé of conditions in Mexico under the regime of Porfirio Díaz. After traveling through Mexico for over a year, his findings appeared first in a series of articles for *American Magazine* in 1909

43. *Ibid.*, p. 62.   44. *Ibid., passim.*

and 1910 and were then published in 1911 as *Barbarous Mexico*.[45] His initial moves in the direction of revisionism came in a series of articles written for the *Nation* in 1919 and 1920.[46] The first of these demonstrated the technique he would use in his major attack on American intervention, *Shall It Be Again?* Turner juxtaposed quotes from statements by President Wilson, some during the election campaign of 1916, some during the war, and some made shortly after the war while Wilson sought to muster support for the Treaty of Versailles. Of course, Wilson's attitude toward the war and the dangers inherent in it varied over the years. For Turner, this sufficed to prove Wilson's deceitfulness. His second article was an attack on the League on the grounds that it would not preserve peace; both the conquered and neutral nations were excluded and the "Big Five" placed in a privileged position. Not without some effort, he also managed to slap at "business" for "its" aims in Mexico and for "its" alleged role in the Lansing-Ishii agreement. The final article was a heavy-handed attack on Wilson's "hypocrisy," based, as was the first article, on the juxtaposition of quotations taken out of context. The substance of each of these articles appeared once more in *Shall It Be Again?*

In 1922 Turner found the war to be "the livest issue of the day, and it will remain an issue so long as future war is in the reckoning. Its lessons hold not only the secret of averting future war, but also the solution of other public questions of a pressing nature."[47] The other "public questions" soon became apparent, having to do mostly with evils Turner believed to be inherent in capitalism.

Early in the book in which he raised almost all of the major questions to be debated by revisionists and their opponents in the years that followed, Turner asked: "Was America ever in danger?" The answer was, of course, a resounding "no." Germany had not attacked nor threatened to attack the United States. The German-Mexican alliance proposed in the "Zimmerman note" had been ex-

45. Chicago: C. H. Kerr, 1911.

46. "A Pledge to the World," *Nation,* CIX (July 5, 1919), 14–16; "Peace League or War League," *Nation,* CIX (August 2, 1919), 140–41; "Standing behind the President—an Impossibility," *Nation,* CXI (October 6, 1920), 370–72.

47. *Shall It Be Again?* (New York: B. W. Huebsch, 1922), p. 5.

pressly contingent upon the United States declaring war on Germany. The Germans had not only not declared war on the United States but had in fact striven to avoid war with the United States. Not only was Germany incapable of invading America in April, 1917, but "Germany would have been physically incapable of invading America even had she possessed no other enemies. This was the judgment of the highest experts in the service of America, sworn to before Congressional committees while this country was neutral."[48] When viewing the alleged threat Germany posed for American security, Turner saw only the immediate situation, a situation in which a threat of invasion was as absurd as he portrayed it. The less immediate problems that might result from a German-controlled Atlantic, German-controlled trade routes, he ignored. By the limits within which he prescribed the matter of "self-defense" he was correct in laughing it off. But he was, in fact, blowing over straw men: the security issue could not be limited to whether or not Germany could have conquered or even invaded the United States in 1917. Within his own framework, however, Turner could conclude that there was no threat of invasion, no threat of any destruction of American institutions, "no immediate and pressing danger of any kind." He was convinced that talk of a Hun invasion was a "gigantic hoax," perpetrated because the element of fear was considered necessary by those attempting to lead the nation into war: the American people had to be frightened before they would allow themselves to be pushed over the brink.[49]

Having disposed of the security argument to his own satisfaction, Turner then faced the interpretation of intervention as a selfless crusade, a war for the extension of American ideals to less privileged peoples. Whereas Bausman had reveled in Wilsonian idealism as the answer to why the United States intervened, Turner ridiculed this interpretation. He argued that "even were a government to be found unselfish enough to assume the fearful cost of war, simply for the sake of extending democracy, the very attempt to impose democracy upon another nation would constitute a violation of sovereignty."[50] But Turner did not believe that the government of the United States had been unselfish, disinterested, or idealistic. The butt of his attack in this instance was President

48. *Ibid.*, p. 14.   49. *Ibid.*, p. 19.   50. *Ibid.*, pp. 152–53.

Wilson. Cleverly extracting numerous excerpts of the President's speeches from 1916 to 1920, Turner asserted that Wilson was guilty of duplicity and hypocrisy: "The great myth of the world war was Wilson idealism. Our noble President was simply a one hundred per cent American politician. The secret of Wilson is hypocrisy."[51] While holding Wilson responsible for involving the United States in the war, Turner did not suggest that Wilson had the power to do this alone. But the President, backed by a power elite, "a minority in control of the finances of the country, the press, and the public offices," could take a course calculated to force intervention.

Repeating arguments long familiar to most Americans, Turner maintained that every American complaint against Germany proceeded from the alleged injury to the selfish interests of "certain" Americans, generally described as the "interests," "Wall Street," or "business." Thus Turner was critical of Wilson because Wilson's path to intervention was paved with issues that were not merely matters of abstract principle but matters of real interest to at least some Americans. He was critical because Wilson was *not* idealistic and because the interests Wilson allegedly served were not those of the majority. But the Turner image of Wilson did not prevail in most subsequent revisionist literature.[52]

In addition, Turner resurrected and endorsed the policies advocated by William Jennings Bryan in 1915. If the American government had really been concerned with preserving American lives it would have notified its citizens that they traveled within the war zones only at their own risk. Turner was most unhappy with the manner in which Wilson and other pro-interventionists had equated the insistence on unhampered trade and travel in the war zone with the defense of national honor. Parodying the "official thesis," he wrote: "Honor is involved with trade and travel because trade and travel are involved with international law, and in-

---

51. *Ibid.*, p. 400.

52. On Turner's influence, Barnes commented: "I was not much affected by the Turner book in judging Wilson, but I did get some unholy glee in citing some of his quotations from Wilson, especially the one in which he expressed the same interpretation of WWI as that for which he sent Debs to prison." Barnes to the author, April 1, 1962.

ternational law is involved with sovereignty. For our own sakes we must maintain our proud position as champion of neutral rights and of humanity." He admitted readily that no one claimed that Americans had an absolute right to trade and travel under all circumstances. The United States declared war on Germany not simply because of German interference with American commerce, but because of the method Germany used when interfering;

> and the method stands or falls by the rules of international law. Of such overshadowing importance is international law, indeed, that we must stand prepared to sacrifice both commerce and lives to it. We must stand prepared to spend even "our last man and our last dollar" in order to maintain the simple right, under international law, of any American to ship the food we need to other countries, or the simple right of the same American to travel anywhere upon the high seas, in pursuit of the patriotic business of causing a scarcity of food and high prices within his own country.[53]

Indeed, to many Americans beside Turner, the right of a few Americans to travel and of another few Americans to make a profit at what seemed the expense of the masses might have seemed meager justification for intervention and the subsequent cost in lives and dollars. When Beard later elaborated on Turner's primitive thesis, he did at least remove the implications of a conspiracy of vested interests and demonstrated that the economic well-being of the entire nation was at stake in the American commerce with which the belligerents interfered.

Turner, and many revisionists who followed him, insisted that the British had been more guilty than the Germans when it came to violations of American neutrality. Taking this argument to its logical conclusion, if our neutrality, our commerce, were what we fought to protect, we should have gone to war with Great Britain. What really guided American policy, Turner maintained, was not principle, but expediency: the fact that the German navy was weaker than the British navy.[54]

Next on the agenda came discussion of the "German Peril" and of the origins of the war. Again the influence of European revisionists was evident as Turner frequently cited Neilson, Morel, and Georges Brandes. Philip Gibbs's indictment of war, *Now It Can*

53. *Shall It Be Again?* p. 103.   54. *Ibid.*, p. 127.

Be Told, provided still more ammunition for the guns of revisionism. Essentially, Turner's treatment of the background of the European conflict was a diatribe against imperialism. All of the great powers were imperialistic. The war was one of rival imperialisms, a rivalry for colonial possessions. England was the worst of the imperialist powers: "every war fought by England within the present generation, as well as by every other great power, although not as plainly so on the surface was . . . a war for business."[55] The Allied powers were as bad as if not worse than Germany in terms of autocracy, secret diplomacy, militarism, and imperialistic ambitions. But while Turner did not believe in the German menace, he made no effort to whitewash Germany. His position was one of standing back and cursing all of the tainted European powers. The United States had no business intervening at such great cost just to place France and England in a position to "overawe Europe." It would have been far better to let them beat each other into the ground. And even if a victory for the Allies was better for the United States, which he doubted, Turner did not believe that American intervention saved the Allies. He argued that a German victory was impossible, that the intervention of the United States destroyed the only chance for the only peace by which America might have gained—a peace without victory. But Wilson, who had used these words, frustrated this peace by dragging his country into the war. Thus, American participation in the World War was "a crime against democracy and permanent peace."[56]

Turner devoted much of the latter half of his book to an indictment of Wall Street and the American imperialists. Wall Street had been enthusiastically in favor of intervention not only in the months immediately preceding the declaration of war, but Wall Street or "big business" had been a "most powerful influence" working toward intervention from the earliest days of the war. In the process of demonstrating the validity of this point he equated the "preparedness" movement with the will to war: those who favored preparedness wanted war.[57]

> At the beginning of 1917, war on the side of the Entente was the one thing that would solve all problems. First, it would ensure another long period of war orders. Second, it would insure Allied

55. *Ibid.*, p. 224.   56. *Ibid.*, p. 236.   57. *Ibid.*, p. 260.

credit. Third, it might be so manipulated as to serve in the attainment of certain other advantages of a permanent nature, toward which Wall Street had been hungrily working. . . .[58]

But he had made Wilson solely responsible for the decision to intervene. How could Wall Street work "its" will through a Democratic president whose New Freedom program was alleged to be anti-big business, anti-Wall Street? To Turner's mind this was easy, although the "interests" were probably more amazed by his explanation than faithful Wilsonians:

> It had always been the policy of President Wilson to serve the special interests of Wall Street, regardless of the general welfare. No American President ever more frankly confessed himself a servant of business than Wilson. No American President ever more completely met the wishes of big business than Wilson.[59]

In a chapter entitled "Wilson Imperialism," much of what Turner meant when calling Wilson the servant of Wall Street became apparent. He was greatly concerned with what he considered Wilson's aggressive interpretation of the Monroe Doctrine, with Wilson's attitude toward the China consortium, with what he considered the imperialistic implications of the Lansing-Ishii agreement. In particular, he was unhappy with Wilson's policies in Latin America, especially with regard to Mexico, but with regard to the Dominican Republic, Haiti, and Nicaragua as well: "Almost from the day Woodrow Wilson took office, the threat of armed force was held over Mexico, with intent to mold Mexico's domestic affairs in accordance with the wishes of Wall Street."[60] In Nicaragua, Turner saw Wilsonian imperialism in action: it was American imperialism "as approved by the controlling element in both the Democratic and Republican parties," and it was not at all different from the imperialism of "England, France, Germany, Japan, or Italy at their worst." With this in mind, Turner insisted that it was absurd to think that Wilson had led the United States to war to put an end to imperialism. It was sufficient, he contended, to point out that Wilson himself was a conventional imperialist before the European war began.[61]

58. *Ibid.*, p. 279.   60. *Ibid.*, p. 335.

59. *Ibid.*, p. 314.   61. *Ibid.*, p. 361.

Having ruled out arguments that the United States intervened in self-defense, or on behalf of democracy, or because of a desire to uphold international law, or in quest of permanent peace, Turner concluded that the "theory of a war for business alone harmonizes with the facts."[62] He found intervention to be undemocratic in every conceivable respect: the way it was achieved, conducted, its burdens distributed, in its "real aims and in its fruits": "we quarreled with Germany, went to war, and negotiated peace, purely in the interest and at the direction of high finance, and at all stages to the prejudice of the general welfare."[63]

The moral Turner drew was that so long as the government of the United States played handmaiden to Wall Street's concern for overseas trade, the United States would constantly be dragged into Europe's wars. Charles Beard was already coming to the same conclusion and spent most of his remaining years elaborating this thesis. But in 1922, Turner was intemperate to a degree that Beard would not equal until he had watched his country suffer through another decade in which the business of government was business, suffer through a depression and through another world war. In *Shall It Be Again?* Turner boldly maintained that:

> The real enemy of America is not autocracy abroad. It is not kings or kaisers or czars. The real enemy of America is our rich fellow-citizen who is willing to plunge our country into war for his own selfish purposes—his political servant without whose voluntary cooperation public war for private profit would be impossible—his intellectual henchman, of the press, the pulpit, and the college, whose function is to identify the national honor with the business ambitions of a small but powerful minority.[64]

Turner's solution to the problems of American foreign policy involved what he considered an "honest" application of Wilson's professed principles. There was, in fact, little difference between Turner's concept of world politics and the concept held by the loyal Wilsonian. If America would only make a sincere effort to act in a disinterested, "idealistic" manner in its relations with other countries, then peace, prosperity, and democracy would be served. Turner's program called for the repudiation of the policy of inter-

62. *Ibid.*, p. 370.   63. *Ibid.*, p. 404.   64. *Ibid.*, pp. 386–87.

vening diplomatically or by force on behalf of American investments in foreign countries; the repeal of the powers which permitted the President to use an arms embargo to assist one side or the
other in a civil war or rebellion; the renunciation of the Monroe
Doctrine; the withdrawal of support of Latin-American dictators
set up by or held up by American favor; the immediate independence of the Philippines, Puerto Rico, and the Virgin Islands. To
carry out this program meant to rid the United States of all the
trappings of imperialism. It meant an end to policies that had involved the United States in friction with other powers and were
likely to be sources of further friction. The program was therefore
one to which all "right-thinking" internationalists, all reform intellectuals, could subscribe. To carry it out meant to right past
wrongs, to remove the sources of fear of the gringo. Do this first,
Turner maintained, and then, and only then, would America be
qualified to propose to the world steps toward permanent peace,
steps which would result in the safety of democracy.[65]

But if Turner's ideas about world politics, about the need to
ease international tensions and to win friends, fell in line with
Wilsonian internationalism, his ideas about America's role in
world affairs would have horrified the Wilsonians, and the more
chauvinistic advocates of a larger American role in world affairs as well. Working from his conviction that it would be
impossible for any European power to take hold in the Western
Hemisphere and dictate its will in American affairs, he called
for a kind of Pan-Americanism that could best be described as
hemispheric isolationism. What he apparently had in mind when
renouncing the Monroe Doctrine was the so-called Roosevelt
Corollary. Once this idea was dropped, the United States and its
hemispheric neighbors—particularly the Latin Americans—could
live together as friends, presenting a united front against Europe
and refraining from meddling in European affairs. To cement
this wall, a constitutional amendment would be passed requiring
a referendum to precede and to determine any decision to use
armed force outside the territorial waters of the United States.[66]

65. *Ibid.*, pp. 406–8.   66. *Ibid.*, pp. 410–17.

In concluding his book, Turner declared:

> The events of the past half-dozen years have demonstrated not only the moral bankruptcy of the political and intellectual leaders that capitalism has given the world, but the inability of capitalism to save the world from periodic disaster. Imperialism is simply a phase of capitalism. Big business government must go, but big business government will not go until big business goes. Only the institution of a new social order, based upon economic equality, will save the world from more and more wars for business.[67]

Basically, Turner was appealing to the idealism and ideology of his audience. He would show how the war had come about, show that American intervention had resulted from the pursuit of selfish interests by a small minority of Americans. From his book most Americans would be expected to see that intervention had been a mistake, that it had not served their interests or furthered their ideals. They would then, it was hoped, act as necessary to remove the source of their difficulties by turning to socialism. Then America could be truly good; and this goodness could be spread throughout the Western Hemisphere and someday throughout the world. Peace would reign supreme because socialist governments would serve the people rather than the "interests"—and the people had never wanted war. This was essentially the enlightenment attitude against which Carl Becker had rebelled in his letter to Professor Dodd in the summer of 1920.

6

During the last half of 1922, Villard's *Nation* continued the fight. A proposal by Lord Balfour for a deal on reparations and war debts provoked an angry editorial article writing off the proposal as a scheme which meant "Europeans be generous with each other, and let Uncle Sam pay."[68] Growing friction over the war debts led to the rapidly growing conviction that the wartime Allies were fair-weather friends; and if they were not to be trusted now, was it not likely that their self-portraits since

67. *Ibid.*, p. 418.

68. *Nation*, CXV (August 16, 1922), 159.

1914 were images not to be accepted at face value? Difficult as it was to fight against the superpatriot's concept of a pure America and to rail simultaneously against iniquitous Europeans, the *Nation* kept trying.

One day Poincaré was overheard declaring that the United States had not been directly menaced by the Germans and, editorially, the *Nation* exulted over the admission and referred their readers to Bausman's book—exaggerating a little his tenure on the Washington Supreme Court and urging that no one be put off by his German name. Then Lewis Gannett, referring to pre-revisionist interpretations of the origins of the war, reported that "They All Lied." The article was a brief survey of revisionist literature in which Gannett wrote of Fay's "New Light" articles, Bausman's book, and other works by E. D. Morel, Francis Neilson, and A. J. Nock. He was generally reserved and objective in his judgments, but nonetheless sympathetic to the revisionists. The time had come to revise the Treaty of Versailles.[69]

In the congressional elections of 1922, Villard was much interested in the fate of the men who had opposed the war resolution in 1917. La Follette was up for re-election, and while there seemed little reason to fear for his success, the *Nation* declared: "If Mr. La Follette is returned to the Senate it will show that the masses of the people are beginning to come out of the hypnotic state in which they were placed by Woodrow Wilson and the war mania, and are beginning to sense how they were lied to, deceived, and misled in the name of democracy and humanity." Back in the days before Villard took over the *Nation*, La Follette's vote against war had been deprecated by the editors; but in 1922 it was remembered that he had made a "noble and justified stand against the war." He had opposed "the madness of war which has cost us so dear, plunged all Europe into misery, and transferred the seat of the worst militarism from Berlin to Paris." When the election returns were in, the *Nation* exulted in the election of men who had voted against war in 1917. To Villard and many reform-minded intellectuals like him, war was, per se, bad. Some had believed that 1917 was different, but as they viewed the postwar

69. *Ibid.* (September 20, 1922), 270; (October 11, 1922), 353–57.

world, they gradually came to believe that they had been deluded. Thus, the men who had opposed intervention had been wiser—and now could be counted upon to work for a better world.[70]

Then on January 11, 1923, French and Belgian troops began the invasion and occupation of the Ruhr district—the ultimate conclusion of Poincaré's determination to collect reparations from the Germans. Senator Borah was outraged, calling the invasion "utterly brutal and insane," and the *Nation* quoted and endorsed Borah's view. Reporters for the *Nation* found French atrocities in the Ruhr comparable to German atrocities in Belgium in 1914 —puzzling, perhaps, in view of the *Nation*'s past efforts to write off the earlier reports as Allied propaganda. But soon there was hope: the British appeared to be repudiating France's Ruhr policy. Perhaps the collapse of the "unholy alliance" was at hand. Perhaps a stop could be put to "an imperialistic and militaristic France bent on dominating Europe and accomplishing what Napoleon failed to effect 110 years ago."[71]

Probably no postwar event aroused American sympathy for Germany as much as the French occupation of the Ruhr. Here was another link in the chain of events that tended to change American wartime attitudes, making them less sympathetic to their former Allies, increasingly sympathetic to the one-time enemy. French activities in the 1920's prepared Americans for the revisionist contentions regarding France's role in precipitating the World War. The villain of 1923 was Raymond Poincaré; and if he was a militaristic warmonger in 1923, was it not likely that he had played the same role in 1914? Thus the mounting list of charges that tended to make Poincaré a greater villain than the Kaiser seemed credible. To many Americans in 1923, the Ruhr occupation established the man's character and sufficed as corroboration of the bits of evidence which suggested that he had plotted the World War. And if pro-German sympathy was now kindled in the United States, it was to be fanned in the months that followed by the growing prestige of the Weimar Republic, by the

70. *Ibid.* (August 16, 1922), 160; (November 29, 1922), 569.

71. *Ibid.*, CXVI (January 24, 1923), 84; (February 14, 1923), 161; CXVII (August 22, 1923), 180.

policies of Gustav Stresemann leading to the Locarno settlement. Throughout 1923 the revisionist pot simmered but never quite came to a boil in the United States. Despite the efforts of Bausman and Turner, the revisionist controversy remained largely the concern of the academicians, well hidden from the public eye. The intellectual atmosphere in which it would bubble over began, however, to expand, as men who had once acquiesced in intervention repented. In Emporia, Kansas, William Allen White asked a few questions: "And, anyway, what has war done for this world that we should try it again? Did it avail humanity anything when the whole world went to war? Who is worse off, the victim or the victors? What creed is established in the world by force? Certainly not democracy. A score of million men are dead and wounded, and for what? Why hug the old delusion that war will make men free?"[72] War is useless—war is useless—how long before the chant murmured here and there by a growing chorus reached the crescendo?

In Detroit, Reinhold Niebuhr, a young Protestant minister accustomed to grappling with theological revisionism, shelved the book he was reading and wrote in his notebook:

> Gradually the whole horrible truth about the war is being revealed. Every new book destroys some further illusion. How can we ever again believe anything when we compare the solemn pretensions of statesmen with the cynically conceived secret treaties? Here was simply a tremendous contest for power between two great alliances of states in which the caprice of statesmen combined with basic economic conflicts to dictate the peculiar form of the alliances. Next time the cards will be shuffled in a different way and the "fellowship in arms" will consist of different fellows.
>
> As the truth becomes known there are however some compensations for the disillusionment. If the moral pretensions of the heroes were bogus, the iniquity of the villains was not as malicious as it once appeared.[73]

72. Editorial, *Emporia Gazette,* January 17, 1923. Quoted in Helen Ogden Mahin (ed.), *The Editor and His People* (New York: Macmillan, 1924), p. 380.

73. *Leaves from the Notebook of a Tamed Cynic* (New York: Meridian Books, 1957), p. 61.

Still early in the year, Ray Stannard Baker's three volumes on Wilson and the Peace Conference were published, and Carl Becker reviewed them for the *Nation*.[74] Again Becker exhibited the high hopes with which many pacifically inclined intellectuals had supported intervention—and the depths to which they could fall when the crusade began to appear like all other wars:

> Having been long engaged in destroying what we are pleased to call civilization, a genuine emotion welled up within us when Mr. Wilson beautifully and positively assured us that war is an abomination, but that this war was different from all other wars because in this war we were fighting to end war and to bring in a New Order of peace and just dealing. The emotion was pleasant and necessary because it enabled us to believe that it was right, in this one case alone, to force millions of young men to go out to kill and be killed. . . . Mr. Wilson was not responsible for the failure, although he was at fault for thinking, and for beguiling us into thinking, that it could have been otherwise.[75]

Becker's words provide a world of insight into why one type of person—the sensitive, humanitarian intellectual—was receptive to the revisionist interpretation of American intervention and why many of those men who represented the best in American civilization became adherents of revisionism. But Becker's disillusionment had carried him farther than most of those who would write "revisionist" books. Becker had lost faith in the efficacy of appeal to reason:

> In the end one rises from a reading of these significant volumes much enlightened; at once amused and saddened, encouraged and depressed; for here on this great stage of the world's history one has witnessed a performance without parallel, in which the animal Man exhibits himself for what he is, a bizarre mixture of wisdom and folly, of cynicism and credulity, of noble aspiration and feeble achievement. One can only say, with Sir Thomas More: "All things will not be well until all men are good, which I think will not be this long time."[76]

74. "Mr. Wilson at the Peace Conference," *Nation*, CXVI (February 14, 1923), 186, 188.

75. *Ibid.*, p. 188.   76. *Ibid.*

Becker's wistful philosophizing did not, however, appease the editors of the *Nation*. In an editorial article they insisted that Becker had accepted Baker's defense of Wilson too readily. Two of them (Villard and Gannett) had been at Paris and they knew better—and a violent attack on Baker's honesty and integrity ensued.[77]

In the summer of 1923, revisionism all over the world received a tremendous boost with the founding of the periodical *Die Kriegsschuldfrage* in Germany. Founded by Alfred von Wegerer, scion of a Prussian military family and himself an officer in the German army during the war, the publication was devoted wholly to the task of reversing the Versailles verdict on war guilt. It meant that writers interested in the war-guilt question who had concluded that any country other than Germany was primarily responsible were virtually assured that their articles would be published. In addition, the founding of *Die Kriegsschuldfrage* formalized and made more effective the exchange of information and ideas between European and American revisionists. Among the early American contributors to the journal were Harry Elmer Barnes, Frederick Bausman, and Sidney Fay. In the United States, however, the first real excitement over the revisionist controversy did not come until 1924.

77. *Ibid.*, p. 166.

CHAPTER THREE

The Ascendance of Harry Elmer Barnes, 1924-1926

Nineteen twenty-four was a vintage year for revisionism in the United States. Not only did the year mark the emergence of Harry Elmer Barnes as the great American champion of the revisionist cause, but both cause and champion succeeded in obtaining considerable publicity in the *New York Times*. Beginning with a review article in the *New Republic*, then an article in *American Mercury*, Barnes ultimately took the controversy to the pages of *Current History*, an auxiliary publication of the *New York Times*. Probably because the *Times* was editorially hostile to Barnes's conclusions, *Current History* followed Barnes's article with a symposium on war guilt. The participants in the symposium included several of America's finest historians and a composite of their judgments would indicate how far scholars had moved away from the judgments of the Creel Committee days.

In 1924, Barnes was thirty-five years old, a professor of historical sociology at Smith College. After graduating from Syracuse University as "probably the ablest student and most tireless worker the Dept History has ever graduated,"[1] he went to Columbia University in 1915 to study with Shotwell, Robinson, Giddings, and Dunning. One year later he was awarded Columbia's top prize in history, the William Bayard Cutting Travelling Fellowship. Although the recipient was supposed to study abroad, the World War interfered and Barnes spent the academic year

1. William Harrison Mace, Head, Department of History, Syracuse University, to Columbia Graduate Faculty, February 1, 1915, Barnes MSS.

1916–17 in Cambridge, Massachusetts, studying at Harvard. This, the year of American intervention in the World War, was also the year in which his interest in world affairs bubbled over and led him to make his views public and to break friendships with friends who disagreed with his view of the proper role of the United States in the World War. Years later he would recall,

> In the winter of 1916–1917 and early spring of 1917, while doing research at Harvard University on a Cutting Travelling Fellowship from Columbia University, I was vehemently interventionist.
> At the request of a local newspaper in my old home town of Fort Byron, New York, the *Port Byron Chronicle* edited by L. H. King, a prominent Republican leader of Cayuga County, I wrote a long article recommending immediate intervention in the European War and bitterly criticizing President Wilson for not getting us in the conflict.
> It was published in two parts and was the longest article the paper had printed in a generation. It was as ferocious in content, policy and language as anything contributed [by] any sane person at the time. It nearly matched the statements on the subject being issued by Theodore Roosevelt and George Harvey.
> Shortly afterwards, I wrote a letter to my closest personal friend in the historical guild [Harry J. Carman?], caustically attacking him for going to Washington to argue before members of Congress against our entering the European War.
> In fumbling through my old papers from time to time I come across this *Chronicle* material to my mingled sentiments of shame, embarrassment and amusement.[2]

Although Barnes was not to receive the call from George Creel, he did make several contributions to the wartime propaganda efforts of the National Security League and the American Defense Society. Before the war was over he received his Ph.D. from Columbia, Dunning noting that "his learning and his capacity for turning out masses of good stuff in incredibly short time is the most striking thing that has come to my attention among our students in thirty years."[3] His first job after leaving the nest was as an associate professor of history at Clark University in Worcester, Massachusetts. A year later, at thirty, he moved to

2. Barnes to author, December 31, 1961.
3. William A. Dunning to G. H. Blakeslee, March 19, 1919, Barnes MSS.

The New School for Social Research as a full professor, then returned to Clark with the same rank in the autumn of 1920. In 1923 he left for Smith where he was to remain until 1930.

Shortly after Barnes reached Northampton, a review copy of Columbia Professor Charles Downer Hazen's *Europe since 1815* arrived at the offices of the *New Republic*. The editors, Herbert Croly and Robert Littell, were unhappy about Professor Hazen's treatment of the origins of the war and, for whatever reason, asked Barnes, then professor of historical sociology, to review the book. Barnes hesitated and suggested that the *New Republic* turn instead to Ferdinand Schevill of the University of Chicago, a historian who had acquired a pro-German reputation. But Croly and Littell feared that Schevill's reputation would "lay him open to a great many irrelevant and hasty come-backs." The editors also feared that a review by Schevill would "result in an exchange of hostilities which would have to be conducted in the correspondence columns to the confusion and boredom of everyone."[4]

Barnes continued to hesitate, at least in part because he believed himself a likely candidate to succeed Giddings at Columbia. He worried about the possible adverse effects on his chances if he published a hostile review of a book by another Columbia professor. Finally, he wrote to Carlton Hayes, also of Columbia, and asked Hayes how he would handle it. Hayes advised him not to worry about Nicholas Murray Butler or anyone else: "If I were you, I would say just what I think about any book, even a colleague's book, feeling reasonably certain that my obvious frankness and honesty would commend themselves even to such persons as might have a kindly personal feeling for the author."[5] And so, Barnes put aside caution and began to write.

"Seven Books of History against the Germans,"[6] primarily a review of Hazen's book, marked both the beginning of Barnes's identification with revisionism and the beginning of his effort to take the war-guilt controversy out of the realm of historians and to place it before the public. Some historians, including Hazen

4. R. Littell to Barnes, January 8, 1924, Barnes MSS.

5. Carlton J. H. Hayes to Barnes, February 6, 1924, Barnes MSS.

6. *New Republic*, XXXVIII (March 19, 1924), Part II, pp. 10–15.

and E. Raymond Turner, protested against his conclusions in the *New Republic*, the *Saturday Review*, the *New York Times*, and in other media more popular than scholarly journals. Barnes and his adversaries exchanged public letters, attacking each other heatedly, and the public took notice. Then, as the memoirs of Americans who played prominent roles in the administration in 1916–17 became available, the focus of the controversy gradually shifted from the question of responsibility for the war to one of why America intervened.

2

Barnes sent the review to the *New Republic*, criticizing Hazen on two counts. First, he found it no longer possible to excuse an interpretation of the war origins which placed exclusive responsibility on Germany, although he admitted to having shared this interpretation in 1917. He insisted that it was no longer reasonable to create an image of a demonic Germany and that objectivity in the writing of history had to return from the depths of the war years. Until objectivity returned, he said, "we shall continue to harbor the myths and delusions that were current in 1917–18, will fail to recognize the futility and needlessness of the horrible tragedy of 1914–18, and will be fatally handicapped in any concerted and intelligent effort to prevent a recurrence of such a cataclysm." Second, he ridiculed Hazen for writing of American intervention in terms like "In such a contest as that the United States belonged, body and soul"; or "We entered the war finally because Germany forced us in." In support of his own "revised" attitude, Barnes cited the work of Sidney Fay and of a number of European revisionists.[7]

After reading the article, Littell wrote that he and Croly were "enormously" pleased. Barnes had done more than demolish Hazen: he had posed an "unanswerable challenge to quantities and quantities of people who have just about the impression of the beginnings of the war and the emotionalism which prevents their gaining anything further than an impression, which is the

7. *Ibid.*, pp. 10, 14.

unfortunate possesson of Hazen." Littell extended his thanks and congratulations for a "singularly admirable book review."[8]

H. L. Mencken, editor of the *American Mercury,* was still more delighted with Barnes's work: "Your neat and complete disembowelment of Hazen gave me great joy. He has been one of my favorite asses for years. I believe that he is much read by newspaper editorial writers."[9]

Bausman, too, enjoyed the review. His letter to Barnes, in addition to commenting favorably on Barnes's "castigation" of Hazen's book, warned of the wiles of the enemy. Writing of his own *Let France Explain* he maintained that while he had taken adverse criticism "very good-naturedly," there were one or two reviewers whom he could not forgive. In particular, he warned Barnes to watch out for Bernadotte Schmitt of Western Reserve.[10]

But for Barnes, a duel with Schmitt remained in the future. More immediately, the enemy appeared in the person of Professor E. Raymond Turner of Michigan. Three weeks after the Hazen review the *New Republic* published a letter from Turner, critical of both Barnes and the journal.[11] Turner was unhappy with both the review of Hazen's book and Barnes's review of Turner's own book two years earlier. The sum of his argument was that because Barnes had been mistaken when he had written for the National Security League, this did not necessarily enhance his claim of greater accuracy now that he had reversed himself. Turner also scolded the *New Republic* for publishing, in his judgment, anything favorable to the Germans or discreditable to the Allies.

Barnes's reply, printed with Turner's letter, contended that new evidence appearing since his review of Turner's book in 1922 had made the Turner-Hazen version of the war preposterous. Turner, however, was not to be put off so readily. Until his death in 1929, he remained Barnes's chief antagonist, writing more letters, and generally less moderate ones, opposing Barnes and the revisionist thesis.

In April the *American Mercury* published Barnes's portrait of

8. Littell to Barnes, February 8, 1924, Barnes MSS.

9. Mencken to Barnes, March 19, 1924, Barnes MSS.

10. Bausman to Barnes, May 2, 1924, Barnes MSS.

11. *New Republic,* XXXVIII (April 9, 1924), 184–85.

Woodrow Wilson, an article which Mencken guaranteed would rank Barnes alongside "Judas Iscariot, Doheny, Daugherty, and Bernstorff."[12] Actually, Barnes was most gentle with Wilson, but he absorbed much of the rest of John Kenneth Turner's answer to why the United States intervened. He felt that while Turner's reasons for American intervention might be correct, it could "be safely held" that Wilson was never aware of the influence of the "interests." Barnes agreed that "we did not actually go into the World War to protect ourselves from imminent German invasion, or to make the world safe for democracy, but to protect our investment in Allied bonds, to insure a more extensive development of the manufacture of war materials and to make it possible to deliver our munitions to Allied ports. . . ."[13] The addition of the munitions "interests" to the forces working for war was Barnes's own contribution: Turner, surprisingly enough, had neglected the "bullet manufacturers." In Barnes's brief statement the essence of Senator Norris' speech on April 4, 1917, had been resurrected.

Barnes's criticism of Wilson differed from Turner's in that Barnes accepted Wilsonian idealism at face value and called it utopianism. Wilson's mistake was in believing that permanent peace could be achieved despite the long history of human perverseness, despite a "half-million years of human savagery and hunting pack ferocity." Here Barnes was echoing Becker's thought, questioning Wilson's faith in reason and progress. Wilson, Barnes contended, discovered too late that the "crimes of two thousand years of European diplomatic and military chicanery could not be effaced in a few weeks by the therapeutic influence of fourteen moral principles." Then Wilson tried his hand at diplomacy, "with the results that would normally attend the entrance of a rural clergyman into a poker game on a trans-Atlantic liner."[14] Here was the image of Wilson created by John Maynard Keynes in his *Economic Consequences of the Peace*,[15] the image of a

12. "Woodrow Wilson," *American Mercury*, I (April, 1924), 479–90; Mencken to Barnes, March 19, 1924, Barnes MSS.

13. *American Mercury*, I, 484–85.

14. *Ibid.*, p. 486.

15. New York: Harcourt, Brace and Howe, 1920.

Wilson who could not be "un-bamboozled," an image which seems destined to survive despite the scholarship of men like Paul Birdsall.[16] It was this portrait of Wilson rather than that by Turner that was to prevail in revisionist literature.

Then George Ochs-Oakes, editor of *Current History*, asked Barnes to do an article for him. It was a ticklish situation for Ochs-Oakes, for while he endorsed Barnes's views on the origins of the war without qualification,[17] the parent organization, the *New York Times* did not. Finally it was agreed that Barnes's article would be accompanied by an editorial comment indicating that it was being published as "an enlightening contribution to this serious question," that Barnes was an impartial historian who had reached his conclusions by impartial judgment as a result of "painstaking and thorough investigation," and that Barnes had no German or Austrian connections, no predispositions toward Germany or Austria.

The article, "Assessing the Blame for the World War: A Revised Judgment Based on All the Available Documents," appeared in May.[18] Barnes argued for a multi-causal, divided responsibility interpretation of the war, an interpretation which of itself might not have offended or provoked any well-informed reader. However, his effort to provide a counterweight to wartime theories of the origins of the war meant playing down Germany's role in the events leading to war while the roles of Russia and France were brought to the fore. In particular, the trumpet of German militarism was muted, while militarism in Russia and France was stressed so as to appear worse in these countries than in Germany. This constituted a sharp departure from Fay's work of 1920–21, but, as Barnes would contend, more documents had become available since Fay had written.

Following a pattern established in the Hazen review, Barnes made frequent references to other revisionists in substantiation of his own thesis: Gooch, A. J. Nock, Max Montgelas, Gouttenoire de Toury, Pevet, and S. Stanojevic. In addition, he invoked the

16. See Birdsall's *Versailles: Twenty Years After* (New York: Reynal and Hitchcock, 1941).

17. Ochs-Oakes to Barnes, March 31, 1924, Barnes MSS.

18. *Current History*, XX, 171–95.

names of prominent American historians who had read and approved his work: William Leonard Langer and Bernadotte Everly Schmitt. Schmitt, however, very soon disappointed Barnes as he had disappointed Bausman. With Barnes's final conclusion, disagreement was probably impossible. He contended that "deeper than any national guilt is the responsibility of the wrong-headed and savage European system of nationalism, imperialism, secret diplomacy and militarism which sprang into full bloom from 1879–1914." He insisted that there could be no hope of permanent peace in Europe until there was general recognition that this system had to be attacked through international co-operation and international organizations.[19] Wilson himself could not have been unhappy with this brief analysis of Europe's plight or with the proposed solution.

But other implications of Barnes's article were grasped by Albert Bushnell Hart of Harvard in his dissent, published with Barnes's piece.

As for the United States, he [Barnes] holds, though this is not stated in so many words, that we were deceived, tricked and duped into our stand in the war, principally by France, but also by England and Italy.

Perhaps without so intending, the author denies the honesty of the Allies and the reality of our appeal to justice and humanity. He makes the American people a set of fools who could not penetrate the secret conspiracy between France and Russia to wreck Europe. . . .[20]

Herein lay the real significance of "war-guilt" revisionism for those concerned with American foreign policy. As Hart went on to declare, if Barnes was right, Roosevelt was wrong, Wilson was wrong, all right-thinking Americans who had supported intervention were wrong; and Barnes was not at all unhappy to have the issue so drawn.

After taking editorial cognizance of the Barnes article on May 4, only three days later the *New York Times* devoted its "Topics of the Times" feature to the Barnes-Hazen controversy. The article left little doubt as to where the *Times* stood:

19. *Ibid.*, p. 194.
20. *Ibid.*, p. 195.

Which of the two knows most about the origin of the war is for the experts to decide a hundred years from now. Meanwhile—well, most of us want to agree with Professor Hazen, for several reasons—one of them being that he does not take himself or his subject with the dreadful seriousness shown by his antagonist, and sincerely tries to prove that historians, like other people, can disagree without calling each other fools, madmen and deliberate—mythmongers.[21]

This was the sort of criticism which Barnes faced continually, a sort of criticism which he could not understand and could not tolerate. Unlike the *Times* writer, Barnes saw the war-guilt question and the question of why America intervened as vital questions, questions of importance for decisions on the present and future foreign policies of the United States, of vital importance to those who truly sought world peace. These were crucial questions, and the quest for the truth could not be hampered by indulging in the requisite niceties of the world of gentlemen and scholars.

If the establishment, speaking through the staid *New York Times*, seemed hostile to Barnes, it was clear that the rebels were with him. Mencken had cheered him on with a personal letter after Croly had published the Hazen review, and Villard supported him with an editorial, "Historians and the Truth." Beginning with "Three cheers for Harry Elmer Barnes," the editorial contained ecstatic praise for the *Current History* article as well as for the Hazen review. The *Nation* took special delight in celebrating "Professor Barnes's smashing of the taboo laid upon historians not to criticize one another."[22] To be sure, if the "taboo" ever existed, Barnes showed little awareness of it.

For a young historian to be in with and praised by the editors of the three periodicals that were in the forefront of the fight against "Main Street" and "Normalcy" was indeed a worthy accomplishment.[23] Additionally, acclaim came from prominent and respected members of the academic world. His friend and sometime colleague, William Langer of Clark University, was "gratified" by the Hazen review: "I . . . hope this roast will act as a

21. *New York Times,* May 4, 1924, Sec. II, p. 6; May 7, 1924, p. 20.

22. *Nation,* CXVIII (May 21, 1924), 576.

23. One might see Barnes as the Arthur Schlesinger, Jr., of the 1920's.

healthy deterrent to others. Teachers ought to protest against such misrepresentation of the facts." George Blakeslee, also of Clark, was pleased by "your thumping and pounding of Hazen's last book. Good for you. He deserves it." Blakeslee's approval of the *Current History* article was, however, more cautious, stressing the advances to ensue as a result of the renewed discussion of the origins of the war. Edwin Borchard of Yale sent congratulations for both the Hazen controversy and the *Current History* article: "You are performing a very noteworthy service in the interests of scholarship and truth." Arthur Schlesinger of Iowa University wrote that the "honors of combat" were with Barnes in the *New Republic* exchanges, adding: "I have not yet read your summarization in *Current History* but I have had rare delight in reading Hart's masterful rebuttal. With all due respect to your polemic ability, I should say that Hart's rejoinder is the best argument that has been yet adduced in favor of your position." For Barnes, perhaps the most satisfying letter came from Charles Beard, who was also pleased by the reviews and articles:

> You delivered terrific blows at the old fiction and came out with flying colors. I am sorry that you were so savage with Hazen, but still his offense against decency was great. It is better to be too savage than a lily-livered creeper around the throne of the great gods in the American Historical Association. Go to it my boy, you have the brains and the drive and you will bust old follies along the line; but subdue your wild steed a bit.[24]

In its June issue, *Current History* contained a symposium on Barnes's article.[25] The participants, including several of the most renowned historians in the United States, were Professors Charles Seymour of Yale, Raymond Leslie Buell of Harvard, William E. Lingelbach of Pennsylvania, A. E. Morse of Princeton, Carl Becker of Cornell, Quincy Wright of Chicago, Lucy M. Salmon of Vassar, G. H. Blakeslee of Clark, Frank Maloy Anderson of Dartmouth, and Bernadotte Schmitt of Western Reserve. While Morse insisted that only a German could be convinced by Barnes's argument, and

24. Langer to Barnes, February 10, 1924; Blakeslee to Barnes, March 31, 1924, May 8, 1924; Borchard to Barnes, May 7, 1924; Arthur Schlesinger, Sr., to Barnes, May 9, 1924; Beard to Barnes, June 28, 1924, Barnes MSS.

25. *Current History,* XX, 452–62.

Anderson suspected Barnes of being anti-French, all except Morse accepted the divided responsibility verdict; Lingelbach seemed unprepared to commit himself, but Seymour, Wright, Blakeslee, and Anderson questioned the "order" of responsibility proposed by Barnes, which at this time ran Austria, Russia, France, Germany, England in descending order of guilt. Schmitt, whom Barnes had originally cited as an authority who had read and approved his article, asserted that several of Barnes's interpretations were inaccurate and dissented from some of his judgments. Buell, who had written to Barnes in April, reporting that he was "gleefully" following Barnes's reviews and fights with Turner, and had announced that he was "thoroughly" with Barnes in the attack on the "Hazen school of historians,"[26] now argued that there was no point in castigating Allied wickedness: war guilt was a question of the past. Now all efforts should be channeled into support of the League of Nations, that Wilson's hopes for peace might be fulfilled.

Salmon and Becker, on the other hand, went all the way with Barnes. Professor Salmon, whose graduate work at Bryn Mawr had been directed by Woodrow Wilson, indicated her conviction that the truth "assuredly lies in the direction pointed out by Professor Barnes." Becker could not find any "material point" on which he disagreed with Barnes. In Blakeslee, Barnes struck the same chord he had touched in Professor Hart—a concern for the implications of the war-guilt controversy upon attitudes toward American intervention. Blakeslee wrote: "The fact that Germany does not bear sole guilt for starting the world conflict can scarcely affect the justice of America's entrance into the war three years later. The United States took up arms against Germany because of what Germany did after the war began."[27] It was, however, Carl Becker who provided, perhaps cynically, a different sort of insight into the budding controversy. More detached than the others, Olympian, Becker suggested that all the weighing of responsibility in which the others indulged really involved the values of those passing judgment. By way of illustration, he wrote:

26. Buell to Barnes, April 16, 1924, Barnes MSS.

27. *Current History,* XX, 459.

Sixty years after the French Revolution, Cobden wrote a long pamphlet proving that, contrary to the accepted opinion among his countrymen, England rather than France was "responsible" for the war of 1793. Everyone who was already of Cobden's opinion judged his pamphlet to be a masterly performance. I am sure Professor Barnes's article will be as widely acclaimed in this country.[28]

3

The friction over the war debts continued to make Americans susceptible to Barnes's opinion. Even the *Nation*, generally reflecting a relatively mild distemper, grew fierce in January and February of 1925. Referring back to when Germany paid for the cost of the postwar occupation, it was noted that "in distributing the billion, the Allies 'overlooked' the United States and calmly pocketed our share." But, as usual, it was France in particular that the editors were after. They were annoyed by the French suggestion that we put France's dead and wounded in the balance and felt that there were a couple of things the French should know:

> First, that the money which our Government lent to the French was not dug out of a gold mine—it is being repaid to the Government by the American taxpayers today. Second, that America was not threatened by Germany as was France, nor did our Government play such a provocative part in the pre-war machinations of Europe as did Messrs. Poincaré and Delcassé. We entered the war when the Allies' fortunes were at low ebb, and turned the scale; when the war was over we asked no colonial compensations or indemnities. . . .[29]

And so revisionism and the war-debts controversy seemed to feed each other. Angered by the Allied attitude toward their debts, many Americans were prepared to believe the worst of the French or British—prepared to accept revisionism. On the other hand, the revisionist contentions provided marvelous fuel for those determined to put the heat on the debtor nations. As long as the two were linked there was little chance of a change in American atti-

28. *Ibid.*, p. 456.
29. *Nation,* CXX (January 28, 1925), 85; (February 4, 1925), 105.

tude toward debt collection, little chance for a change in American policy.

After a lull of several months, Barnes created another stir. In March, 1925, he gave a talk on "Disarmament and Security" in which he continued to discuss world politics in Wilsonian terms. He contended that disarmament was in itself of no particular significance, that some form of collective security would likely be more "constructive and salutary." Eventually, of course, he came to the matter of war guilt and announced that he had been forced, by new evidence, to modify the conclusions of his *Current History* article; he now found that France and Russia were tied for first place in his responsibility scale. At this point in his talk, a bit of commotion occurred. There was in his audience a Frenchwoman, a Professor Marguerite Clement of the University of Paris. Professor Clement leaped to her feet to oppose Barnes's conclusions. The Germans had raped French girls, and while she apparently numbered herself among the unraped, she had seen enough to be indignant about any suggestion that the French were worse than the Germans. Barnes might have preferred to debate Hazen or Turner, but the choice was not his. While the audience cheered and hissed, an argument ensued between Barnes and the Frenchwoman. Just before the meeting broke up, a new antagonist, Professor Alfred L. P. Dennis of Clark, rose and pronounced Barnes's statements to be "rubbish."[30] Although Dennis participated briefly in the public discussion of Barnes's work, his ablest thrust came in a letter to Barnes. Barnes had written to Dennis, chiding him for the diplomatic language he had employed in contesting Barnes's conclusions. Dennis replied by complaining about the mild tone of Barnes's letter:

> If one desires to be notorious, one naturally prefers to be malodorous than not to smell at all. I hope, therefore, for my own satisfaction that you will be good enough to respond to this letter by a more sincere and studied effort. Be virile, be boorish, be ruffianly but above all avoid the gaucherie of imitating the style and manners of a gentleman. In other words, so far as you consistently can, as one of the great brood of little henry menckens, be yourself.[31]

30. *New York Times,* March 15, 1925, p. 6.
31. Dennis to Barnes, June 4, 1925, Barnes MSS.

In the May issue of *American Mercury*, Barnes put his revised order of war guilt into print.[32] Simeon Strunsky, editorial writer for the *New York Times*, was both irritated and amused by this new effort:

> This revision is all the more striking because it is contained in an article entitled "The New History." It was the vice of the old method of writing history that it concentrated "primarily upon trivial personal anecdotes, party intrigues and diplomatic chicanery" against which J. R. Green, Rambaud, and McMaster were among the first to rebel. Yet the startling thing about Professor Barnes's analysis of the problem of war guilt is that it concentrates precisely on the diplomatic "chicanery" of which the old history was so fond. . . .[33]

It would have been difficult to counter Strunsky's complaint, and Barnes, in replying, did little more than note that he had read the "able and good-natured editorial."[34] Strunsky had, however, noted something which suggests why Barnes's insistence that revisionism was a digression from the main stream of his historical writing conflicts with the view of so many later students who identify him almost exclusively with revisionism. In much of his historical writing after 1925, Barnes would eventually reach a discussion of the origins of the war and present the conclusions of the extreme revisionists. Even his *History of Historical Writing* was to contain an attack on the "epic mongers."[35]

The editors of the *Nation* kept pace with Barnes, viewing the battle as part of the effort of all right-thinking men to oppose the American Legion, the Ku Klux Klan, and the DAR. General Robert L. Bullard was overheard suggesting the likelihood of French atrocities during the World War and the *Nation* warned that the general would be lucky if he did not bring down upon himself the "wrath of the Daughters of the American Revolution and all our other patriotic societies." A few weeks later, the *Nation* celebrated its sixtieth anniversary and Mencken pointed up the journal's

32. "The New History," *American Mercury*, V, 68–76.

33. Unsigned editorial, *New York Times*, May 3, 1925, Sec. II, p. 4. Strunsky was identified by John B. Oakes, editor of the editorial page, *New York Times*, in a letter to the author, November 28, 1961.

34. Letter to the Editor, *New York Times*, May 9, 1925, p. 14.

35. Norman, Okla.: University of Oklahoma Press, 1937.

leadership in the good fight: "Is the Creel Press Bureau theory of the war abandoned? Is it possible to find an educated man today who is not ashamed that he succumbed to the Wilson buncombe? Then thank the *Nation* for that deliverance."[36] Implicit in these statements was first the idea that anyone who opposed revisionism was siding with the patrioteers, and second, that he was a Main Streeter, a buncombe-swallowing member of the "boobocracy." Here was *one* reason why few historians took up the challenge presented by Barnes—why few historians opposed revisionism. So long as Barnes and the other revisionists were sponsored by the journals of the intellectual elite and opposed by organizations that were anathema to other intellectuals, that very alignment virtually guaranteed the revisionists against open attacks from those best able to cope with them.

In August the *Times* ran an editorial entitled "Simple-Simon Psychology" which was essentially a severe criticism of Barnes's *New History and the Social Studies.*[37] When replying, Barnes took advantage of the opportunity to stir the revisionist controversy. He graciously conceded the kind treatment accorded him by the *Times* and *Current History* over the previous two years and denied any feelings of resentment "over your amusing yourself at my expense." He professed that he would be able to "bear with complacency the prospect that Charles Downer Hazen and Alfred P. Dennis may write you congratulatory letters." Finally, he declared the edtorial to be the product of a cultivated mind, "not obviously the achievement of a literary thug, as has too often seemed true of your most respectable metropolitan competitor."[38] Here was a way to arouse public interest in revisionism. It took two sides to have a controversy and Barnes had to have enemies to keep the controversy going. Whatever else may have been said about Barnes, he knew how to goad his opponents. Once criticize Barnes and one might be involved in the debate for life—and after.

In October, 1925, Barnes began a series of articles in *Christian Century* under the general title, "Was America Deluded by the

---

36. *Nation*, CXX (June 10, 1925), 641; *Baltimore Evening Sun*, July 6, 1925 (reprinted in *Nation*, CXXI [July 22, 1925], 130).

37. *New York Times*, August 2, 1925, Sec. II, p. 4.

38. *Ibid.*, August 6, 1925, p. 18.

War?" By way of introduction, an editorial declared: "Among
American scholars, Professor Barnes has taken front place not only
for his objective mastery of the data but for his courage in giving
forth the truth to which the data points."[39]

The series ran to eleven articles, and in them, Barnes's conclusions became more extreme than ever before. In 1922 he had argued that responsibility for the war was divided. By 1924, although
he still held Austria primarily responsible, he had moved France and
Russia ahead of Germany in his guilt scale. Earlier in 1925 he had
concluded that France and Russia were tied for first place, but now
he suggested that France and Russia were *solely* responsible for
the war. He declared that he realized it would be easier to convince
people of divided responsibility than to prove to them the sole responsibility of France and Russia, "but the writer is not running
for Congress on the issue of war-guilt." He claimed that his only
interest was in advancing the cause of truth and that he believed
it would be better to make slow progress in this cause than to be
"quickly successful in disseminating a benign influence."[40]

In reaching this conclusion he maintained that it was impossible
for any "honest and unbiased" student of the existing documents
to deny that the German civil government did not will war in
1914, but opposed it; nor could any "fair-minded" student deny
that Germany possessed better reasons than any other major European power for desiring a large army for protection. And Barnes
found that it was "perfectly clear" that the Kaiser did not desire
a European war. If one recognized that the German civil government had lost control of the military, that German ambitions relative to the *status quo ante bellum* were greater than those of the
"have" powers, that the Kaiser would gladly have achieved any
of his ends diplomatically rather than militarily, then Barnes's argument, while not exonerating Germany, was probably valid. In
fact, Barnes never actually contended that Germany was wholly
guiltless. This was what Becker would call Barnes's "sledge hammer" approach: offering an extreme thesis to catch the public eye,

39. "Professor Barnes on War Origins," *Christian Century*, XLII (October
8, 1925), 1231.

40. "Russia and France Start the War," *Christian Century*, XLII (November 5, 1925), 1375.

making frequent overstatements that seemed ridiculous out of context, but which were in fact qualified by the text as a whole. If for a historian this technique was reprehensible, for a publicist avowedly concerned with arousing public interest it was undoubtedly invaluable.

By the time Barnes turned to the question of "Why America Entered the War,"[41] there was little doubt that he would conclude that intervention had been a terrible mistake. While the reasons for intervention were admittedly complex, they were not incomprehensible. Earlier,[42] he had noted that the willingness of the United States to intervene "was considerably enhanced by the American jealousy of German commercial and industrial expansion." Now he went on to declare that he was himself "no fervent believer in the universal validity of the economic interpretation of history," nor would he guarantee the correctness of recent attempts to demonstrate that the United States intervened solely on behalf of American financial interests in the Allies, *but* "unquestionably from 1915–1918 the enormous power of American finance and industry was directed almost solely toward the defense of the allied powers and the support of their subtle propaganda."[43]

In terms of individual responsibility, Barnes singled out Walter Hines Page as the number one culprit. Asking himself why Wilson had not put a stop to British "lawlessness" at sea, Barnes maintained that the most powerful influence had been, "unquestionably," the "virulent pro-English attitude of Ambassador Page. . . . If we had possessed at London a competent, fair-minded and judicious ambassador the story of American foreign policy from 1914–1919 would have been far different from what it was."[44] Unlike most other revisionists, Barnes was even critical of William Jennings Bryan and condemned Bryan for the pacifism "which made him opposed to strong and vigorous language in our protests to England."

Barnes concerned himself briefly with the influence of Allied propaganda, but unlike others similarly concerned, he generally

41. *Christian Century,* XLII (November 19, 1925), 1441–44.
42. "Germany and Europe, 1870–1914," *Christian Century,* XLII, 1239.
43. "Why America Entered the War," *Christian Century,* XLII, 1443.
44. *Ibid.,* p. 1441.

stressed the reasons why Americans, particularly President Wilson, were receptive to this propaganda. He argued that Wilson knew and cared little about the culture of any European country other than England: "All of his great heroes in literature and political science were English authors." Barnes did, however, find that Allied propaganda prevented Americans from understanding the German mind in 1916 and 1917 and kept from Americans any "adequate knowledge of the very real desire for peace in Germany at this time."

Continuing his analysis of Wilson's shift from "far-sighted neutral" to "vigorous partisan of the allied propaganda," Barnes brought to bear the tools of the social sciences. Demonstrating a manner in which the historian might use some knowledge of psychology, he referred to "the matter of his [Wilson's] courtship and his marriage with the second Mrs. Wilson. The psychology of the long-suffering pacifist is not well adapted to the conventional behavior pattern, attitudes and techniques of the suitor and bridegroom."[45] Once again Barnes had used an approach that would inevitably appall historians, but as an attention-getting device, the coincidence of Wilson's courtship and his shift to advocacy of preparedness provided a delightful ploy. Then Barnes turned to Wilson's "vanity" and concluded that there was no doubt that it had been enormously inflated by the popularity of his tour on behalf of preparedness late in 1915. He claimed that there were many who argued that Wilson's decision was affected by the conviction that he could assume world leadership only if he led the United States into the war. And in Wilson's actions in the spring of 1916 and after, Barnes found evidence which lent "much plausibility to this hypothesis."[46]

Barnes then contended that if Wilson had replaced Page with an "honest, courageous and legally-minded" ambassador, and had observed "strict neutrality," the war would have ended by December, 1916, followed by a peace treaty "infinitely superior in every way" to the Treaty of Versailles. In support of this contention he wrote of the very real desire for peace in Germany, of the "highly reasonable and statesmanlike" nature of German peace overtures,

45. *Ibid.*, p. 1443.
46. *Ibid.*, p. 1444.

peace overtures which included terms more to the advantage of the world than those subsequently imposed at Versailles. In sum, Barnes had reversed his position of 1916–17; now he accepted many German contentions at face value and scoffed at all Entente contentions. Following this reversal it was only logical for him to conclude: "If we honestly face the facts we shall probably have to agree that the entry of the United States into the world war was an almost unmitigated disaster, not only to us but to Europe."[47]

If Barnes the revisionist was Barnes the publicist rather than the historian, what was his cause? In 1925 at least, it was not revisionism per se. His effort to "Liquidate War Time Illusions" was not simply an effort to get at the "truth," the historical "facts" regarding the origins of the war, but an attempt to influence foreign policy on two counts. First,

> the guilt for the world war having been distributed, the expense of indemnifying the sufferers should likewise be distributed. The United States might well use its undoubted financial power to induce France and England . . . to forego all notion of any reparations from Germany and to adopt the program of a mutual sharing with Germany of the burdens of reconstruction and rehabilitation. The United States could with great propriety indicate its goodwill and intentions in the circumstances by cancelling the debts of the European powers on the above condition.[48]

This program for getting Europe out of the morass of unpaid war debts and reparations may have been utopian; it may well have been the program of a man who had become pro-German. But there was hardly anything sinister about either program or advocate, and it would seem likely that efforts along the lines indicated by Barnes would have been more salutary than the efforts to reconstruct Europe which were based upon the war-guilt clause.

Secondly, Barnes was attacking the concept of the "just" war— war in which the masses are taught that it is less sinful to kill when one is fighting to make the world safe for democracy or to create a world in which peace will be perpetual if only the evil present in the enemy is first expunged. Here was Barnes the convert, a man

47. *Ibid.*

48. "The Revisionist Viewpoint Corroborated," *Christian Century*, XLII (November 26, 1925), 1478.

who had so very recently called shrilly for a holy war, seeking in the same flamboyant manner for personal expiation.

If we can but understand how totally and terribly we were "taken in" between 1914 and 1918 by the salesmen of this most holy and idealistic world conflict, we shall be the better prepared to be on our guard against the seductive lies and deceptions which will be put forward by similar groups when urging the necessity of another world catastrophe in order to "crush militarism," "make the world safe for democracy," "put an end to all further wars," etc.[49]

In November, the editors of the *Christian Century* asked their readers to nominate a historian to reply to Barnes. Ultimately, the readers nominated over three hundred scholars, statesmen, and churchmen. The names of the top twelve candidates were then placed on a cut-out ballot for a final selection by the readers. The twelve were Frank Malloy Anderson of Dartmouth, Carl Becker of Cornell, Charles Seymour and Edwin Borchard of Yale, Herbert Adams Gibbons of the Army War College, Albert Bushnell Hart of Harvard, Carlton Hayes and Charles Downer Hazen of Columbia, James Shotwell, Director of the Carnegie Endowment for International Peace, Frank Simonds, journalist, Ferdinand Schevill of Chicago, and Barnes's good friend, E. Raymond Turner, then of Michigan. In January, 1926, however, the editors announced that they had sent successive invitations to the eight with the highest vote, but all had declined. Subsequently, the remaining four, including Becker, also declined. For various reasons no one attempted to refute Barnes's conclusions.[50]

The reasons for Becker's refusal to criticize Barnes's articles came out in a letter he wrote to Barnes shortly thereafter: "I was in *essential* agreement. I am, so far as the brute facts are concerned and that means that it is no longer possible to lay upon

49. "Liquidating War Time Illusions," *Christian Century*, XLII (December 3, 1925), 1506.

50. In a letter to Barnes, February 19, 1926, Borchard wrote that he had declined on the basis of his belief that Barnes's interpretation was "probably substantially correct." E. Raymond Turner refused, declaring: "I do not think any historian of established reputation will much care to compete with the sensationalist effusions of this writer." Quoted in a letter from C. C. Morrison, editor of the *Christian Century*, to Barnes, February 3, 1926, Barnes MSS.

Germany the responsibility for the war." Becker then proceeded to indicate where he differed from Barnes, and in so doing, indicated again his loss of faith in both the enlightenment view of man and in appeals to reason.

> Where I differ from you is in this: you are inclined to believe that some special persons are criminally responsible in somewhat the same sense that a man is criminally responsible when he commits a murder for personal advantage, and you are inclined . . . to think that by exposing the criminals the world can be enlightened and induced to take a radically different attitude towards wars. I on the other hand can't see either of these things. . . . You said yourself here that Poincare et al no doubt were or thought of themselves as being honest, highminded gentlemen who were doing their duties to their countries and therefore to the H. Race— and that if we were in their positions with their training and traditions we would doubtless have done as they did. That is exactly what I think . . . if that is the case I don't quite see how they can be held responsible in the sense in which you hold them so.[51]

Here was Becker outdoing Barnes in an endorsement of environmental determinism, relieving man, the subject of history, from both responsibility for his acts and the dignity of rational choice.

Becker was also underlining a contradiction or dualism in Barnes's *Weltanschauung*—a dualism which pervaded almost all of Barnes's work. Barnes was at once a firm believer in environmental determinism and a believer in the rationality of man, the ability of man to make choices. Again and again in his revisionist writings he would refer to the need for a new kind of "conditioning," a change in man's environment which would remove tendencies toward war. And in the same articles and books he would single out the individuals who were "responsible" for the war or for American intervention. Becker alone raised the question of how Barnes could in one sentence maintain that a man's actions were determined by his training and the traditions of his country and in the next sentence hold that man "criminally responsible" for the war. In Barnes's hands, then, revisionism was an appeal to reason by a man whose faith in reason was sometimes limited. Ultimately, the contradiction appears to have been resolved by a kind of elitist

51. Becker to Barnes, February 21, 1926, Barnes MSS.

thought: those who accepted the revisionist thesis were capable of being rational; the other poor creatures remained victims of their environment.

4

During the winter of 1925–26, James T. Shotwell, under whom Barnes had studied at Columbia, brooded about his former student. Shotwell's sympathies were not with Barnes in the revisionist controversy, but his main concern seemed to be with what he feared was the failure of his own teaching about historical method. And so, as all teachers should, Shotwell wrote a kindly letter of advice to the younger man, apologizing for sounding like an old professor talking to a graduate student:

> Your attitude in estimating that you have the truth in this matter seems to me . . . not like the statement of an historian but more like the controversial assertions which one can find in the theological controversies of the 16th and 17th centuries. Feeling strongly as you do, it has, I regret to say, led to a certain carelessness in your method of dealing with facts. . . . Speaking strictly from the historical standpoint, I find a number of fallacies in technique in your method of dealing with the data before us. . . .[52]

No one could reasonably challenge the adequacy of the training to which Barnes had been exposed at Columbia and at Harvard; probably it was the best training available to a young historian in the second decade of the twentieth century. But the implication of Shotwell's letter was that credentials were no substitute for performance: once Barnes had met Shotwell's standards and presumably he could meet them again at will. Despite mounting criticism from his colleagues, however, he stayed with his "sledge hammer" approach.

While Barnes was achieving a degree of fame in some circles— and notoriety in others—Alfred Knopf, the publisher, asked him to rewrite the *Christian Century* articles for publication in a single volume. The result was *Genesis of the World War* which appeared in the summer of 1926. In his preface, Barnes argued that the problem of war responsibility was not an "esoteric matter of erudite historical scholarship" but one of the "livest and most impor-

52. Shotwell to Barnes, February 18, 1926, Barnes MSS.

tant practical issues of the present day." Unhappy about the existing conditions in Europe and in the world, he blamed the "unfair
and unjust" peace treaty which he contended had been based upon
an "uncritical and complete acceptance of the grossest forms of war
time illusions." The study of war guilt would, he maintained, aid in
understanding and preventing war. Again he launched an attack
upon the concept of a just war. Once he had believed, but now he
would know better—listen to the confessed sinner, "learn the great
lesson here embodied" and "we shall have a powerful argument
with which to meet the propaganda of those who will announce the
necessity and idealism of the next war."[53]

The text of *Genesis* differed from the *Christian Century* articles
primarily in tone. The book was apparently written for a less
learned audience and filled with the sort of hyperbolic statements
one might hope would appeal to the public. For example, early in a
chapter devoted to blaming France for the war, he declared:
"There is little if anything to follow in this chapter to which any
honest and informed Frenchman out of political life would not
subscribe."[54] Moving from hyperbole to fantasy, Barnes repeated
a story attributed to the wartime Chief of the Intelligence Division of the British General Staff. This officer had boasted of switch-
ing the title of a picture of a trainload of dead German horses being
taken to a fertilizer plant to a picture of dead German soldiers being taken to the rear. Allegedly, the picture was then circulated in
China where the ancestor-worshipping Chinese were outraged by
this evidence of German desecration of the dead. Barnes then swal-
lowed years of sophistication and declared that the photograph
"had a great deal of influence in inducing the Chinese to enter the
World War on the side of the Allies."[55] Obviously, this book was
not meant to be a contribution in the form of "erudite historical
scholarship."

In his discussion of American intervention Barnes contended
that John Kenneth Turner's *Shall It Be Again?* was, "in spite of
its animus and bias," the ablest book written on the subject. While
Barnes's treatment of Wilson was not as hostile as Turner's, he

53. *Genesis of the World War* (New York: Knopf, 1926), p. xii.
54. *Ibid.*, p. 399.
55. *Ibid.*, p. 293.

did appear to be moving closer to the Turner image of Wilson. On the one hand Barnes believed that Wilson was "a man who loved peace but was drawn into war by a false conception of the facts and issues involved. There is no doubt that he was a pacifist at heart, but he viewed the conflict as one in which England was upholding the cause of civilization."[56] Here was Wilson portrayed as a well-meaning but mistaken man who believed that the United States would have to intervene if England could not otherwise win the war. But on the next page Barnes wrote of another Wilson —of a Wilson who was as determined as Roosevelt was to enter the conflict. But Wilson was more subtle, more skilful than Roosevelt in mustering popular support for intervention. He succeeded in giving the country the impression that he was "a long-suffering and much abused pacifist who had resolutely stood out against war until no other alternative presented itself."[57] Once having discovered the hypocritical Wilson, Barnes then concluded that Bryan's work to get Wilson the Democratic nomination in 1912 was Bryan's most tragic achievement: Champ Clark would never have taken the country into war. Then came the claim that Wilson had decided in favor of intervention "by the close of 1915." Thus the resumption by the Germans of submarine warfare provided merely an excuse, for Wilson "secretly conveyed to England his intention to enter the war on the side of the Entente nearly a year before . . . if Germany would not accept terms of peace which only a conquered state could be expected to accept."[58]

Carl Becker regarded *Genesis* as the most effective presentation of the revisionist case, "a marvelously straight, swift, cogent presentation of facts and conclusions." He suspected that Barnes had oversimplified the psychology of Poincaré and Grey, but concluded that "substantially the fundamentals are right, and this simplification will do no harm since without it you could not get the attention of many readers."[59]

Although *Christian Century* had been unable to get Ferdinand Schevill to reply to Barnes's articles, the editors were successful

56. *Ibid.*, p. 614.
57. *Ibid.*, p. 615.
58. *Ibid.*, p. 658.
59. Becker to Barnes, undated, Barnes MSS.

in their effort to get him to review *Genesis*.[60] As is often the case
with reviews, the reader was given perhaps more insight into the
mind of the reviewer than into the book being reviewed. Schevill
portrayed Barnes as a human gadfly, stinging the "sluggish conscience of his countrymen." He noted that in academic circles,
"supposed to be partial to enlightenment," Barnes was considered
"a good deal of a nuisance." But Barnes had to become a gadfly,
partly because "he feels the strong urge of the convert." Schevill
also noted that Barnes was, with James Harvey Robinson, "a
leading exponent of that new doctrine of salvation loosely com-
prehended by the term 'social intelligence.' "

> Not only was he in his capacity as a scholar prompted to revise
> his erring views but also, because of his long established faith in
> the directive role in human affairs of the enlightened mind, he was
> fairly impelled insistently to raise his voice against a mass of ab-
> surdities and falsehoods which helplessly poisoned the interna-
> tional situation and paralyzed and would indefinitely continue to
> paralyze every program and movement looking toward a more
> gracious order of society than the one we have on our hands.[61]

This insight into Barnes's mind may not have been as astute as
Becker's was, but Professor Schevill's position in the revisionist
controversy was readily apparent.

He went on to note that the book had not been written for
scholars, that "dry-as-dust scholars will not fail to complain that
the book lacks that air of frozen detachment which is their fetish
except when under the illicit inspiration of other idols they grind
out wisdom for Mr. Creel's bureau of information."[62] Barnes's
dismissal of the charges of German responsibility for the war did
not impress Schevill: this was no longer original. Barnes was merely
associating himself with all other serious scholars concerned with
the origins of the war: "In short, there are today among reputable
historians only revisionists."

Finally, Schevill placed Barnes at the head of the "radical revisionists," men who rejected the thesis of divided responsibility

60. "Professor Barnes on War Guilt," *Christian Century*, XLIII (June 17,
1926), 778–80.

61. *Ibid.*, p. 778.

62. *Ibid.*

and placed full responsibility for the war on the shoulders of the French and the Russians. Examining this "radical" thesis, Schevill found that the case presented by Barnes "must in all its essential features be held as proved."

W. J. Ghent, writing in Theodore Roosevelt's old organ, *Outlook*, reacted rather differently than Schevill had. His outrage was given voice in an article entitled "Menckenized History."[63] Barnes, he claimed with some justice, had used every trick and device common to the jury lawyer. No good could come of this—but wait, "perhaps one happy outcome will be the arousing of the timid or somnolent historians who have left this subject almost wholly in the hands of the 'revisionists.'" Ghent complained that the revisionists, supported by the "parlor radicals," had succeeded by "noise, aggression and concert of action" in intimidating the opposition. Then he astutely called attention to the place of revisionism in the intellectual currents of the twenties: "Vociferous and sweeping denunciation of existing beliefs, customs, standards, and institutions is the current mode, and 'revisionism' is merely one of its phases."[64] Ghent's insight was still another indication of the basis of the success of the revisionists in the 1920's. Those Americans who because of pro-German sympathies, antipathy to one or more of the Allies, pacifism, or other reasons had opposed intervention were easily "won over" to the conclusions of the revisionists. And for the young intellectual seeking to distinguish himself from the masses, to become a "little henry mencken," revisionism provided one answer. The close ties between Barnes and Mencken, between revisionism and the *American Mercury* had, then, significance beyond the fact that all concerned appeared to be Germanophile. If the popularity of the *American Mercury* during the 1920's is recognized as an indication of the alienation of many intellectuals from American society during those years, revisionism was a weapon used against that society. What better way could there have been for the younger generation to undermine the pretensions of the previous generation than by demonstrating that the cause for which their elders had been willing to fight and die had been worthless, a fiction created by "myth-

63. *Outlook*, CXLIII (July 28, 1926), 286–90.
64. *Ibid.*, p. 286.

mongers." Men who had been so easily, so readily deceived, could hardly be trusted to establish the values, the standards of the country.

The reviewer for the *New Republic*, G. Lowes Dickinson, grumbled a bit about propaganda and counterpropaganda, noting that "both alike travesty that cold gray fact which is the truth."[65] But Dickinson also declared that he did not wish to pick a quarrel with Professor Barnes, for he considered Barnes "one of those to whom we are indebted for dispelling the myth" of Germany's sole responsibility for the war.

The editors of the *Nation* tipped their hands by asking Frederick Bausman to review *Genesis*. Bausman noted that opinion had changed since he had written *Let France Explain* and been unable to publish it in the United States. For the change he credited Barnes's "brave attacks." Privately, he worried Barnes, voicing his suspicions as to Knopf's reasons for publishing *Genesis* in such a cheap-appearing volume.[66]

In a review article for *Current History*, Charles Beard drew the limits of his own adherence to revisionism.[67] He felt that Barnes had made a real contribution to the study of the origins of the war, that one could not read *Genesis* without agreeing that the war-guilt clause was an erroneous verdict. He refused, however, to accept Barnes's thesis with respect to American intervention. The crucial difference was that to Beard the question of who would be morally or legally condemned for starting the war was irrelevant. What was relevant was the significance of the war's outcome for the United States. Beard might have changed his mind about Germany's role in starting the war, but this had not seriously modified his contempt for Germany. He indicated no doubt whatever but that a triumphant Germany "astride" Europe would not have paused long before going after the United States. He took issue, also, with Barnes's treatment of Wilson and particularly with his acceptance of the story of the "Sunrise

65. *New Republic,* XLVII (July 28, 1926), 284–85.

66. *Nation,* CXXIII (September 1, 1926), 198; Bausman to Barnes, November 8, 1926, Barnes MSS.

67. "Heroes and Villains of the World War," *Current History,* XXIV (August, 1926), 730–35.

Conference" when Wilson had allegedly tried to get Democratic congressional leaders to endorse intervention. It was upon Wilson's role at this conference, supposedly held early in 1916, that Barnes had based his belief that Wilson's pacific attitude in the election of 1916 was hypocritical. Beard also disagreed with Barnes's interpretation of the House-Grey memorandum, stressing the fact that the American commitment to intervene, as indicated in the memorandum, was contingent upon German acts and was further qualified by Wilson's insertion of the word "probably": the United States would "probably" intervene if Germany acted in a specified manner. To Beard, this was not commitment enough to support a claim that the memorandum indicated that the decision to intervene had been made.

Beard's conclusions were essentially in the realm of *Realpolitik:* "It is decidedly the interest of the United States to help prevent the rise of any European power to a dominant position." If American intervention had resulted in an Entente victory followed by a situation in which the Entente allies were at each others' throats, the results were salutary. The Entente victory was desirable, not because the Entente powers were good and the Central Powers bad, but because the Entente victory prevented the emergence of one dominant power. Americans "should regard with cold blood all the quarrels of Europe." This was not a call for an "isolationist" or "non-interventionist" foreign policy, but for a policy based on national interest rather than on sympathies.

Beard's article brought into sharp relief the attitudes of Barnes toward world politics and toward the role of the United States in world affairs. Though the two men would one day join forces in the fight against American intervention in another war, there would never be agreement in their approaches to problems of foreign policy. Barnes never renounced idealism as a basis for foreign policy. He remained committed to Wilsonian ideas of internationalism until the day when being an "internationalist" meant advocating intervention in another war. His argument with regard to World War I was essentially legalistic and moralistic. The Entente had not been pure: its case was not morally and legally perfect; its cause was not idealistic. A crusade on behalf of the likes of Grey, Poincaré, and Izvolsky was necessarily a false crusade, a hoax. Regardless of whether or not America gained by intervening, it had been morally wrong to do so. Similarly, to have advocated intervention in an unjust cause was morally wrong. Barnes himself sought salvation through revisionism, a process of exorcising his own guilt by shining a spotlight on those who had played a more significant role in the steps leading to war and to American intervention.

Unlike Beard, Barnes did not see the likelihood of Germany posing a threat to the United States. Once, to be sure, he had seen and written of such a threat, but soon after the war, for whatever reasons, he came to feel that the threat had not existed. For Beard, such a conclusion would probably have sufficed to end all thought of intervention. For Barnes, however, the question of the legitimacy of the Entente cause was relevant. Despite his strictures on "just wars," his argument that American intervention had been a mistake rested heavily upon his conviction that there had been no just cause, no just war involved. From his own conclusions about the origins of the war and the reasons for American intervention he came to the point where he believed that there could be no just war. Again the dichotomy was apparent between his faith in "social intelligence" and the determinism inherent in his belief that man being the sort of animal he was, war had never been and never could be justified.

There were several other reviews of *Genesis,* two of which elicited strong responses. The first of these was by Professor Schmitt, who had refused to permit Barnes to use his name as one of the authorities approving the conclusions presented in *Genesis.*[68] Reviewing several books on the origins of the war,[69] Schmitt concluded with a long discussion of Barnes's book. In sum, he found the book to be a "grievous disappointment." He suggested that Barnes had not read the documents himself and that he had neglected to apply his critical faculties to secondary sources. The second of these reviews, written by Henry W. Nevinson, appeared in the *Saturday Review of Literature.* The review began: "Shameful and disastrous as was the whole Treaty of Versailles, there was one clause in it that surpassed all others in shame. It was

68. See letter from William L. Langer to Barnes, undated, Barnes MSS.
69. "July, 1914," *Foreign Affairs,* V (October, 1926), 132–47.

Article 231." In general, Nevinson agreed with Barnes, but he did suggest that the pendulum was swinging too far in Barnes's portrait of Germany. When he concluded that "we all stand for revision if we have any sense at all," he was not giving *Genesis* a blanket endorsement.[70]

E. Raymond Turner, however, read Nevinson's review and became enraged. Writing to the editor of the *Saturday Review,* he indicated his lack of respect for Nevinson, then quickly turned on Barnes:

> Among the scholars whom I know in this country I find no one who regards Professor Barnes as an historian of standing with respect to this subject; and avowedly, I believe, he attempts to be a sociologist, not an historian. It appears to me that he is primarily a journalist, with strong tendency towards sensationalism. If he were able to overcome certain temperamental defects and resist the temptation to write hastily and rashly on so many and such various subjects, it would still be necessary, I think, before he could give anything of worth on the causes of the War, for him to devote several years to study of the documents and the sources, something that I conceive he has not yet had opportunity or inclination to do.[71]

The response to Schmitt's review came, of course, from Barnes himself. The significance of Barnes's attack on Schmitt lay not in his efforts to refute Schmitt's criticism, but in the tone of the rebuttal. Hitherto, Barnes's opponents had been open to charges of being unfamiliar with the relevant documents. Schmitt could not be challenged on these grounds. Moreover, in his review of *Genesis* he had noted that the book was based not on the documents but on secondary sources. He had been critical of Barnes's work because it was a synthesis of revisionist writings which had not been verified by original research. Schmitt had looked at Barnes as a historian and found him wanting.

In reply, Barnes ignored the methods generally used by historians when opposing the interpretations offered by other historians. Rather than raise questions about the use of evidence,

70. "The Great Revision," *Saturday Review of Literature,* III (November 20, 1926), 309–11.

71. *Saturday Review,* III (December 11, 1926), 428.

he again turned to psychoanalysis. Schmitt had been a revisionist in the early postwar days. Why had he "become progressively more anti-revisionist about in direct proportion to the increase of documentary evidence supporting the revisionist viewpoint?"[72] Barnes concluded that the answer involved Schmitt's fear of identification with the Teuton, his English sympathies, and his desire for academic security and prestige:

> There is the very important fact that Mr. Schmitt seems to live in daily dread of being mistaken for a member of the detestable Teutonic breed. . . . Like his compatriot, the late Walter Hines Page, Mr. Schmitt was reared in our Southland, so noted for its altogether commendable esteem for the culture of our mother country, Great Britain. . . . Unquestionably, Oxford thrilled this Tennessee schoolboy quite as much as the Court of St. James filled Mr. Page with a divine afflatus. . . .[73]

After suggesting that Schmitt moved up from Western Reserve to Chicago as a reward for opposing revisionism, Barnes provided his readers with an insight into his own views on the historical profession:

> Had I been angling for a promotion in academic historical circles I should not have chosen any subject bearing upon the war-guilt problem, but would have written with the most immaculate restraint and the most approved indecisiveness upon some such highly relevant and stirring problem as scutage, knight-errantry, the Legend of the Year 1000 or the historiography of the Donation of Constantine.[74]

Schevill thought Barnes's reply a good piece of work which did not go beyond the limits of propriety, but Barnes was uncertain, perhaps too readily accepting a rumor that Schmitt had sent a circular to the membership of the American Historical Association, condemning him. Even some of his usual supporters were critical of his reply to Schmitt. Knopf affirmed his hearty sympathy for

72. "Mr. Bernadotte Everly Schmitt and the Question of Responsibility for the Outbreak of the World War," *Progressive*, December, 1926. Reprinted in *In Quest of Truth and Justice* (Chicago: National Historical Society, 1928), pp. 298–331.

73. *In Quest of Truth and Justice*, pp. 301–2.

74. *Ibid.*, p. 329.

Barnes in his controversies with Turner, but thought "the article in the Progressive likely to do you more harm than it will Schmitt." Preserved Smith wrote, "with the frankness of a friend and admirer," that he did not care for the *Progressive* article. First of all, it had been discourteous. Secondly, "I esteem the question of Schmitt's complexes and motives of very slight importance and irrelevant to the question of war guilt. Prove the truth of your assertions without going into the problem of what warps Schmitt's judgment of the facts." Finally, he compared Barnes's rebuttal of Schmitt with Berkeley's refutation of Newton's work on the ground that Newton was an atheist.[75] But Barnes was too much the polemicist to hold back for very long.

And so the tone of much of the controversy between the revisionists and their opponents was set. Little time or space were devoted to academic discussions of evidence and the use of evidence, much time and space to name-calling and questioning of motives. Perhaps it could have been no other way. Two honest, well-trained scholars examined the evidence and came to conclusions diametrically opposed. Frequently the opposing interpretations come generations apart. This time they appeared simultaneously. How do scholars, let alone laymen, explain such a controversy?

75. Schevill to Barnes, June 13, 1928; Knopf to Barnes, January 11, 1927; Smith to Barnes, January 18, 1927, Barnes MSS.

CHAPTER FOUR

The Controversy Begins To Focus on American Intervention 1926-1929

After rejoicing in the fact that revisionist literature could at last be published in the United States, Judge Bausman produced a second volume, *Facing Europe,* which appeared late in 1926.[1] He reiterated his earlier judgment on the origins of the war, but permitted Great Britain and the American Anglophiles to share top billing with his favorite culprits of 1922. Despite having read John Kenneth Turner's *Shall It Be Again?* and much of Barnes's work, despite having discovered the role of the "interests," he continued to view American intervention as a selfless crusade led by a well-meaning but badly advised, ill-informed President. He portrayed Wilson as an honest, skeptical man, imbued with the correct ideals but buried under Allied propaganda and harrassed constantly by Anglophile advisers:

> To the credit of the president be it forever remembered that, even though his feelings were on the side of Great Britain, he perceived the mass of falsehood which was permeating our very souls . . . the feeling of all the people in high political and financial circles was intensely hostile to Germany. It was by these people that the president was immediately surrounded. Such a voice as Bryan's was no longer in his council. He had to fight it out alone. . . . The marvel is that Wilson stood out so long. . . .[2]

1. New York: The Century Co., 1926.
2. *Facing Europe,* pp. 77, 83.

Bausman's travels around the country during the years 1915–16 left him with impressions that facilitated his acceptance of Turner's indictment of the "ruling class," if not Turner's image of Wilson. He had found, as he recalled in 1926, that

> the banking class were nearly unanimous for war; the manufacturing class were by a large majority for war; the food manufacturers seemed to be divided. The farmers were almost wholly against war, as well as the small shop keepers, the clerks and general workmen. . . . Wilson's difficulty was that the voices which reached him every hour, the faces, the demeanors, the undisguised feelings, were all those of the class that controlled powerful newspapers; the class that he had to chat with, to mingle with, a more or less wealthy class, at all events a ruling class, were all, all, for war. . . .[3]

Years before, Bausman had supported Wilson's domestic program, and now he restated the value he placed upon Wilson's domestic achievements. But who had driven this great leader to war—who but the very "interests" against whom Bausman and Wilson had once fought, the "interests" that dominated the Atlantic coast, all pro-British. Wilson himself had almost to the last been unwilling to go into war, "before as after his reelection, so that such of his admirers as called him nobly insincere in the first period, or regarded him as impatiently awaiting a warlike feeling among our populace, were mistaken."[4]

Bausman devoted chapters to both Colonel House and Walter Hines Page and in these chapters found an area for agreement with Barnes. He declared House and Page to be rabidly pro-British, obsequious—in sum, bad influences on the beloved Wilson. In terms quite similar to those found in *Genesis,* he maintained that "nobody can doubt" that an impartial ambassador and "no Colonel House" would have meant a policy which would have forced Great Britain to revise her "sea policy" so as to remove the pressures that forced Germany to resume her unrestricted submarine warfare.[5]

Finally he returned to what might be considered his favorite point: the United States had intervened altruistically. He could

3. *Ibid.,* p. 78.
4. *Ibid.,* pp. 83, 159–61, 174.
5. *Ibid.,* p. 222.

not understand how people could persuade themselves that the United States had intervened for gain, and he referred all to Colonel House's diary for proof of American altruism. Again, "the Allies beguiled us into this war by false propaganda, concealing both the origins of the war and their secret profits, while we did everything we could to aid them and got nothing by way of compensation." Closing with a peek into the future, Bausman revealed that America's next war would be with Great Britain.[6]

In the scholarly journals, *Facing Europe* was received ungraciously. In the *Political Science Quarterly,* for example, Arthur B. Darling declared: "Packed with inaccurate statements, prejudiced views, and illogical conclusions, this is an extremely dangerous book to place in the hands of uninformed and unthinking men."[7] But in the journals of opinion, especially those designed to appeal to the reform intellectual, Bausman's work received a more cordial reception. Ernest Henderson, writing for the *Nation,* was pleased particularly with the chapters on Wilson, Page, and House, and offered as his only criticism the thought that Bausman did not go far enough.[8]

For the *New Republic,* Robert Morss Lovett, one of the editors, added to Bausman's laurels while using his review as a vehicle for a general defense of revisionism. Lovett contended that no one who had looked at the "facts," "with the exception of a few professors zealous of their vested interests in textbooks [Hazen and Turner?]," believed in Germany's "sole guilt"; that the "disinterested search for the chief author of the War leads to many questions which only France can answer." He saw as Bausman's main argument the idea that the United States could have ended the war without intervening and concluded with the suggestion that Bausman's "system of education, unpleasant as it is and wounding to national pride, may prove the best preparation for the future."[9]

Before his death in 1931, Bausman made two other notable public appearances, both in 1927. In these appearances he ex-

6. *Ibid.,* pp. 321–22.

7. *Political Science Quarterly,* XLII (September, 1927), 441.

8. *Nation,* CXXIII (December 1, 1926), 564.

9. *New Republic,* XLIX (November 24, 1926), 22.

hibited positions which could not readily be generalized as "revisionist." On the other hand, the Anglophobia and chauvinism that were revealed in Bausman were traits or attitudes toward which revisionism could easily lead. Conceivably Bausman might have been both Anglophobe and chauvinist when writing his two books, but it would seem more likely that these were feelings and attitudes that followed his commitment to revisionism. Only in the late 1920's did his writing indicate any animus toward Great Britain and then only after he came to the conclusion that British propaganda and American Anglophiles had been responsible for American intervention on behalf of an unjust cause. Writing for Mencken's *American Mercury* in the fall of 1927, Bausman again indicated the extent to which he had been shaken by revelations of British propaganda campaigns in the United States, by British efforts to avoid paying their war debts.[10] Most of all he was upset by what he viewed as the pro-British, anti-patriotic attitude of America's upper classes:

> Was ever a country so bedeviled as ours? Has there ever been one in all history in which the class most powerful in controlling government and public opinion was determinedly bent on giving away enormous sums of the country's money to nations already heavily armed and openly expressing contempt for a sacrifice [American intervention] which they would accept only as their due. . . . It is an actual fact that in many circles of wealth and fashion in this country one who takes his country's side in these debates is put to shame at dinner tables. . . .[11]

In the same month that Bausman's article appeared on the newsstands, Bausman himself appeared as a witness for the prosecution in the trial of William McAndrew, suspended Superintendent of Schools in Chicago. McAndrew had been suspended in a controversy over his alleged authorization of un-American, pro-British textbooks. Bausman had been invited to testify as an expert on the nature of the British threat. He reminded his audience that "England beguiled us into war, took all the spoils of it and did not want to pay her debts." The great conspiracy was the "deliberate

10. "Under Which Flag?" *American Mercury*, XII (October, 1927), 195–203.

11. *Ibid.*, p. 196.

work of human minds, aided by financiers of England, who seek, first, the full cancellation of England's war debt to the United States and, second, the placing of the Union Jack wherever now flies the Stars and Stripes." Asked if he had seen evidence of British propaganda in the United States, he replied affirmatively: "I thought there was a great deal of it in the schools . . . in the public libraries; in literature generally." Asked what evidence of British influence he had noted in the libraries, Bausman produced an American Library Association pamphlet, "The Europe of Our Day," prepared by Herbert Adams Gibbons of Princeton. Bausman testified that Gibbons recommended books that were contemptuous of the United States, including a book by Carlton Hayes of Columbia, "whose history has recently been condemned by the Veterans of Foreign Wars."[12]

As his performance drew to a close, Bausman, who had once studied at Harvard, testified: "I know that the wealthy classes of Europe have a tremendous influence at Columbia and Princeton." And with his last words he revealed what lay behind the work of the opponents of revisionism: "England fears that if America gets to know England was a guilty party in the causes of the World War, America no longer will fawn at her feet as some do."[13]

Here was one road revisionism could follow. Blame Lombard Street and British propaganda, Wall Street and the Anglophiles for American intervention in a war that was no affair of the United States, and then spend the rest of your life attempting to exorcise these influences in this country. It was an easy road to follow if one belonged to an ethnic group hostile to Great Britain, easy if one was imbued with a tradition of hostility to the upper class of the effete East—since that class was pro-English and had been pro-war. The desire to oppose the "ruling group" and to oppose war made it relatively easy to learn to hate the English. So often, decisions of that sort are made on the basis of who is on what side.

And so it was that attitudes that had permeated American reform movements since the 1890's, attitudes deeply rooted in the

12. *New York Times,* October 20, 1927, p. 2.
13. *Ibid.*

Middle West, came to serve as a basis for an ultranationalistic reaction to American intervention in the World War—as a basis for pressures against subsequent involvement with Europe. In the years that followed, there was, to be sure, a tinge of Anglophobia to revisionism, but it is more significant to note how *little* of this there was, how *little* connection there was between Anglophobia and the work of men like Barnes, Beard, Grattan, and Millis. The crusade against the "interests," however, continued to loom large.

While Bausman was demonstrating that revisionism could lead to an accord with the American Legion, the main currents of revisionism swept by him. Barnes kept on with his running battle with E. Raymond Turner, stopping now and again to catch a blow from one of the *New York Times* editorial staff. Beard, having once made clear the extent to which he dissented from Barnes's conclusions, gradually blurred the differences. C. Hartley Grattan debunked the historical profession with an article on the wartime activities of a number of historians, and everyone who cared about the *Kriegsschuldfrage* edged forward in anticipation of the "definitive" word which Sidney Bradshaw Fay's study was to provide. Then slowly the focus shifted from *Kriegsschuldfrage* to the question of why America had intervened in the war.

2

Posterity may not regard E. Raymond Turner as a great historian, but a more dogged opponent of revisionism there was not. In January, 1927, he returned to the barricades with a sharp attack against Barnes in particular and the revisionist interpretation in general:

> A number of individuals with bias stronger than attainments, various radical publications, and certain monthlies and weeklies have asserted repeatedly that the Treaty of Versailles was foolish and unjust, and that Germany was not as responsible for the war as were Russia, France and Great Britain. . . . Also they say that the United States was deceived into joining the Allies.
>
> In this country the most vociferous advocate of these absurdities is H. E. Barnes, "Professor of Historical Sociology." His seeming

inability to deal with evidence is equalled by capacity for going to
extremes and constantly and rapidly writing something more. . . .[14]

Turner also noted that Professor Schmitt had reviewed *Genesis*
with the "reserve and moderation that a gentleman and scholar
employs." The implication was, clearly, that Barnes's reply to
Schmitt in the *Progressive* was rather an ungentlemanly piece.

Barnes replied, of course, and did not overlook Turner's jibe
at his academic title. He suspected, probably with some justification, that he was being opposed for his role as pioneer in the
application of the social sciences to the study of history as well as
for his revisionism. First he quoted G. P. Gooch, the English historian, in defense of his revisionist work: "No other American
scholar has done so much as Professor Barnes to familiarize his
countrymen with the new evidence which has rapidly accumulated
during the last few years, and to compel them to revise their
wartime judgments in the light of this new material"; and then
he went on to defend his multi-disciplinary approach and his
preparation for historical research.[15]

In the summers of 1926 and 1927 Barnes went to Europe to
continue his search for the truth about the origins of the war.
While in Europe, he read in the archives, interviewed various
statesmen, and not infrequently gave speeches in which he offered
his conclusions on the *Kriegsschuldfrage*. To no one one's surprise,
Barnes's views proved to be agreeable to German audiences. But
all the while, a representative of the *New York Times* watched.
"Barnes Declares Germany Guiltless" read the caption over a
little squib one day. The *Times* reported that Barnes had spoken
at a banquet in Berlin and while his views had been greeted with
acclamation, "there was a feeling that in his white washing of
Germany so completely [he] had gone a step too far"—for the
New York Times if not for his Berlin listeners.[16]

Shortly afterward, Barnes returned to the United States and
was greeted by another barb from the *Times*. In "Topics of the
Times" the subject was Harry Elmer Barnes, "More Popular
Abroad."

14. *Ibid.*, January 2, 1927, Sec. VIII, p. 12, Letter to the Editor.

15. *Ibid.*, January 9, 1927, Sec. VIII, p. 8, Letter to the Editor.

16. *Ibid.*, July 22, 1927, p. 4.

It is obvious that Professor Harry E. Barnes carried with him a most attractive article of export when he went to Germany. His views on "German war guilt" were of a sort to receive the welcome which they did when he presented them in Berlin. . . .
It is to be noted, however, that when his pleasing commodity for the German market was reimported here it did not meet with universal favor. . . .[17]

That same summer, Charles Beard was stepping up his crusade against foreign investments, demanding heavier income and inheritance taxes to pay for rural roads, schools, and electric power, calling for the diversion of the "surplus of plutocracy" from foreign investments to domestic use. In illustrating his argument before a meeting of the Institute of Politics, he declared:

> Incidentally . . . this would reduce our chances of becoming mixed up in the next European adventure in Christian ballistics. If the present rate of foreign investments keep up, every village skin-flint from Maine to California will soon have a hundred-dollar foreign bond paying 8 per cent instead of the 6 per cent local rate, and thus inspired will be by a holy zeal for righteousness, justice or whatever the next warlike device may be, which means at bottom a lust to get the money back with interest.[18]

Perhaps "Uncle Charlie" was just being cynical, as on occasion he liked to seem. But the last "European adventure in Christian ballistics" had been the World War, and he seemed to be implying that American involvement in that war might not have been as salutary or as necessary as it had appeared to him in 1917 and again when he had reviewed Barnes's *Genesis*.

Then in 1927, the Beards' *Rise of American Civilization* appeared.[19] Richard Leopold has suggested that the version of why the United States intervened presented by the Beards in Volume II of this work "would have satisfied most Wilsonians."[20] The Beards contended that it seemed "plain that, until the United

17. *Ibid.*, July 26, 1927, p. 18.

18. *Ibid.*, August 3, 1927, p. 9.

19. Charles and Mary Beard, *The Rise of American Civilization* (2 vols.; New York: The Macmillan Company, 1927).

20. "The Problem of American Intervention, 1917: A Historical Retrospect," *World Politics*, II (April, 1950), 409.

States entered the war, Wilson . . . looked rather coldly on the pretentions of both the embattled forces, being inclined to regard the conflict as a war of commercial powers over the spoils of empire." The Beards contended also that even after Wilson had made the decision to intervene he remained convinced that England's primary interest in the war was commercial and imperialistic. They found no evidence to indicate that Wilson had ever surrendered his conviction that, "as far as the causes and objects of the war were concerned, there was no ground for assuming that either party to the conflict had any special merit of righteousness to be accepted at face value."[21]

In effect, the Beards were arguing that Wilson's decision to intervene and his subsequent decisions on war strategy did not stem from any illusions fostered by Allied propaganda. But this did not answer the question of "why" the United States intervened, nor did the Beards attempt to meet his question head-on. They did ask and attempt to answer the question of what changed Wilson from a man "who 'didn't wish either side to win' into an ardent advocate of war 'without stint' against Germany"—the latter position approximating that of Charles Beard in 1917. Well, there had been the decision by the Germans to resume unrestricted submarine warfare. There had been the fear that the Allies might lose. And there had been the financiers and other selfish factions: "No doubt the war dirge raised by these selfish factions was adequately financed, astutely managed, and effectively carried into strange out-of-the-way places as well as into the main highways."[22] At this point, the faithful Wilsonian might have paused and sniffed suspiciously: what were the Beards suggesting?

The Beards granted that the letters and papers of Wilson's contemporaries supported the image of a Wilson who was skeptical about the contentions of Europe's warring powers and who chose to aid the Allies only after the revival of the submarine issue, only after he began to fear that the Allies might lose, only after he had been subjected to the "war dirge" of selfish factions. But they added that it could not be denied that there was authentic evidence for another view of the case, "namely that the President,

21. *Rise of American Civilization,* II, 627, 629.
22. *Ibid.,* p. 631.

having come practically to the end of his rope as regards domestic policies—as he himself confessed to Colonel House on September 28, 1914—reached the conviction in 1915 or early in 1916 that he could play a masterful role on the international stage by taking the United States into the war on the side of the Entente Allies, irrespective of German submarine tactics."[23]

To support the latter case, the Beards resurrected the "Sunrise Conference," which Charles Beard had apparently buried in his review of *Genesis*. Now there was "convincing proof" of a conference in February, 1916, during which Wilson contemplated war and "sounded out his party in Congress to see whether his project was acceptable." At very least, the Beards maintained, "it cannot be denied that while 'waging peace,' President Wilson was revolving in his mind the question of his leadership and mission in world affairs, and kept revolving it until he finally broke with the German Empire."[24] If, as Professor Leopold has suggested, most Wilsonians were satisfied with the Beard interpretation of American intervention, most Wilsonians had come a long way since 1917.

3

In August, 1928, as a reluctant Secretary of State yielded to the chorus of voices that insisted that war was useless, the United States joined numerous other nations in condemning recourse to war as a solution to international controversies. In November, Al Smith was defeated in his effort to become President of the United States. Also in 1928, Harry Elmer Barnes, skeptical about the Kellogg-Briand Pact, ardently supporting Smith and the promise of more beer, produced two new books. One of these, *Living in the Twentieth Century*, while not an addition to Barnes's revisionist output, provided some interesting insights into Barnes's attitudes toward world affairs. In his scale of values, he placed "social reform" at the top and then attacked war and militarism as the chief obstacles to programs for social reconstruction. Because of wars, there were always "preparedness" programs and people were always burdened by taxes for armaments—never leaving

23. *Ibid.*, pp. 631–32.
24. *Ibid.*, p. 633.

sufficient funds for social reconstruction. Moreover, "man needs all of his intelligence and resources in the task of solving our social problems within national boundaries. There is little hope that man will be able to cope successfully with the complexities of the modern age if his efforts are thwarted and destroyed by the periodic intervention of war, destruction and confusion."[25] Obviously, the next step was to seek a way to end war. While Barnes's deterministic conception of human nature had led him to conclude that there could never be a "just" war, somehow he was optimistic enough about the ability of men to alter their environment to believe that a world without war might be brought about. Thus, in the same volume in which he wrote, "It is probable that adrenalin played as large a part as pan-Slavism in Saznov's decision upon war in July, 1914," he could and did outline a program for the elimination of war. There was nothing particularly original or exciting about Barnes's program. What was significant was that it was the program of a man whose attitudes toward world politics were, in 1928, essentially the same as those held by Woodrow Wilson in 1917 and 1918.

Barnes began with an attack on nationalism, political and economic. He compared the citizen of the modern nation state to the primitive savage of the "tribal group" and found little to choose between them when it came to "crude emotions when the matter of national pride is involved." He called the European system of "differential" tariffs the most significant factor, excepting possibly the struggle for overseas markets, in "bringing on" the World War. He saw the creation of a large number of small independent states on the ruins of the Austro-Hungarian Empire as a backward step—unless some method of international control was established.[26]

Barnes also stressed the importance of avoiding one-shot panaceas for preventing war. The movement for the "outlawry" of war was grand, but it could only succeed if the causes of war were eliminated. And Barnes was not at all hesitant about defining causes: "The causes of war may be summarized as: biological,

25. *Living in the Twentieth Century* (Indianapolis: Bobbs-Merrill, 1928), p. 340.

26. *Ibid.*, pp. 315 ff.

psychological, social, economic, political and ethical." Now, on to their elimination: Barnes called for an international organization with the "power and inclination to enforce peace." First, the world had to be shown that the nation state was but a stage in political evolution, like tribalism or feudalism. Ultimately, the nation state would be followed logically by a world organization, without which "no plan for eliminating the causes of war can be complete." Taking cognizance of the fact that others had had this idea before him and had actually done something about it, Barnes wrote: "We now have the League of Nations in conception and structure. It remains to transform it from a league of victors into an organization honestly devoted to undoing the injustices of the past and to promoting fair-dealing in the future."[27] The story has but one moral: Barnes's attitudes toward world politics were essentially Wilsonian. His criticism of the conduct of American foreign policy under Wilson's direction was based simply on his belief that Wilson's judgment had been bad and that Wilson had not succeeded in doing the job perfectly. Intervention had been a mistake because the Allied cause had not really been just. The League of Nations was not really any good because it was not a league of all nations. If Barnes had had the reins, nearly all of the foreign policy decisions made by Wilson would have been made on the same basic principles. The decisions, presumably, would nonetheless have been different and a better world would have evolved.

Barnes's other publication in 1928 was *In Quest of Truth and Justice,* a collection of the controversies in which he had participated and a summary of his views on war guilt and American intervention. In addition, he included the article Grattan had written for Mencken on the historians at war, but as originally written rather than as previously published. The letters of E. Raymond Turner were assembled under the title "Pedantry and Pomposity"; the exchange with Schmitt was collected under the title "Timid and Vacillating Revisionism: Bernadotte Everly Schmitt"; and in a discussion of other opponents of revisionism, Barnes referred to William Stearns Davis as the "distinguished historical novelist of the University of Minnesota."

27. *Ibid.,* p. 345.

Unquestionably, *In Quest of Truth and Justice* was not a scholarly contribution. The preface, however, left no doubt as to why Barnes had prepared the volume. His *Genesis of the World War* had not sold and he was trying desperately to make his views known to the public. He declared that despite the "very unusual courage" of his publisher and the especially generous expenditures for advertising, despite a kindlier reception from reviewers than had been anticipated, *Genesis of the World War* had not "attained to the degree of distribution which was hoped for." A major difficulty, he found, had been "the unwillingness of booksellers to cooperate, even when it was to their pecuniary advantage to do so." He suspected that the booksellers had presumed to "censor their customers' reading in the field of international relations as in the matter of morals." He claimed that booksellers had even discouraged customers who sought to have his book ordered for them.[28] Another theory, offered years later by Carl Becker, was that no matter how much Barnes tailored his histories for a mass audience, the public would still prefer the *Saturday Evening Post*.[29]

In his preface, Barnes again emphasized his belief in the didactic purpose of written history. If the writing of history did not contribute to the improvement of man and the conditions under which he lived, it was a useless exercise. The test of good history was, then, essentially pragmatic in the sense that good history would be defined as that which served a useful purpose. Thus, the work of the historians studying the war-guilt question or seeking the reasons for American intervention would be sterile if their discoveries did not lead to a better world.

Quite candidly, Barnes expressed his belief that the moment was one in which "esoteric research" had to be sacrificed in favor of "popular exposition." In another frank admission he declared that he regarded himself as "better adapted to general synthesis and controversy than to obtuse and detailed research."[30] With this last statement few of his critics would have disagreed.

In discussing the reasons for American intervention and in ap-

28. *In Quest of Truth and Justice,* pp. v–vi.

29. "What Is Historiography?" *American Historical Review,* XLIV (1938), 22.

30. *In Quest of Truth and Justice,* p. v.

plying his conclusions on the *Kriegsschuldfrage* to questions of American foreign policy, Barnes contended that the only point about American intervention that could be stated "clearly and dogmatically" was that the resumption by the Germans of unrestricted submarine warfare was the "occasion and not the reason for our becoming a belligerent."[31] The historical lesson was equally clear: "An understanding of these facts certainly should do much to make us less ready to pull the chestnuts out of the fire for any European nation or coalition whatever in the event of another European conflagration."[32]

Then Barnes sat back and hopefully read Sidney Bradshaw Fay's *The Origins of the World War*. Like everyone else who had taken a stand on the war-guilt question, Barnes sought vindication in Fay's work. Fay was a universally respected historian whose scholarship and objectivity were unquestioned. The reaction to his two volumes was varied and strange, but no stranger than the varied reactions of the scholars who had studied the documents available on the origins of the war. The opponents of revisionism worried through most of the study and then joyously waved about Fay's conclusions: The Austrians may have been the guiltiest, but the Germans were not much better, and at any rate the preponderance of guilt remained with the Central Powers. Barnes, on the other hand, was delighted with Fay's contribution until he reached the conclusion. The conclusion, he insisted, was a *non sequitur:* Fay's evidence had relieved the Central Powers of the bulk of the responsibility for the war. Thus both sides of the controversy found cause for rejoicing and cause for regret in Fay's work—perhaps as good an indication as any of Fay's objectivity and of the human capacity to find what is being sought.

Barnes, of course, claimed Fay's study as a victory for the revisionists. Two contemporary reviews prepared by Barnes were entitled "The Twilight of the Myth-Mongers" and "The Revisionists Vindicated."[33] In the first of these, Barnes claimed that Fay was, because of his standing in the profession, "absolutely invul-

31. *Ibid.*, p. 98.

32. *Ibid.*, p. 3.

33. *Living Age*, CCCXXXV (December, 1928), 270–71; and *Current History*, XXIX (December, 1928), 443–48.

nerable" to the "specious" criticisms levied against other revisionists. Fay's "espousal of an advanced version of revisionism will in itself prove a landmark in the history of the war guilt controversy. All of the timid but sincere and candid brethren in the American Historical Association can now clamber aboard the revisionist toboggan with the utmost good taste and a minimum of trepidation."[34] In the second review, for *Current History*, Barnes, writing in the same vein, contended that "the great majority of Professor Fay's closest friends and associates in the historical profession desired, above all else in the world," to have Fay use his reputation in opposition to revisionism and "to vindicate the timid, the evasive, the slothful and the somnolent."[35] Barnes declared that "Fay does not stand with those absurd revisionists who contend that the Central Powers were innocent lambs,"[36] but Fay had taken a position which he, Barnes, claimed as vindication of the non-absurd revisionists like himself. Barnes concluded with an expression of hope that "Professor Fay will soon recover from any feeling of timidity which may depress him, and from any regret that he was unable to please those of his profession who are more interested in preserving their prejudices and *amour propre* than they are in arriving at accurate historical conceptions."[37]

4

As the decade of the twenties drew to a close, interest in the *Kriegsschuldfrage* waned in the United States and the primary focus of the revisionist controversy shifted to the question of why America had intervened. In the newer revisionist interpretations of the story of American intervention, the implications of the war-

34. *Living Age,* CCCXXXV, 270.

35. *Current History,* XXIX, 444.

36. *Ibid.,* p. 445. This statement was subsequently incorporated into a review of Fay's work included in Barnes's *World Politics* (New York: Knopf, 1930), with one interesting modification: in 1930 Barnes substituted the word "extreme" for the word "absurd." Barnes considers the 1930 piece the best review he wrote during the interwar period. Letter from Barnes to the author, January 31, 1962.

37. *Ibid.,* p. 448.

guilt controversy were usually present, but were more often than not of far less significance than they had been to Harry Elmer Barnes.

The first important figure in the shifting focus of revisionism was C. Hartley Grattan whose *Why We Fought*[38] was the first documented analysis of the events leading to American participation in the war. Of especial interest in Grattan's background was the fact that he had studied with Harry Elmer Barnes at Clark University —although it is worth noting that while Barnes introduced him to intellectual history it was with George Blakeslee that he studied international relations. Thus, while Grattan's subsequent close relationship with Barnes permits an image of him as the apprentice, carrying the work of the master to a new area, it should not be surprising that his approach to revisionism and to world affairs differed markedly from Barnes's.

Born in Wakefield, Massachusetts, in 1902,[39] Grattan had been too young to play any part in the movements for or against intervention. Entering high school at New Bedford in February, 1916, he became, briefly, a member of the ROTC. His subsequent resignation from the corps concluded his military career. Many years later he felt he had resigned because his mother had instilled in him a dislike of soldiers. When he graduated from high school in 1920, he gave the salutatorian's address, "Why War?" which he remembered as an anti-war tract. Then, in the autumn of 1920, he entered Clark University, where he studied under Barnes, his "favorite professor." In the years after graduation, he could best be described as a writer with three primary areas of interest: literary criticism, Australia and the Southwest Pacific, and American foreign relations. As a literary critic, Grattan was a radical in much the same sense Bourne had been a decade before. Much of his work was devoted to defending the "alienated" intellectuals, the literary figures whom Archibald MacLeish later castigated as "The Irre-

38. New York: The Vanguard Press, 1929.

39. Possibly because of the volume of Grattan's writing about Australia, he is occasionally referred to as "Australian-born." See, for example, the reference in Ernest May, *American Intervention: 1917 and 1941* (Washington, D.C.: American Historical Association, 1960), p. 4.

sponsibles."[40] The debate over whether or not the intellectuals of the twenties were in fact alienated from American society may go on forever, but there is little doubt that Grattan was himself much concerned with the political issues which confronted American society—particularly issues of international politics.

Early in 1925 Barnes was shopping around for someone who would write an article "debunking" Walter Hines Page. Edwin Borchard agreed that the article was desirable, that analogies could be found between the activities of Page and Benedict Arnold, but he had not the time to prepare the article himself. Grattan had graduated from Clark and was struggling along with about as much luck as most young writers. Barnes brought Grattan and Mencken together and it was agreed that Grattan would write the Page article for the *American Mercury*.[41]

Since 1922, B. J. Hendrick's volumes, *The Life and Letters of Walter Hines Page*,[42] had been appearing, and as in many such documents the importance of the central figure in the events in which he had participated was much exaggerated. Both Page and Page's biographer held exalted views of Page's influence on Wilson's decision to intervene. In 1925 there were few people, and Grattan was not among these, who knew how little respect Wilson had had for Page and Page's judgment. Years later, after Charles Seymour[43] and others had documented Wilson's mistrust of Page, those revisionists who sought a villain would turn to Robert Lansing.

Grattan argued that Page had really been a traitor who had served Great Britain rather than the United States, had served British interests rather than American. But Grattan was also quite harsh with Woodrow Wilson, certainly harsher than Barnes had been in his Wilson article of 1924. Writing of Page's influence on Wilson, Grattan found it probable that "Wilson's desire to appear

40. See Grattan (ed.), *The Critique of Humanism* (New York: Breever and Warren, 1930); "Modern Critic's Point of View," *Nation*, CXXX (April 30, 1930), 514–17; "New Voices: The Promise of Our Younger Writers," *Forum*, LXXXVII (November, 1932), 284–88.

41. Borchard to Barnes, April 7, 1925, Grattan MSS.

42. Garden City, N.Y.: Doubleday, Doran, 1922–26. The work is in three volumes.

43. See Seymour's *American Diplomacy during the World War* (Baltimore: Johns Hopkins University Press, 1934).

as the messiah of the new day" had been at least as important a factor in Wilson's decision to intervene as were Page's constant efforts to drive him in that direction. With a veiled reference to the "Sunrise Conference," Grattan wrote of the "little known fact that Wilson wanted to enter the war before the election of 1916, and was only prevented from doing so by the Democratic leaders of Congress. . . . Wilson began to see that he could not be a messiah through peace activities, so he turned to war."[44]

In 1925, then, Grattan's view of why America fought centered upon Wilson's decision in favor of intervention. Asking himself why Wilson had made that decision, he put aside the matters of war guilt, the submarine issue, and national security, and assumed that the decision had been a mistake. Implicit in this approach was, obviously, the idea that the war had been of no concern to the United States and that nothing had occurred which merited a decision to fight. The United States had intervened because a traitorous ambassador had put constant pressure upon a President who was seeking some means to satisfy his messianic complex.

Borchard, who had seen the article in manuscript, liked it, and Grattan received other indications that his portrait of Page had been well received. Claude Bowers, then editor of the New York *Evening World,* wrote of his pleasure in reading "your article on that intolerable English lickspittle" and noted that he had received corroborating information from Colonel House via Professor Dodd and from William McAdoo. Perhaps the pleasantest surprise came from Albert Bushnell Hart who requested permission to use the article in a book of readings he was preparing. Curious, Grattan asked why, and Hart's secretary replied that "your views coincide in many points with Professor Hart's." In the years that followed, Grattan's view of Page prevailed, and Page's role ceased to be an issue between the revisionists and their opponents.[45]

Again, in 1927, as Grattan was beginning to make progress in the literary world, Barnes came to him with an idea for an article

44. "The Walter Hines Page Legend," *American Mercury,* VI (September, 1925), 51.

45. Borchard to Barnes, May 3, 1925, and August 28, 1925; Bowers to Grattan, November 9, 1925; John Gould Curtis to Grattan, January 22, 1927, Grattan MSS.

for the *American Mercury*. Mencken had long been after "George Creel's herd of 2,000 historians," and Barnes was prepared to assist Grattan in working up the desired study. While this was to be as much a contribution to the revisionist controversy as the Page sketch, it was a contribution of a very different sort. "The Historians Cut Loose"[46] was a description of the wartime contributions of scholars employed by Creel, by the National Security League, and by the National Board for Historical Service. The effect of the article was to weaken the position of opponents of revisionism. Carl Becker, who had come to regret the Creel Committee days and who was viewed by Barnes as a staunch supporter of revisionism, was exempted from Grattan's attack: he had probably written with certain "philosophical reservations." But Charles Downer Hazen, Albert Bushnell Hart, and others who had either openly opposed revisionism or had written of the war years in a manner rather out of tune with revisionism, came in for a goodly share of ridicule. In sum, the article was an early playing of the "court historian" theme.

Grattan's major contribution to the revisionist literature, *Why We Fought,* came in 1929, a year in which he also published two other volumes, including a biography of Ambrose Bierce. On the title page of *Why We Fought* appeared Randolph Bourne's words demanding that the war not be permitted to pass into "popular mythology" as a "holy crusade." In the text, Grattan did what he could to keep Bourne's words from having been in vain.

Unlike Barnes, Grattan attempted to avoid polemic and gave every appearance, from careful documentation to cautious conclusions, of being as judicious as a professional historian. He began with a discussion of the European background of the war, and on the question of war guilt he took what Barnes would call a "mild revisionist" position or what was essentially a general agreement with Fay's position. He denied that Germany's role in the prewar crises indicated any particular moral deficiency, but he noted that Germany had given Austria a free hand in a game that led to war. Like Barnes and Beard he contended that it was "now established" that mobilization makes a declaration of war a "mere formality," and, believing this, he maintained that if Austria's actions had

46. *American Mercury,* IX (August, 1927), 414–30.

made a European war possible, "Russia was fast making it inevitable." But Grattan did not follow Barnes in exchanging heroes and villains. Essentially, he saw the war coming out of international anarchy with Germany and all the rest just players in the game.[47] Even this "mild" *Kriegsschuldfrage* revisionism of Grattan's was, however, significant in his interpretation of why the United States intervened. If Germany had not been "morally deficient," if responsibility for the war's origin was really divided, it was difficult to see American participation in the war as an effort on behalf of the forces of light against the forces of darkness. And, if America had not fought for all that was good against all that was evil, if there had been no moral grounds for intervention, why had she fought at all?

Grattan then turned to a study of the influence of propaganda and here he benefited from the pioneering work of Harold D. Lasswell.[48] Rather than claim, as Bausman had, that the United States had been drawn into the war by a combination of the deceitfulness and effectiveness of British propaganda, he noted that "an important condition of propaganda success is of course a favorable disposition amongst the people to be attacked. It is beyond question that the British propagandists . . . had little to do beyond confirming and elaborating prejudices already pretty firmly set in the American mind." Grattan was not contending that British propaganda had nothing to do with American intervention; he was suggesting that the British were successful because they entered a fertile field, because Americans were not neutral in thought from 1914 to 1917, but were already predisposed in favor of the Allies. He was, however, opposing Bausman's emphasis on the deceitfulness and the insidiousness of Allied propaganda. Americans were not beguiled into the war on the side of the Allies. Rather Americans had wanted to accept the argument of the Allies, wanted an excuse to intervene against Germany. Responsibility for intervention was domestic, American, and could not be put off on the Allies.[49]

47. *Why We Fought,* pp. 4–19.

48. *Propaganda Technique in the World War* (New York: P. Smith, 1927).

49. *Why We Fought,* p. 39.

Similarly, Grattan noted the traditional hostility of the United States toward Germany. Instead of stressing American sympathy with Germany during the Franco-Prussian War, he focused on the conflict of interests in Samoa, American suspicion of the intent of the German fleet at Manila and of German intentions during the Venezuelan incident. With a sophistication frequently lacking in other revisionist treatments of the influence of propaganda on the decision to intervene, Grattan's treatment noted the existence of German as well as British propaganda and suggested that propaganda per se was not as significant as traditional sentiments of sympathy or hostility.

On one point, however, Grattan seemed to feel that pro-Allied propaganda had been influential in leading the United States along the road to war. He found that the threat of a German victory occurred persistently in the "propaganda" of the supporters of the Allies. From that "remarkable" premise, these people "proceeded to evolve wonderful arguments about what would happen to the United States in such a case." They concluded that the United States had better be prepared for these eventualities and, "of course, in being prepared, the United States would be in a position to help the British defeat Germany before she overran the world."[50] Presupposing that Germany had never had a chance to win and would never offer a threat to the United States, Grattan viewed the preparedness campaign as a means by which those interested in the cause of the Allies could maneuver the United States into a position of backing up Great Britain. As for Wilson, "opposed as he was in the beginning to all efforts to increase the army and navy he soon came to think that the dominant bandwagon was the one playing the Preparedness tune."[51] Thus Wilson's political opportunism gave the "Preparedness" campaign the necessary further impetus and official endorsement.

Grattan then turned to the economic influences on the decision to intervene. He noted judiciously the absence of an "absolute stimulus-response relation between economic facts and political conduct" but followed this with a puzzling statement: "To accept such a position [of economic determinism] is to ignore the capac-

50. *Ibid.*, p. 117.
51. *Ibid.*, p. 119.

ity of mankind to rationalize its conduct in ways more flattering to its self-esteem than a frank admission that dollars and goods rule."[52] The second statement and Grattan's subsequent remarks suggested that he himself relied heavily upon an economic interpretation of history. He pointed to the "economic foundation" of the World War and of "every" other war. "The flag," he wrote, "follows trade, the politicians follow the flag, the propagandists follow the politicians, and the people follow the propagandists."[53] Grattan was contending that although man could fool himself into thinking that he would fight only for noble causes, he really fought only for cash. This had been true in all wars and Grattan did not postulate an exception for America's decision to fight in 1917.

Grattan was not, however, always consistent with his apparent acceptance of economic determinism. His analysis was not the work of a doctrinaire socialist like that of Nearing or John Kenneth Turner. If the facts as Grattan saw them did not square with economic determinism, doctrine was subordinated to the evidence. He took issue, for example, with the prevailing revisionist thesis that the bankers became pro-Ally in direct proportion to the increase in their investments in England and France. Grattan argued that this contention neglected "the fact that the bankers were pro-Ally *before* they began to get fat by battening on the body of Mars."[54] And his explanation for the bankers' early pro-Ally sentiments included "social connections" among the reasons.

After this side glance, Grattan went on to note that between 1913 and 1917 the economic ties of the United States increased rapidly with the Allies, while they all but disappeared between the United States and Germany, adding, "that this should be without effect on American sentiment is simply a position that cannot be maintained." It followed that "it was to Germany's interest to sink the vessels of her enemies. It was to America's economic interest that nothing be placed in the way of landing her goods in Allied countries. When the two interests clashed, we followed the direction of our economic interest. We tried to prevent the Germans using

52. *Ibid.*, p. 127.
53. *Ibid.*
54. *Ibid.*, p. 131.

their submarines."[55] Thus Grattan accepted readily the existence of a conflict of interest between the United States and Germany. It was this conflict of interest rather than any scruples about the niceties of international law that had led to American intervention when Germany resumed unrestricted submarine warfare.

Similarly, when discussing the possibility of the United States Government imposing an embargo on all shipping, Grattan granted that such an act not only would have disrupted foreign trade but would have wrecked the domestic economy as well.[56] But to Grattan this was not sufficient reason to forego the measure. Herein lay the real significance of Grattan's interpretation. To be sure, his interpretation was economic, and this insinuation that Americans had fought for other than the purest of patriotic reasons assured the alienation of the American Legion and the DAR. But most important was the fact that despite his recognition of a conflict between German policy and American economic interests, he saw no reason for war. Despite his realization of what an embargo in 1917 would have meant to the American economy, if the embargo would have kept the United States out of war it should have been imposed. To Grattan, the most obvious point of all was that these economic interests were not worth fighting for.

Although Grattan was convinced that Wilson wanted to lead the country into war, he was extremely cautious in his indictment of Wilson. Other revisionists had and would make much of the "House-Grey Memorandum" of February, 1916. Grattan, with somewhat less vigor than Beard, indicated his reservations about the extent of the American commitment. He noted that Wilson had inserted the word "probably" when discussing the course of action to be taken by the United States in the event Germany refused to consider peace proposals: "Should the Allies accept this proposal, and Germany refuse it, the United States would *probably* enter the war against Germany." Grattan believed that Wilson's insertion of "probably" was intended to protect him from embarrassment in the event that the agreement became public, but he also noted that Wilson had been "hesitant" to commit himself absolutely.[57]

55. *Ibid.*, pp. 135, 164.
56. *Ibid.*, p. 171.
57. *Ibid.*, p. 360.

Then Grattan turned to the legend of the "Sunrise Conference" which other revisionists, Grattan himself in 1927, used to demonstrate Wilson's desire to take his country into the war. Grattan examined the evidence for the existence of the conference and, like Beard in 1926, found the evidence unconvincing:

> While the Sunrise Conference has been accepted as authentic by such diverse figures as Harry Elmer Barnes and William Allen White, the writer feels that Dr. Charles Beard's attitude must be his own: "The story of the meeting with Clark, Flood and Kitchin is at present very shadowy, and until it is made more precise and authentic, it must remain in the form of dubious evidence."[58]

In a footnote, Grattan also quoted a statement he had received from Ray Stannard Baker, Wilson's biographer, indicating the absence of evidence in Wilson's papers proving the occurrence of the Sunrise Conference.[59]

Despite his refusal to use "dubious" evidence in support of his case, Grattan retained the conviction that Wilson wanted intervention. With this conviction came the implication that only an "articulate minority" shared Wilson's desire. These feelings led Grattan to the point of grave concern over what he considered the irresponsibility, to Congress and to the electorate, of the directors of American foreign policy. Wilson could and did make policy decisions without consulting his Cabinet. Wilson "conducted the foreign policy of this country to the point where war was the way out. He did not ask Congress to render an opinion on his conduct of foreign affairs. He presented them with a *fait accompli*."[60]

The belief in executive irresponsibility in America's foreign relations subsequently became particularly important when efforts were made to apply the "lessons" of revisionism to the conduct of foreign policy. Although the issue of whether or not intervention had the support of a majority of Americans was never resolved, not even *among* the "revisionists," many of those who accepted the "revisionist" interpretation sought to limit the President's power—to prevent him from leading the United States into war against the will of the majority of the people.

58. *Ibid.*, p. 364.
59. *Ibid.*
60. *Ibid.*, p. 181.

Seeking the "essence" of Wilson's foreign policy, Grattan concluded that it was

> an effort to realize the American ideals of peace and disarmament by agreement between the dominant powers of the world. The expansionist impulses of the great nations were to be directed into socially desirable channels such as the development of backward areas. The policy, in the eyes of its proponents, necessitated the extention of democracy as the most beneficent and righteous governmental form known to man. It also allowed for the economic penetration of small and backward states, thus providing full scope for the American genius. During the war it found its chief expression in efforts to arrange a peace among the warring powers.[61]

Grattan agreed readily that this seemed an "admirable" policy, but he contended that in the hands of inexperienced diplomatists, men "incapable of viewing nations in arms dispassionately," it soon evolved into "a movement to eliminate from the list of Great Powers, the nation opposed to that group which engaged their sympathies. It eventually became a crusade against Germany."[62] Ultimately, the government of the United States failed to maintain the balance between the belligerent groups. The interests of the United States became entangled with those of the Allies and Wilson's entire program went for naught. Finally, through German "stupidity," the "efficient emotional excuse" was provided and the American people could be "persuaded to war."[63]

The reviews of *Why We Fought* that appeared in the *Nation* and *New Republic* reflected the general endorsement of revisionism by reform intellectuals.[64] For the *Nation*, McAlister Coleman wrote that Grattan's book served "the useful purpose of reminding us once more that democracy's Achilles' heel is its foreign relations."[65] Coleman, like Grattan, was voicing the growing feeling that governments, not peoples, willed war; that Wilson, not the

61. *Ibid.*

62. *Ibid.*

63. *Ibid.*, p. 176.

64. The book was not reviewed in any of the scholarly journals. Leopold suspects that review copies were never sent.

65. *Nation*, CXXX (March 26, 1930), 368.

American people, willed intervention; and that war could be prevented if the people were given greater control over foreign policy.

Harold Lasswell reviewed the book for the *New Republic* and claimed that "Grattan may have begun his volume as a disillusionist, but his thorough scholarship and temperate tone entitle him to a place among the objectivists."[66] If nothing else, this at least meant that Lasswell agreed with Grattan.

But Grattan and his former teacher, Barnes, were to be greatly saddened by a review written by Sidney Bradshaw Fay. Fay was, of course, the man Barnes felt had done more than any other single man to shake Barnes's own wartime beliefs, the man who had really begun the revisionist controversy in the United States. But Fay would have no part of the revisionist interpretation of American intervention. Reviewing *Why We Fought* for the New York *Herald Tribune,* Fay wrote:

> Mr. Grattan has not risen fully to his opportunity. Perhaps he is too anxious to debunk the current American Legion notion that we gloriously fought to make the world safe for democracy. With the advantage of the hindsight afforded by the course of subsequent events and by the present abundance of memoirs and documents, it is easy for him to rail at the selfishness, stupidity or deceptions of the leaders in Washington and the Allied capitals. But he does not take adequately into account the psychological fact that these men of 1914–1917 were ignorant of much that we now know; and he does less than justice to the undoubted idealism of Colonel House and President Wilson. . . .[67]

Fay was also critical of Grattan's organization which was essentially topical rather than chronological: "This has its advantages, but it tends to obscure the essential fact of the gradual evolution of opinion on the part of President Wilson and the American people between 1914 and 1917." Then, after admitting that he found the book "interesting" and "lively," Fay concluded by expressing "fear" that the reader might finish Grattan's book "without knowing precisely why we fought."

In fact, Grattan did not answer the question posed by the title of his book. This had not been his intention. He was much more

66. *New Republic,* LXII (March 12, 1930), 104.

67. *Herald Tribune,* Books, January 12, 1930, p. 5.

interested in demonstrating that there was no reason for the United States to have fought; more interested in demonstrating that previous interpretations of American intervention were oversimplified. Grattan's approach was unlike that of any of his predecessors, but was rather a forerunner of what a later generation would call "realism" in the analysis of foreign policy. A nightmare to historians of Rankean attitude, Grattan's method was one of "second-guessing" Wilson and his associated decision-makers, seeking not to describe events but to determine what went wrong. As for obscuring the role of public opinion, Grattan could not have cared less. The possibility that public opinion in democratic America might have permitted Wilson no alternatives to the policies he pursued—a possibility which Grattan would not have conceded—was still no excuse if these policies were detrimental to the nation's interests. For Grattan, as a more eloquent speaker later declared in the same context: "History does not forgive us our national mistakes because they are explicable in terms of our domestic politics. . . . A nation which excuses its own failures by the sacred untouchableness of its own habits can excuse itself into complete disaster."[68]

First, Grattan asked if it had been morally imperative for the United States to intervene. With regard to the origins of the war he had found no moral basis for intervention. He had no special affection for the Germans, no particular desire to apologize for their role in the days or years immediately preceding the war. In fact, he found that on several occasions the Germans had acted stupidly. He had not, however, found any evidence to indicate that the Germans were morally inferior to any other participant in the war; nor did he see events occurring during the war itself as indicative of peculiar German immorality. He viewed submarine warfare "cold bloodedly" and could not bring himself to believe that it was any less moral than a food blockade or any other means of killing non-combatants. Increasingly, it became apparent that Grattan did not believe moral issues led to American intervention, but that he viewed them rather as abstracts painted by ideologists to obscure less altruistic concerns. He was

68. George F. Kennan, *American Diplomacy, 1900–1950* (New York: New American Library, 1960), p. 65.

not, however, implying the existence of a conspiracy to deceive the masses. Too sophisticated for conspiracy theories, yet unable to accept idealism as sufficient motivation for human action, Grattan implied that the discovery of moral issues, the cloaking of interest in idealism, were the necessary, although unconscious, rationalizations of moral man in an amoral world.

Like most of his contemporaries, Grattan could not conceive of a German victory in the World War as a threat to the security of the United States. But unlike Bausman and Barnes, he readily conceded that intervention had arisen out of a genuine conflict of interest between Germany and the United States. The Germans had to stop American shipments to the Allies; the American economy could not survive a trade stoppage. Here was a case of war in the national interest, but this was the point at which the limits of Grattan's realism were reached. He was realist enough to see and to demonstrate the extent of American economic interest in the Allied cause—and to contend that this interest was not worth the price of war to the country as a whole. But like so many other reform intellectuals in the years following the war, and unlike the "realists" of the Theodore Roosevelt breed, Grattan could cut only one way—always to deny the usefulness of war—never to justify it; to note the economic realities of international politics, but never the realities of power.

With Grattan unable to accept the economic interests involved in international trade as worth a war, the next logical step was for someone to demonstrate that shoring up the American economy in 1917 had been a mistake. Before October, 1929, and the crash, this would have seemed an unlikely argument. But after several years of the Great Depression, first Charles Beard and then Grattan himself proceeded to contend that it would have been best to have permitted the economy to collapse in 1917.

CHAPTER FIVE

The Application of Revisionism to American Foreign Policy 1930–1934

On Tuesday, October 23, 1929, the tickertape at the New York Stock Exchange ran 104 minutes late before the day ended. The Market, which had been wavering since September, took a severe drop. On the twenty-fourth, the bottom dropped out and the panic was underway. The Great Depression had begun its withering course. Grattan's *Why We Fought* appeared in November and sales were not enhanced by conditions following the crash. But the climate in which an economic interpretation of historical events would be readily accepted was gradually evolving. In the following decade, economic concerns—heightened by the depression—dominated society, shaping the assumptions, hopes, and aspirations of all men. And like American attitudes toward all other aspects of human existence, American attitudes toward foreign policy, toward the late World War, could not escape the clouded lens of the depression through which they were filtered.

As the decade of the twenties came to an end, Americans tended to view the war-guilt question as ancient history, and Harry Elmer Barnes was pretty well reconciled to treating it as such himself. In his massive *World Politics in Modern Civilization*,[1] he declared that he had devoted "altogether too much time and attention to the question of the causes of the outbreak of the World

1. New York: Knopf, 1930.

120

War" and suggested that he was ready to return to his own academic interests. He repeated his conclusions and maintained that the continuing flow of documentary evidence justified still more extreme revisionism. Writing as historiographer, he categorized the writers who had dealt with the *Kriegsschuldfrage*. First, there were the "bitter-enders," including Professors Hazen, E. Raymond Turner, William Stearns Davis, and Frank Maloy Anderson. These men, Barnes contended, held to the wartime views of the exclusive responsibility of the Central Powers for the World War. Then there were the "salvagers," including Schmitt and Seymour. They were the kind who cited all the latest documentary evidence but still held the Central Powers primarily responsible. Finally, of course, there were the "revisionists" of the "moderate," Fay, variety, and the more uncompromising group led by Barnes.[2]

He recognized, however, that the history of American intervention was a fertile field in which to continue the revisionist controversy: "The realistic history of Wilson and the World War in America and Europe has not even been attempted, though much preliminary evidence has been suggested by the courageous, if exaggerated and one-sided, book of John Kenneth Turner, and in the New York *Nation*."[3]

Barnes also provided a few of his own thoughts on why the United States had intervened. As he had indicated, his view was not very much different from that of John Kenneth Turner. We fought not to protect America from the threat of German invasion, not to make the world safe for democracy, but "to protect our investment in Allied bonds and to insure a longer period and more extensive development of the manufacturing of war materials."[4]

He was, to be sure, critical of Wilson, but time and again he would reach back to defend Wilson against the latter's more extreme critics. Wilson was "personally incorruptible," and he "really felt that Great Britain and her Allies were fighting for

2. *World Politics*, pp. 452–53, 471, 475–76.

3. *Ibid.*, p. 376. Apparently Barnes had not seen Grattan's *Why We Fought* at the time he was writing.

4. *Ibid.*, p. 378.

civilization." Barnes found Wilson pro-British and "intensely vain," but he "was not a hypocrite." "Mr. Wilson had a great capacity for verbal auto-intoxication and in the process of elaborating the war epic in his remarkable speeches he seems in part to have convinced himself."[5]

It was Wilson whom Barnes labeled "the supreme architect of the Holy War Legend," the man who put intervention in moral terms. But almost as he criticized Wilson's idealism, Barnes revealed the extent of his own commitment to that idealism:

> It was Wilson's creation and engineering of the League of Nations which left the only heritage of good from the days of the Holy War propaganda and furnished the only real hope of achieving a better day. Finally, the vestiges of the Wilsonian idealism have made it more difficult for the European diplomats to abandon all pretense to peace and justice in their post-War dealings. . . .[6]

Turning to his own country, Barnes blamed the reaction against Wilson for the "sordidness, materialism, corruption, and isolation which have characterized American politics since 1921." However, "the Wilson legend has kept alive American idealism and the support of the League of Nations."

Sharing Wilson's attitudes toward world politics, but unhappy with Wilson's casting of the American role in world affairs, Barnes left the stage to Charles Beard, who had little objection to American intervention in 1917, but was appalled by Wilson's concept of the nature of world politics. While Barnes tried to return to his real interest, intellectual history, Beard dominated the revisionist controversy. Nonetheless, as one familiar with Barnes's energy and tenacity would have expected, Barnes could not refrain from quarterbacking a few more thrusts at the defenses of the "salvagers" and "bitter-enders." But the big play fizzled. Barnes called upon Professor M. H. Cochrane of Missouri, ofttime critic of the revisionists in general and Barnes in particular, to "devastate" Schmitt's Pulitzer Prize-winning *Coming of the War, 1914.*[7] Cochrane produced a book-length critique, *Germany Not Guilty in 1914.*[8] Barnes wrote the foreword, and the book jacket con-

5. *Ibid.*, p. 411.   7. New York: Scribner's, 1930.
6. *Ibid.*, p. 367.   8. Boston: The Stratford Company, 1931.

tained a statement expressing the belief that further discussion of the causes of the war would not be necessary. The next ploy was to obtain for the book a suitable review in the *New Republic*. The editors of the *New Republic* tried, but months passed without success. Finally Malcolm Cowley gave up and told Barnes what Barnes had been prepared to believe for some time: "I must say that in a case like this American history professors seem to be a pretty chicken-livered bunch. They all say that you are right and Schmitt was wrong, but each one finds a new excuse for not entering the argument."[9] Beard, however, had never been accused of being "chicken-livered."

2

Charles Beard had been an active supporter of American intervention in the World War. He had voted for Charles Evans Hughes in 1916 because he himself had not felt "too proud to fight." After the United States intervened, he contributed to the war effort as a publicist, as with his article on behalf of the Liberty Bond drive mentioned earlier.

In 1918, with Frederick Ogg, Beard wrote *National Governments and the World War*.[10] In his share of the volume, Beard discussed at length the reasons for American intervention, and while endorsing the reasons offered by Wilson he added particular stress to the threat posed for the United States by a victorious Germany.

It was against a government conceived in military despotism and dedicated to the proposition that kings can do no wrong, that President Wilson asked his country to take up arms. To say that the outcome of the war in Europe was of no concern to the United States was to ignore forty years of German history. Thousands of peaceful citizens, though looking with horror upon the thought of war, were slowly and reluctantly driven by events to the conclusion that a German victory in Europe would imperil democracy in the United States in the coming years. They *realized* that, with Great

9. Cowley to Barnes, February 26, 1932, Barnes MSS.
10. New York: Macmillan, 1919.

Britain beaten and her colonies annexed by Germany, America would not be spared by a power founded on the sword.[11]

To these Americans, with whom Beard identified, two centuries of progress, and perhaps even faith in progress, seemed to be at stake: "To them, the triumph of the German war machine, dominating all Europe, would make vain and foolish two centuries of struggle for popular government, for popular control over the power of kings and aristocracies, for the extension of the suffrage and the advancement of democracy."[12] And thus America went to war "to aid in overthrowing militarism and imperialism and in preventing their return to plague the earth's weary multitudes."

Beard felt that Wilson in calling for a declaration of war had proved that the United States would be, "in very truth," going to war in response to transgressions already committed against the United States. Beard's attitude toward submarine warfare was very different from the attitude subsequently exhibited by Grattan. In 1918, Beard was not acting the part of "hard-headed realist": "Even if established law had not forbidden the wanton killing of non-combatants, the dictates of humanity would have prevented such outrageous conduct."[13]

Beard contended that Germany was "the one power of the earth" that had opposed a union of nations against war—because Germany, "under her imperial and military masters," was "bent upon designs of conquest and subjugation." For this reason, "far-seeing men" had realized that before a concert of nations could arise, "the sword of the German military masters would have to be broken." He wrote that it "was in reality in response to a war against war that the American people so quickly rallied to the call to lay aside the ways of peace and embark upon the trying and costly enterprise of beating German militarism on the field of battle, thus throwing down imperialism to make way for the union of nations against war."[14]

It would appear that in 1918 Beard had no doubts as to why America had intervened, no doubts as to the righteousness of America's cause. Only five years after he shocked the country

---

11. *National Governments and the World War*, pp. 13–14, italics added.

12. *Ibid.*, p. 14.   13. *Ibid.*, pp. 556, 559.   14. *Ibid.*, p. 562.

with his *Economic Interpretation of the Constitution,* Beard came up with a host of reasons for American intervention and not one of these was economic. The United States fought to end war, to save democracy, to wipe German militarism and imperialism off the face of the earth before America itself was threatened. And in their inhuman use of the submarine, the Germans did indeed seem peculiarly immoral to Charles Beard.

All this was before the secret treaties of the Allies were revealed, before Beard saw the Treaty of Versailles, and and before Sidney Fay wrote his "New Light" articles for the *American Historical Review.* In the early 1920's, Beard seemed disillusioned about the origins of the war, less certain about the reasons for American intervention. But in 1926, in his review of the *Genesis of the World War,* he took issue with Barnes's interpretation of American intervention and expressed anew his earlier conviction on the necessity of intervention. Then in 1928, in *Rise of American Civilization,* his conviction seemed to waver. He might not bring himself to accept the revisionist interpretation of why the United States went to war, but he had to admit that the evidence for the revisionist case had become impressive.

Early in 1929, Beard wrote a pair of articles for *Harper's,* dealing with matters of war and peace. In the first of these he made clear his acceptance of war-guilt revisionism, but left ambiguous his position on American intervention. He contended that Poincaré was "at least" as responsible for the war as any other single individual and condemned the war-guilt clause as a factor, like armament races and commercial rivalries, leading to the next war. He added that not a single "outstanding" scholar in France, England, or the United States believed in the "Paris doctrine that the Central Powers and their Allies must bear the sole responsibility for plunging Europe into hell." He also wrote of the "Carthaginian" peace and made several cynical references to the war for democracy. His attitude toward American intervention in 1917 seemed to have changed considerably, but he had not yet declared intervention a mistake.[15]

In the second article for *Harper's,* Beard concerned himself with

15. "Bigger and Better Armaments," *Harper's,* CLVIII (January, 1929), 133–43.

the outlook for peace.[16] He examined the League of Nations, conceded "all" criticism of that organization, and then argued that all powers including the United States had to recognize its presence and co-operate with it, directly or otherwise. Arguments of this sort, matched by Barnes, make it difficult to label either man an "isolationist" and make it difficult to equate revisionism with "isolationism."

The most suggestive argument put forth by Beard was that international capitalism was the best hope for peace.[17] Beard maintained that the international bankers had the power to prevent war and that enlightened self-interest would lead them to work in that direction. Referring back to the World War, Beard had no doubt that the bankers could have brought it to a halt at will, simply by agreeing to end credits to the belligerents.

Drawing implications from arguments by Beard is hazardous work at best. It would seem safe to guess that Beard was being impish in contending that his expectations of peace rested upon his faith in the international bankers.[18] On the other hand, it would seem likely that Beard did believe that international capitalism had influenced the course of the World War and had the power to affect the existing peace. But it would be rash to read into Beard's statement a suggestion that the bankers had caused the war or made the decision of the United States to intervene. At most Beard implied that the bankers had permitted the war to run longer than enlightened self-interest had dictated, had allowed the United States to intervene when they might have prevented intervention.

Beard, like Grattan, had recognized that in 1917 the United States had economic interests which could be protected only by intervention. The question that seemed to run through his mind in the 1920's was whether or not these economic interests had been worth fighting for: might it have been better to permit the econ-

16. "Prospects for Peace," *Harper's,* CLVIII (February, 1929), 320–30.

17. *Ibid.,* p. 327.

18. Thomas C. Kennedy suggests that Beard may be taken seriously here. He contends that long before World War I, Beard "began to perceive the possible amelioration of national rivalries through international trade and finance." See Kennedy's "Charles A. Beard and American Foreign Policy" (unpublished Ph.D. dissertation, Stanford, 1961).

omy to collapse in 1917 and then to try to restore it on a firmer foundation—a foundation unaffected by the vicissitudes of international trade. Long hostile to "dollar diplomacy," to internationalism based on international trade and the exploitation of underdeveloped countries, Beard poked around in quest of evidence with which to demonstrate that international trade did not pay—evidence that might also suggest that the war had not been worth fighting. Then, beginning in October, 1929, the pieces began to fall in place, and before the Great Depression had run its course, Beard thought he had found what he had been looking for.

3

Between Charles Beard and the Navy League no love was lost. Unlike Samuel Eliot Morison, Beard's heart was cold to the men who went down to the sea in ships. While others, watching a new ship launched, thrilled at thoughts of romantic adventure in distant exotic lands, Beard could think only of the cost, of funds that could have been spent on domestic improvement; could think only of the naval officers who had presumed to make foreign policy in the past, of gunboats protecting the interests of the United Fruit Company or of the Standard Oil Company. Much of Beard's work in the years of the Hoover Administration was devoted to opposing the efforts of the Navy League to create a navy "second to none." Every now and then, something would occur to him that seemed relevant to American intervention in the World War and he would be found drawing striking parallels with the revisionist interpretation of that act: "President Wilson came to the conclusion in 1915 that the United States should have a navy second to none—perhaps because he had already come to the personal decision that he would in due time take the country into the World War on the side of the Entente Allies."[19]

Then Beard proceeded to demonstrate that his quarrel with the Navy League did not relieve his skepticism regarding the peace movements of the day. In an article for *Harper's,* he argued that the primary problem in American foreign policy was one of national security, which he defined as the ability to protect the

19. "Big Navy Boys," *New Republic,* LXIX (January 20, 1932), 261.

country against invasion.[20] Of both the pacifists and the Navy League he was critical because they failed to see the issue in these terms. To him it was apparent that most advocates of peace were thinking not in terms of national defense "but of overcoming the growing war machines by pledges and promises of friendship and good will among nations." He sympathized with the hopes of such as these, but insisted that "the central issue of national defense is not clarified by the spread of sweetness and light."[21] Beard followed this with a reminder to the Navy League that striving for naval hegemony was not the answer either: Japan and Great Britain would never permit the United States to gain such status. Pointing to the World War he noted that Great Britain had not waited "until von Tirpitz had the trident in his hands. She joined the combination that smashed him and ruined his country."[22] With increasing regularity, Beard turned to the lessons of the World War in support of his foreign policy proposals, and these lessons became increasingly similar to the lessons found by Barnes and Grattan.

On those rare occasions when Beard neglected to publish his thoughts, the *New York Times* might be counted on to write them up for him. Late in February, 1932, the *Times* quoted a brief but loaded statement. Beard was concerned still with national defense. He found everyone participating in wordy discussions of war and peace without considering the "substance of defense." Hoover had said that the purpose of the army and the navy was to prevent an invasion. To Beard this meant "that national defense means defense of our continental heritage, not defense of every American dollar in every part of the world against any and all powers, no matter what the issue."[23] Again, it is easy to read too much into Beard's words and tempting to contend that Beard was referring to the circumstances of 1917 and preparing to argue that the United States should not have fought to protect its trade when such trade was upsetting a life-and-death struggle in Europe. Indeed, Beard did in after years make these very points, but to try

20. "Our Confusion over National Defense," *Harper's*, CLXIV (February, 1932), 257–67.

21. *Ibid.*, p. 260.   22. *Ibid.*, p. 266.

23. *New York Times*, February 28, 1932, Sec. II, p. 4.

to make the Charles Beard of 1933 fit the revisionist mold is to miss the subtle manner in which Beard and revisionism came together. Unlike Barnes and Grattan, Beard first worked out an elaborate concept of national interest and then a still more elaborate plan, "continentalism," for combining domestic and foreign policy. In arguing for his policy he found the revisionist interpretation of American intervention a valuable tool. As the possibility of American intervention in a second world war grew imminent, as Beard's efforts to foster his own "continental" policy grew more frantic, his acceptance of revisionism increased strikingly. Revisionism suited Beard's policy and Beard's policy suited the revisionists. By 1939 the integration was complete.

4

In November, 1932, Franklin Delano Roosevelt was elected President of the United States. Here was a man whose fine phrases brought real hope to Charles Beard and many another American who strained toward that "rendezvous with destiny." Earlier in the year, Beard had received a grant of $25,000 from the Social Science Research Council to assist him in a search for a precise definition of the "national interest."[24] As he proceeded with his study he was particularly pleased by Roosevelt's activities in the realm of foreign policy. Roosevelt seemed to be following precisely the lines he would have drawn. Yes—the New Deal had real promise, and hopefully Roosevelt would not jeopardize it by worrying overly about the problems faced by the rest of the world. Like the *philosophes* of the Enlightenment, Beard clung tenaciously to the idea that there were times when foreign relations played too great a role in the political affairs of the nation—when the playthings of princes had to be set aside to face the mundane necessities of the nation.

The first product of his research was *The Idea of National Interest*,[25] probably the dullest book Beard ever wrote. For the most part, the book read like an encyclopedia: example after example of the way "thinkers and statesmen" had used the term "national interest." All of these men seemed to conceive of interest "as a real-

24. *Ibid.*, March 23, 1932, p. 23.   25. New York: Macmillan, 1934.

ity open to human understanding and as a kind of iron necessity which binds governments and governed alike." However defined, national interest "cuts across the social divisions reflected in political parties and compels 'a united front.' "[26] Anyone who had been following Beard's wars against "dollar diplomacy" and the Navy League needed to read no further to know what he was up to. He had quickly and unostentatiously set up a criticism of the existing concept of *national* interest as representative merely of the interests of small groups—and probably detrimental to the country as a whole.

Soon Beard came to a discussion of what he considered to be the Republican as opposed to the Jeffersonian concept of national interest: whereas the Jeffersonian party had emphasized the "national" in national interest, being "essentially isolationist in outlook," the Republican party chose to emphasize "interest" in its foreign policy. At the close of the nineteenth century, Beard saw the Republicans developing a " 'new' *Realpolitik*": "A free opportunity for expansion in foreign markets is indispensable to the prosperity of American business. Modern diplomacy is commercial. Its chief concern is with the promotion of economic interests abroad." This Beard described as the "instrumentalities and implications of dollar diplomacy by which the national interest was to be actively fostered and achieved."[27]

Beard noted that governmental action on behalf of commercial expansion, regardless of source or origin, was justified on the ground of national interest. He found the conception of national interest revealed in American state papers to be "an aggregation of particularities assembled like eggs in a basket." Markets for agricultural produce and for industrial commodities were in the national interest: "naval bases, territorial acquisitions for commercial support, an enlarged consular and diplomatic service, an increased navy and merchant marine, and occasional wars were all in the national interest. These contentions were not proved; they were asserted as axioms, apparently regarded as so obvious as to call for no demonstration."[28]

Beard went on to complain that the "whole weight" of govern-

26. *The Idea of National Interest*, p. 3.
27. *Ibid.*, pp. 87, 107.   28. *Ibid.*, p. 167.

ment activities was brought to bear to safeguard the American stake in international commerce, "on the hypothesis, and no doubt the conscientious belief, that the 'national interest' is thereby advanced." Then came the master stroke—the link between revisionism and Beard's policy—the union soon to be consummated in the neutrality legislation of the 1930's. The United States, he wrote, had not been entangled in the alliances which fixed the lines for the World War. Nonetheless, the nation was drawn into the war "under conceptions of interest and moral obligation." Then he quoted Curtis Wilbur and let the Secretary of the Navy make the point. Wilbur declared that "the World War furnished a clear instance of violated commercial right and our defense thereof. We fought not because Germany invaded or threatened to invade America, but because she struck at our commerce on the North Sea, and denied to our ships and to our citizens on the high seas the protection of our flag."[29]

Beard granted that Wilbur's statement might have oversimplified the case, but "it at least expresses substantial truth; no commerce, no violation of rights, no entanglements of diplomacy and war."[30] "No commerce," "no war," wrote Charles Beard in 1934. Everything for which he had thought he was fighting in 1917 and 1918 was forgotten. "No commerce," "no war," wrote Charles Beard in 1934, and soon thereafter, when the second world war loomed on the horizon, this thought became law, the neutrality legislation which circumscribed American foreign policy in the late 1930's. Thus was revisionism applied to the formulaton of American foreign policy.

Letting up, briefly, in his attack on international commerce, he turned to another late-nineteenth-century phenomenon: the development of the feeling of "moral obligation to embark upon projects for uplifting, civilizing, or Christianizing other peoples beyond the confines of the country."[31] The United States began getting involved in "moral adventures" in diplomacy, even to the extent of employing force "for the purpose of doing good to other peoples by interfering with their domestic and international quarrels." Beard made no specific reference to the World War, but he did write of the pre-eminence of moral values among the underlying

29. *Ibid.*, p. 313.   30. *Ibid.*   31. *Ibid.*, p. 358.

assumptions of Wilson's foreign policy and of Wilson's belief that democracy was a "decided good" whose attainment by other nations was worthy of American assistance. Beard's own preference was to see democracy spread by "weight of example," but "this swelling passion to do good, to impose inherited principles of government and civilization on other peoples" had been given a fixed place in American diplomacy; "under skillful leaders it may make crusades and holy wars." Beard could even think of occasions when moral obligation seemed to require forcible intervention in the affairs of other countries. Again, Beard had forgotten or put aside his own wartime thoughts, forgotten his own crusade for democracy.

Beard then raised the question of who was to interpret the national interest. In a discussion of the power of the President to do the interpreting, Beard referred again to American intervention in the World War: "By common consent President Wilson could have kept the country out of the World War, perhaps as easily as he took it into the War. Practically considered, the determination was his own."[32] Thus Beard ignored the overwhelming congressional vote for war, ignored the pressures exerted by Charles Beard and others throughout the country, which were driving Wilson toward calling for intervention. In terms of future policy this interpretation of the decision to intervene would lead to efforts to take away from America's chief executive his alleged power to involve his country in war.

In his lectures at Dartmouth in 1922, published as *Cross Currents in Europe Today,* Beard had described the United States as an industrial and trading country with a trade empire reaching all over the world. He found the United States dependent upon foreign trade, "if not for a livelihood, at least for what is called prosperity."[33] In 1934, Beard was convinced that the experience of the depression had undermined the theory that international trade was salutary for the American economy. He was convinced that the various policies based upon this theory had at least aggravated the depression.[34] He argued that loans abroad, for example, had been to the interest of the banking houses transacting them and had been neither directly nor indirectly of benefit to the nation. He in-

32. *Ibid.,* p. 417. 33. *Cross Currents,* p. 242.
34. *The Idea of National Interest,* pp. 490–91.

sisted that businessmen worked on only one principle, the search for profit, and he could find no evidence that those concerned with international commerce made their transactions with anything else in mind—not even the advancement of the "national interest." The core of Beard's thought in 1934 was his belief that the United States had become involved in the World War and had been forced to intervene in that war because of American commercial interests. Like Grattan, he saw a conflict between the economic interests of the United States and Germany's determination to win the European war. More clearly than Grattan, Beard recognized the importance of these economic interests. But he could and did try to demonstrate that these interests were interests of the few and not of the country as a whole. When he had done this to his own satisfaction he was certain that the desires both for social reform at home and for a means to keep the United States out of the next war could be satisfied by extensive limitation and control of America's external commerce.

Beard expressed his high hopes for Franklin Delano Roosevelt as a man who would use the presidency to foster the national interest as Beard himself conceived it. He believed Roosevelt was concerned with "things constituting national interest" which were not related to the "implications of empire or to any duty owed by the United States to 'benighted peoples.' " In Roosevelt's campaign speeches of 1932, Beard found no indication of concern for "so-called 'international issues' or 'world interdependence' ": "Without doubt he [F.D.R.] expressed an essentially 'national' point of view, which, while not denying a place to international aspects, nevertheless clearly indicated that they were secondary and largely incidental to the 'intranational' approach to the solution of domestic problems."[35]

Beard was also pleased by what he interpreted as attitudes of the "dominant" group within the Democratic Party. To this group the possibility of a distinctively American character and way of life, as "envisaged by Jefferson," remained a "living and vital force." These men emphasized domestic issues, and to them "the fact that foreign trade is less than 10 per cent of the total United States trade activity does not represent the margin between mere

35. *Ibid.*, pp. 526–29.

existence and prosperity, but it illustrates the importance of the domestic market and shows how little we are dependent upon foreign countries."[36]

Roosevelt's "torpedoing" of the London Conference excited Beard, and he quoted Roosevelt with unabashed glee: "The sound internal economic system of a nation is a greater factor in its well-being than the price of its currency in changing terms of the currencies of other nations." This, wrote Beard, was the "national attitude" which regarded internationalism as incidental to "a strong national solidarity based upon a distinctive conception of American society and its interest." This, wrote Beard, was a "resurrection" of the relationship between nationalism and internationalism which the authors of the Federalist Papers had had in mind, which Washington had contemplated in his Farewell Address, and which had been the cornerstone of Jeffersonianism.[37]

Beard felt that Roosevelt and he had learned the same lesson from the crash of 1929. Together they had come to see that it was both possible and desirable to have a high standard of "national well-being" with minimal reliance on foreign trade. Their conception of national interest indicated that economic recovery would come not from adjustments made at international conferences or from outward thrusts of commercial power, but from the "collaboration of domestic interests with a view to establishing the security which may come from integrated economic activities and a more efficient distribution of wealth or buying power."[38] Beard did not want this "new nationalism" confused with any of the predatory varieties he had attacked in the past. If it ran counter to the Cobden-Bright internationalism of laissez faire, it was also "far from being the old nationalism of imperialism based upon *Machtpolitik*, which supports outward thrusts of American economic power and sustains them by diplomacy and arms."[39] Beard wanted to be certain that his readers understood that this was to be a nonimperialistic nationalism.

As much as Roosevelt pleased him, Beard could not relax. Roosevelt liked the navy and gave no indication of letting up on naval expenditures. Roosevelt liked playing power politics. These were

36. *Ibid.*, p. 534.
37. *Ibid.*, pp. 541–42.
38. *Ibid.*, p. 545.
39. *Ibid.*, pp. 545–46.

things that made Beard uneasy. He could see Roosevelt's little games "resulting in a grand diversion—a diversion that might not be unwelcome, should the domestic recovery program fall far short of its aims."[40] Thus were the seeds of World War II revisionism sown.

In the *Yale Review*, Carl Becker failed to suppress a chuckle over Beard's pretense to objectivity, his claim to be presenting nothing but the relevant facts and leaving for a companion volume the business of interpretation. Becker reminded his readers that there was probably no one who knew as well as Beard "that facts acquire relevance only when arranged in a pattern from which some significance emerges." Becker found the pattern in which Beard arranged his facts "revealing enough by itself," but noted that the author was always at hand, "for any reader who needs a little help, to run his pointer over the essential features of the design."[41]

An interesting contrast with Becker's review appeared in the *Nation*, a product of the pen of Harold Laski. Laski felt that no one could read *The Idea of National Interest* without real enthusiasm and constant illumination. Unlikely as this may have seemed to any who picked up the book, it was credible—a matter of taste. But Laski added that he was disappointed that Beard had refrained from interpretation—that there was hardly a chapter that did not "cry out" for interpretation.[42] And so it seemed *The Idea of National Interest* would have to be added to the list of books that Harold Laski had never really read.

Another example of the ability of men to find what they seek in a book was provided by the reviews of Edwin Borchard in the *New Republic* and Tyler Dennett in the *American Historical Review*. Borchard made the astounding discovery that Beard had rejected the assumption that all political motivation is economic, while Dennett found Beard merely "illustrating" the economic basis of politics—although he clearly suspected Beard of having attempted to "prove" the economic basis. Dennett made one other point of considerable significance: he believed the book might be expected

40. *Ibid.*, pp. 547–48.

41. *Yale Review*, N.S., XXIII (June, 1934), 814–17.

42. *Nation*, CXXXVIII (April 25, 1934), 479–80.

to "introduce into the study of American diplomatic history a needed note of realism."[43] This, of course, was Beard's great hope. Before the end of 1934, Beard's *The Open Door at Home* was published.[44] This was the promised companion volume to *The Idea of National Interest*. He contended again that in *The Idea of National Interest* he had presented "theories and facts, without criticism, as far as humanly possible." That had been the "fact statement" and *The Open Door at Home* was to present Beard's personal view of a policy designed in the national interest.

The concern of the reform intellectual for cleaning house in the United States before attempting to save the world permeated the book. Beard contended that the national interest would be served best if more emphasis were placed on eliminating backwardness at home "than on effort to wrest new 'benighted' areas from Great Britain, France, or Japan for the purpose of securing more moral obligations to other races." He noted that "those who are deeply moved in the virtuous sense implied by 'the white man's burden' can, in view of the condition of several million Negroes in the United States, probably find extensive outlets for their moral urges at home."[45] For those to whom domestic opportunities seemed too few, Beard recommended that "sacrificial virtues" be exercised by bringing the United States into the League of Nations where they could administer mandates, "thus aiding powerfully, if indirectly, in the process of spreading 'order, civilization, and Christianity.' "

Beard seemed extremely sensitive to the label "isolationist" and made several careful efforts to separate himself from a breed to whom he would apply the label. Those *he* would call isolationists believed in keeping the American government from entering into any agreements leading to peace "which would interfere with American capitalists in the enjoyment of protective tariffs, in pushing foreign trade and investments, and in enforcing their interests abroad by engines of coercion, by war if necessary."[46]

Whatever one cared to call Beard's policy, it was quite different from the "isolationism" he described. His desire to be free of

43. *New Republic,* LXXVIII (April 4, 1934), 220–21; *American Historical Review,* XXXIX (July, 1934), 742.

44. New York: Macmillan, 1934.

45. *The Open Door,* p. 55.   46. *Ibid.,* p. 130.

commitments to other countries was not conceived out of any desire to permit would-be American imperialists to run rampant.
Beard was concerned primarily with avoiding commitments or entanglements which might result, as in 1917, in the United States
becoming involved in quarrels and wars which were unrelated to
American policy aims and which diverted American energies from
the pursuit of the national interest. For Beard, the "supreme" interest of the United States was "the creation and maintenance of a
high standard of life for all its people and ways of industry conducive to the promotion of individual and social virtues *within the
frame of national security.*"[47] Toward this goal the nation had
been moving until 1917. Then came intervention, an action which
might or might not have been necessary, but an action which was
taken without consideration of national interest. Using a revisionist argument, Beard contended that it was "highly doubtful whether the United States would have entered the World War 'in defense
of democracy' if American nationals could have sold munitions
and supplies as freely to the Central Powers as to the Allies, and if
the Germans had not preyed upon American commerce."[48]

Beard's attitude toward war played an important part at this
stage of his argument, and his attitude was markedly different from
that of Barnes. He was disgusted with American "thought" on the
subject, disgusted with uncritical slogans: "War is evil"; "War
never settles anything"; "Preparation for war leads to war";
"War is an outcome of capitalism." He was equally irritated with
military slogans and mottoes. War was not, Beard insisted, a "pri-
mordial force, independent of national policy and will." On the
contrary, he contended, "the majority of wars known to history—
all great wars—have been associated in origin with policy" and, he
added, "with the more or less conscious purposes of the leaders,
governments or ruling classes that have precipitated them."[49]

Beard's concern over American intervention, in the last war or
the next, had, then, nothing to do with whether the war was "just"
or not. The problem as he described it was one of entering or staying out "on grounds of policy conceived in the national interest as
here defined." On these grounds he was uncertain whether intervention in the World War had been well advised or not. Would it

47. *Ibid.*, p. 210.   48. *Ibid.*, p. 173.   49. *Ibid.*, p. 248.

have been more desirable for the United States to have remained neutral? Beard saw no way of securing an unequivocal answer.[50] It was the manner in which the United States became involved in the war that disturbed him. In a different context, he wrote: "To encourage by State action American nationals to develop private interests in historic war zones beyond the effective control of American military and naval power is a betrayal of national interest conceived as supreme public interest."[51]

In sum, Beard did not claim that intervention was a mistake: this was the unknowable. He did suggest that the United States had stumbled into the war because its actions in the years 1914 to 1917 were not taken as part of a broad design of national policy, but rather as *ad hoc* reactions to steps taken by the belligerents. In this way American foreign policy became geared to the policy of the belligerents, particularly to German submarine policy, and effective control of the decision of whether or not the United States would intervene was turned over to the Germans.

Now Beard called for intensive reconstruction at home and asked that the United States make "no commitments that cannot readily be enforced by arms," that the United States refrain from giving other nations "moral advice." He called for a policy of "fair and open commodity exchange" with other nations and for a military establishment adequate to defend "this policy." Under these conditions the United States might "realize maximum security, attain minimum dependence upon governments and conditions beyond its control."[52]

Such a policy, Beard insisted, did not preclude "constant and sympathetic collaboration and cooperation with other nations so minded."[53] He opposed "passionate hostility" toward the League of Nations and the World Court, but he did expect "friendship" with these organizations to be discriminating. If other nations repressed predatory interests and conducted their policies in a way similar to that prescribed by Beard for the United States, then international co-operation could be most fully realized.

Finally, Beard returned to thoughts of the next war and to the lessons of the last war: "Since insistence on historic neutral rights

50. *Ibid.*, p. 244.
51. *Ibid.*, p. 269.
52. *Ibid.*, pp. 273–74.
53. *Ibid.*, p. 274.

in the next general war, and on the right to sell supplies and munitions to belligerents, will, as sure as fate, involve the United States
in that war, the only way to avoid being drawn into the holocaust
is to establish positive restraints on such rights now by legislation."[54] Then came the substantive proposals, drawn from an article by Charles Warren in the April, 1934, issue of *Foreign Affairs*:
(1) a ban on the sale of munitions and on their shipment in American bottoms; (2) the exclusion of armed belligerent vessels
from United States ports; (3) exclusion from American ports of
all vessels of belligerent powers which permit the flying of the
American flag as a *ruse de guerre* (4) exclusion of belligerent
prizes from American ports; (5) exclusion from American waters
and territory of all belligerent submarines and aircraft; (6) seizure
of belligerent vessels that remain in American waters beyond a
brief period of time; (7) prohibition of loans to belligerents; (8)
prohibition of belligerent recruiting in the United States; (9)
prohibition of American enlistments in belligerent armed forces;
and (10) prohibition of American travel on belligerent supply
ships. Beard contended that with these restraints on the activities
of private interests "clearly and firmly established in advance, the
Government of the United States could then decide, on the merits
of the issue as public interest, whether to enter or stay out of the
war."[55]

Beard's support of this program, soon to be substantially accepted in the neutrality acts of the 1930's, was obviously not based
on any a priori anti-interventionism. Other revisionists might be
charged with opposing American intervention in World War II
long before the war began, long before the issues of the war became
apparent; Beard, however, was concerned primarily with preventing any future intervention from occurring as haphazardly as had
intervention in 1917. For Beard, the neutrality legislation would
preclude the possibility of war resulting from a number of issues
he considered spurious, issues generally involving neutral rights.
In a sense, he was providing a particularly salutary service for the
American people. He was attempting to change American attitudes
toward world politics and America's role in world affairs. He was
trying to get the American people accustomed to discussing foreign

54. *Ibid.*, p. 286.   55. *Ibid.*

policy issues in terms of national interest rather than in terms of profit, honor, or moral obligation.

Samuel Flagg Bemis read *The Open Door at Home* for the *American Historical Review*. He finished feeling a bit skeptical about some of Beard's scholarship—the contrasts seemed too sharp, the selection of evidence something of a problem. Unlike Beard and the majority of the reform intellectuals, Bemis was not enthusiastic about the prospect of a planned economy. But he did find large areas of agreement with Beard—a little flag-waving was always a good thing. Reporting a rumor that President Roosevelt was already using the book as a guide, Bemis expected it to have tremendous influence in the United States.[56]

The caption for Maxwell Stewart's review in the *Nation* read "Beard Turns Nationalist," and Stewart went on to reproach Beard, gently but firmly, for being carried away with the flag-waving. The *New Republic* succeeded in getting Secretary of Agriculture Henry A. Wallace to write a lengthy review of Beard's blueprint. To what extent Wallace's views reflected those of Roosevelt or the administration may never be known, but it was clear that Wallace personally was not about to give Beard's ideas his unqualified approval. He declared that Beard wrote with "more intelligent patriotism than any other American" he had ever read, but he was not impressed with Beard's economic theory—finding him "not quite so good an economic technician as he is a historian."[57]

Perhaps the most interesting review of *The Open Door at Home* was written by Herbert Agar, southern journalist and recent convert to the philosophy of the Southern Agrarians. The Southern Agrarians were a group of southern intellectuals, including Allen Tate, John Crowe Ransom, Robert Penn Warren, and Frank L. Owsley, who were in rebellion against the persistence of the idea of progress in American thought—in rebellion against the glorification of industrialization and science, against the values of American society in the decade preceding the depression. Ultimately, these men and their movement were concerned with ending the

56. *American Historical Review,* XL (April, 1935), 541–43.

57. *Nation,* CXXXIX (November 28, 1934), 625; *New Republic,* LXXI (January 2, 1935), 225–27.

subservience of the South to the rest of the nation. In the 1930's, when men like Agar joined them, they were attempting to come up with a positive program to alleviate their grievances. Their answer was "Distributism," an ode to the virtues of life on the land—a program which demanded regional self-sufficiency, the redistribution of property as well as income, and an end to free trade. And Agar was delighted with Beard's book: Beard was with them; liberals could be "Distributists"; Beard's program fitted the Distributist program for America. In their common belief that commercialism was largely responsible for the evils in American society, Beard, sometime apostle of progress and industrialism, and the Agrarians, who distrusted industrialism and knew better than to believe in progress, came together.[58]

Commercialism, however, provided a still stronger link between the Agrarians and revisionism. If these southern intellectuals were prepared to blame commercialism for social evils in general, the revisionists were in the process of indicting commercialism for the specific sin of having involved the United States in the World War. And this revisionist argument was not lost on Frank Owsley, who wrote it into the final chapter of his interpretation of Civil War diplomacy.[59] Why had Europe failed to intervene to save the South? The answer was commercialism—war profits—the unwillingness to risk the profits derived from neutral trade. In this strange way revisionism could appeal to the southern intellectual —as the southerners found in revisionism an argument useful for a reinterpretation of the Civil War, for a restoration of southern pride.

5

While Beard held the reins in the application of revisionism to American foreign policy, Barnes and Grattan remained active. In an article discussing Woodrow Wilson's failure to create a viable peace at Versailles, Grattan seemed to be resolving his own ambivalence toward economic determinism by absorbing much of Hob-

58. *American Review,* IV (January, 1935), 297–309; for the most famous statement by the Southern Agrarians, see *I'll Take My Stand* (New York: Harper and Brothers, 1930).

59. *King Cotton Diplomacy* (Chicago: University of Chicago Press, 1931).

son's thought on imperialism. He contended that Wilson had failed to appreciate the "economic aspects" of the power of nationalism. Wilson had failed to realize that an international community of interest was impossible "while the nations of the world were based on a type of capitalist economy which is only healthy as long as it is capable of indefinite expansion and which can only expand by invading the rights and privileges of other nations." Grattan added his own belief that nationalism was in "its last stages," that internationalism would triumph in the end, "though only when the nations of the world operate on radically different economic bases." Shortly afterward, further evidence of Grattan's rapid drift to the left appeared in his criticism of Roosevelt as a "rentier" who was trying to save capitalism.[60]

In May, 1934, Grattan wrote an article closely paralleling Beard's efforts: "Why America Will Go to War."[61] The article was an obvious bid for legislation to prevent the situation Grattan was predicting. Drawing upon the lessons of the World War he declared that it was inevitable that the United States would participate in future wars in Europe and Asia. The one possibility of avoiding this was to block, by legislation, the recurrence of the entangling incidents of 1914 to 1917. Like Beard, Grattan was suspicious of Roosevelt, and to the dangers revealed by the "lessons" of 1917 he added the danger involved in the fact that Roosevelt was a convinced navalist.

In July, 1934, Barnes delivered an address at the University of Virginia's Institute of Public Affairs. If he was suspicious of Roosevelt he kept his suspicions to himself. First, he declared that "the war which was to make the world safe for democracy actually made democracy less safe in the world" than at any time since 1848. He then proceeded to laud Roosevelt and the New Deal as the only hope for the country. He argued that if the business leaders of the country had any sense they "would rally to his program with more loyalty than the profiteers rallied about Woodrow Wilson in 1917–18." He declared the depression to be a greater

60. "The 'Failure' of Woodrow Wilson," *North American Review,* CCXXXVII (March, 1934), 263–69; review of *The Roosevelt Omnibus* by Don Wharton (ed.), *Nation,* LXXXI (January 9, 1935), 256.

61. *Scribner's Magazine,* XCV (May, 1934), 321–26.

threat to democracy than "Prussianism or the last Kaiser." Roosevelt was the last hope of capitalism and democracy in the United States: "If the New Deal collapses, we have the stark realities of Fascism and then Communism staring us in the face. It is the New Deal, castor oil or the firing squad. Let the Steel Trust put this in its pipe and smoke it."[62]

But Barnes, too, was already moving to the left of Roosevelt, and, before long, concern over Roosevelt's foreign policy would limit his enthusiasm. Before that happened, a "revisionist" interpretation of American intervention in 1917 would appear as a Book-of-the-Month Club best seller.

62. *New York Times*, July 3, 1934, p. 7.

CHAPTER SIX

The United States Will Not Stumble into War Again
1935–1936

Early in 1934, while Beard was preparing to offer his views on national interest and foreign policy, the manufacturers of war materials were subjected to an intensive muckraking. There appeared almost simultaneously H. C. Engelbrecht and F. C. Hanighen's *Merchants of Death* and an article in *Fortune*, "Arms and Men," which demonstrated skilfully that arms manufacturing had become an international racket.[1] To introduce their book to the public, the authors of *Merchants of Death* called upon Harry Elmer Barnes. Barnes obliged, and in the foreword he attempted to define the role of the armament manufacturers. He insisted that they were not the chief menace to peace and that the authors were conscious of the "broader forces" that played a larger part in "keeping alive the war system." Barnes contended that armament manufacturers "never exerted so terrible an influence upon the promotion of warfare as did our American bankers between 1914 and 1917. Through their pressure to put the United States into the War these bankers brought about results which have well nigh wrecked the contemporary world."[2] For Barnes, it was still open season on bankers, but Frank Simonds, prominent newspaper authority on world af-

1. New York: Dodd, Mead and Co., 1934; *Fortune*, IX (March, 1934), 53–57 ff.

2. *Merchants of Death*, pp. vii–viii.

fairs, thought otherwise. Reviewing *Merchants of Death*, Simonds predicted that despite the intent of the authors the book would lead to a crusade based upon the erroneous assumption that the armament industry was responsible for war.[3]

In Congress a resolution calling for an investigation of the arms industry had already been introduced in the Senate and buried in committee. The new publicity given to the industry, however, facilitated favorable action on the resolution. By the fall of 1934, a special Senate committee, chaired by Senator Gerald P. Nye, began to hold hearings. Nye ultimately made all sorts of sensational discoveries, generally confirming his own presuppositions, but the public curiosity was permitted to mount until well into 1935 before the committee's preliminary report was turned over to the newspapers.

2

Back in 1931 a young journalist, Walter Millis, had written a highly readable account of the Spanish-American War.[4] When the reader finished Millis' book, there was not much left of the glory and romance of the adventure of 1898. Almost the entire war was depicted as a vast comedy, bungled from beginning to end. Whatever one thought of the book, it was obvious that Millis had rather a different view of the war than Theodore Roosevelt had and that Millis had rather less respect for martial virtues than Teddy had.

Millis was born in Atlanta, Georgia, in 1899. Barely eighteen when America declared war on Germany, he was sent to officer candidate school and commissioned as a second lieutenant in the army before the war was over. But Lieutenant Millis never saw any action, never left the United States, and later confessed that he had never had too much faith in the official versions of the reasons for intervention.[5] The whole experience was not an unusual one, but Millis became fascinated by "war." Upon completion of his studies at Yale in 1920, he devoted most of the rest of his life to the study of war.

3. "An International Racket," *Saturday Review of Literature*, X (April 28, 1934), 657–58.

4. *The Martial Spirit* (Boston: Houghton Mifflin, 1931).

5. "The Faith of an American," in Stephen Benét (ed.), *Zero Hour* (New York: Farrar and Rinehart, 1940); see pp. 219–21.

When *The Martial Spirit* was published, Millis had already established himself as a world affairs commentator of some note for the New York *Herald Tribune*. In 1932 he was invited to participate in a conference on armament limitation held under the auspices of the Foreign Policy Association. His comments at the conference indicated that he was moving in approximately the same direction as Charles Beard. Millis began by asking what a navy was supposed to do and ultimately concluded that the size and purpose of the navy should be limited to "those objectives which there is some reasonable likelihood the navy will succeed in holding within a cost commensurate with the advantages to be derived." Like Beard, he was arguing that there was no virtue in a big navy for its own sake—but he was also condoning implicitly the use of force as an instrument of national policy. In the next breath, however, he opposed "world dominion" as an objective and contended that other objectives should be pursued "only in so far as they can be achieved by diplomatic or moral effort." While his ambivalence toward force was confusing, Millis was himself quite certain where the application of his principles would lead: the United States would abandon "the idea of interdicting Japanese policy in Manchuria and even of physically defending the Philippines."[6] Obviously, Millis did not believe that the Japanese could be stopped in Manchuria without the use of force; nor did he appear to believe that the Philippines were worth defending. He was in favor of moral suasion, but apparently unimpressed by the dictates of international morality as applied to Japanese aggression.

Then, just a few weeks before the Nye Committee report was released, Millis' study of American intervention in the World War appeared on the book stands.[7] As in *The Martial Spirit*, so in *Road to War*, Millis "debunked" war and concentrated upon demonstrating, at least to his own satisfaction, that the United States had stumbled into the war, that the decision to intervene had not been an integrated part of an over-all foreign policy for America. Woven into the narrative was a second, less obvious, theme: resort to force is futile; the ends for which the United States fought could not be achieved by force.

6. *New York Times,* July 30, 1932, p. 14.

7. *Road to War* (New York: Houghton Mifflin, 1935).

For Millis, the *Kriegsschuldfrage* was of virtually no significance. In a few brief references to the origins of the war he called the Kaiser's "casual assurance" to Austria "the most important link in the long chain of causation" and pointed to American ignorance of the background of the war, American neglect of the importance of Russia, and the American tendency to view the initial crisis "in the conveniently simple terms of a wanton Austrian attack upon 'Little Servia.' " In sum, Millis viewed the origins of the war much as Bernadotte Schmitt had, and others whom Barnes had labeled "salvagers."

Unlike Grattan and Barnes, Millis did not seek to demonstrate that the United States had erred in intervening in the war. His primary objective appeared to be one of proving that the United States had blundered into the war in such a way as to guarantee that intervention would be futile. Whether or not American intervention was necessary or advisable was a question that Millis, like Beard, realized could never be answered with certainty. But again like Beard, Millis believed that it was relevant to raise the question of whether or not the United States had intervened for the right reasons—and more clearly than Beard, Millis replied in the negative. The United States had fought without reason and had drifted into the war as a result of a national psychological binge rather than as a result of deliberate national policy.

Millis began by suggesting that the drive toward intervention came out of the reform currents that had swept over the American scene in the years preceding the war: "It simply accorded with tradition when a mood of evangelical reform at home expressed itself, from time to time, in superior admonition to foreign powers whose governments oppressed their benighted peoples under the chains of militarism and reaction." The reform movement was every day in every way making the United States a better place in which to live; couldn't something be done for these other less fortunate peoples? In practical terms, the reformers had given little thought to foreign policy: "The New Freedom preferred merely to assume that the United States would always be found upon the side of righteousness in world affairs." In this combination of reform zeal, self-righteousnes, and naïveté, Millis saw the ingredients necessary for a crusade: "It was not, in those early days, the conservatives . . . who saw in the Allied cause a holy crusade for the rights of humanity. It was the liberals, the progressives, the leaders of reform and the standard bearers of the New Freedom."[8]

Millis depicted Wilson and his administration as unprepared to deal with foreign policy issues. He felt that Wilson simply based his foreign policy on domestic ideals: "If idealism and democracy, 'good' government and social justice were principles adequate to the solution of domestic problems, they should be enough for foreign policy as well."[9] However, this sort of "ethical" foreign policy, as practiced in "watchful waiting," seemed to lack the glamor of *Realpolitik* or the saber-rattling of Theodore Roosevelt.

Here Millis had observed something that no one but Harold Stearns had touched upon. Grattan and Beard noted the growth of interventionist sentiment in the United States in the years following the start of the war and were suspicious, as were Nearing and John Kenneth Turner, of the role played by the "plutocracy" in the growth of this sentiment. Grattan and Beard were, to be sure, more sophisticated than Nearing and Turner and did not postulate conspiracies, but for all four, economic forces seemed to predominate. Turner was, in addition, highly suspicious of Wilson, as was Grattan in his early articles. Barnes came closest to Turner in his own explanation of the growth of interventionist sentiment. Bausman, of course, blamed the Entente. It remained for Millis to blame the American people.

Millis had set up this indictment of the people by pointing to the lack of "glamour" in Wilson's foreign policy. Then, for a moment, he put aside the World War and turned to Mexico: "Suddenly and unaccountably—for was it not the people who suffered in war and was not a democracy like the United States therefore peace-loving by definition?—there had developed a powerful popular pressure for military action in Mexico."[10] Here, then, was something new in revisionism: the thought that ordinary "peace-loving" people make war rather than criminally insane statesmen or "economic vultures"—and that these people need not have an economic interest in the war.

"War," said Millis, "is terrible," but "it is also glamorous, and because of its appalling terror it exercises a compelling fascination. Americans might thank God for the Atlantic Ocean; they might

8. *Ibid.*, pp. 9, 45.   9. *Ibid.*, p. 11.   10. *Ibid.*, p. 16.

tremble at the sight of Europe—and yet experience a strange temptation to imitate her."[11] To this feeling, Millis related the "Preparedness" campaign. The "unparalleled virtue" of "Preparedness," preparedness against war, was that it enabled Americans to share the European experience while convincing themselves that their efforts were designed to spare America from the horrors of the European war: "It provided the thrill, at the moment that it promised to prevent the damage."

Millis focused again on Mexico for another illustration of his idea. He noted that there had been much discussion of the private and political pressures for intervention in Mexico against Pancho Villa. But he felt that there was still more involved, that the newspapers had been filled for too long with the horror and heroism of the war in Europe, "with pictorial glamours of war and with the fascination that war irresistibly exerts." He suspected that a "strange, haunting feeling had been growing that the United States had been missing something." Then came Pancho Villa and Americans had a chance for a war of their own; "could we fail to take it —more especially since it wouldn't be a real war and promised to be all but bloodless?"[12] And still again, Millis found an incident with which to challenge those who found "the people" ever peace-loving and only their leaders conjuring up excuses for war: "And when May [1916] brought the New York demonstration, it must have been very hard for even a Progressive to retain his faith in the pacific foresight and self-restraint of the people."[13] Thus, while suggesting that the administration had been unwise in permitting the country to drift into war, Millis nonetheless found the administration "unquestionably representative."

In terms of application to policy, Millis' interpretation had implications significantly different from those derived from the interpretations of other "revisionists." Much had been made by others of the alleged executive irresponsibility in foreign affairs, yet Millis ignored this issue and focused on the pressure of public opinion. Thus, while the work of Grattan and Barnes, for example, suggested the need to curb the President's authority in foreign affairs, as was subsequently done in the neutrality legislation, nowhere in *Road to War* was there any attempt to demonstrate that limiting

11. *Ibid.*, p. 93.   12. *Ibid.*, pp. 283–84.   13. *Ibid.*, p. 304.

executive power would have made a difference in 1917 or would keep America out of the next war.

Turning to the influence of propaganda on the growth of interventionist sentiment, Millis followed Grattan's lead. The importance of propaganda was not in its deceitfulness or its insidious effect, but in its value for indicating the actual prejudices of allegedly neutral Americans. Millis noted that despite a long "popular tradition" of Anglo-American hostility, the American public was, in the years 1914 to 1917, markedly receptive to the British viewpoint. He found that the "educated leaders of the New Freedom," unlike the "old fashioned" politicians, were steeped in British literature and traditions. Thus, "the Allies had only to play upon an opinion overwhelmingly disposed in their favor." Like Grattan, Millis did not overlook the fact that the Germans, too, had made an enormous effort to sway American opinion. But "the Allied propaganda . . . enjoyed the inestimable advantage of being self-financing. Our public clamored for the books, articles and motion-picture films which conveyed it. . . . Those who voiced the German side of the case found no such markets."[14]

The logical conclusion of Millis' analysis of the influence of propaganda was that the United States had not been lured into the war by propaganda. The American people had believed what they wanted to believe and had selected that propaganda which conformed most closely to their presuppositions—and those presuppositions favored the Allies.

There were several points, however, on which Millis agreed with the prevailing revisionist interpretation. Like all the revisionists except Beard, Millis laughed off the thought of a German threat to the United States: "The Secretary of State saw even more clearly than the President that there was not 'the slightest danger' of a Teutonic invasion; but this very obvious piece of common sense served only to convince House that Mr. Bryan was as 'innocent' as 'my little grandchild, Jane Tucker.' "[15]

Similarly, Millis treated America's commercial involvement with the Allies in the usual revisionist fashion. He cited with obvious approval the position of Representative Towner of Iowa, who had "clearly foreseen" the danger. Towner had warned that shipments

14. *Ibid.*, p. 202.   15. *Ibid.*, p. 96.

of clothing and food to England and France would aid the Entente war effort. Once the United States began filling the supply function for the Allies, the country would be fortunate to avoid being drawn into the war. But, Towner had insisted, encouragement of even commercial exports to one group of belligerents, while the other had no access to American markets was, simply, inviting the entanglement of the United States. Writing of Towner, Millis declared: "His fate was that of other Cassandras; few saw the relationship between these lucrative new markets and our own neutrality, and the Allies' commercial purchases mounted rapidly." While clearly favoring Senator Hitchcock's bill for an embargo on munitions, Millis nonetheless indicated the breach between his assumptions and those of other revisionists. Rather than harp on the evils of munitions manufacture or manufacturers, Millis restricted his complaint against the munitions trade to the extent to which this trade involved the United States in the conflict: "Unfortunately, the [embargo] movement was presented as one of humanitarian idealism, rather than as a severely practical way of preserving the United States from involvement in the war."[16]

Despite this picture Millis was painting of a country inadvertently drawn into war because of commercial involvements, he himself raised questions which qualified this thesis. The extent of America's economic involvement in the war was a generally appreciated fact. Revisionists usually argued that without this involvement there would have been no American ships attacked by German submarines and thus, no war. Opponents of revisionism argued that American trade with the Allies did not justify Germany's inhuman use of the submarine. Millis asked whether trade and the submarine were all that important: "Would the United States, however, have permitted Germany to win in any event?"[17] The question was, of course, unanswerable, but by raising it, Millis suggested that there might have been more to American participation in the war than the members of the Nye Committee were then considering.

Nonetheless, Millis' discussion of America's economic involvement in the war was such as to support the growing pressure for legislation to prevent a subsequent economic involvement from

16. *Ibid.*, p. 99.   17. *Ibid.*, p. 373, footnote.

entangling the United States in a future world war. Millis has recalled correctly that while he wrote a "good deal" about neutrality legislation he was never an "ardent advocate" of such legislation.[18] In *Road to War,* however, he had endorsed Representative Towner's contentions and Hitchcock's munitions embargo bill and thus implied that if the efforts of these men had been successful, the United States might not have been forced to intervene in the war. While Millis himself could not be accused of so simple a view of the meaning of history as to see a direct analogy in the 1930's, it was not likely that many of his readers could be granted his degree of sophistication. Even Samuel Flagg Bemis, one of the foremost American diplomatic historians of the day, saw little difference between the interpretation offered by Millis and that put forth by Grattan in *Why We Fought.*[19]

Millis' treatment of the primary figures in the making of American foreign policy, 1914–17, was consistent with his argument that the people rather than their leaders make war. Bryan was not lionized, but he had seen "more clearly" than Wilson that there was no danger of a "Teutonic invasion," and "only the much despised Mr. Bryan seems to have had the common sense to understand that 'the responsibility for continuing the war is just as grave as the responsibility for beginning it.' "[20] On the other hand, Page was spared the condemnation he had received at the hands of those who accepted his own estimate of his influence. The worst Millis would say of Page was that he, "like most American diplomats . . . in the opening years of the twentieth century—knew almost nothing about European diplomacy." In terms of Page's influence on Wilson, Millis noted that lack of agreement between the two men was obvious by September, 1916, and that Page had actually been frightened by Wilson's expression of hostility toward the Allies.[21]

It was Colonel House who received the harshest treatment at

18. Millis to the author, November 25, 1961.

19. See his *Diplomatic History of the United States* (New York: Henry Holt, 1955), pp. 590–91, footnote: "This book [*Road to War*], undocumented, reflects conspicuously the labors of research embodied in the earlier, carefully documented work, of similar tendency, by C. Hartley Grattan, *Why We Fought. . . .*"

20. *Road to War,* pp. 78–79.   21. *Ibid.,* pp. 20, 337.

Millis' hands, largely on the grounds of his naïveté. But Millis constantly separated House's views from Wilson's and in no way suggested that House had been responsible for the decision to intervene. Millis laughed at House for contending that Bryan was "innocent" for refusing to believe that the Germans might one day attempt to invade the United States. He accused House of "suffering from that fatal tendency of the negotiator to imagine that with a word here, a hint there and a few quiet little conversations over the coffee cups the destinies of peoples might be transformed and the mighty torrents of human history channeled to any desired end."[22]

Millis wrote of House's "naive faith" that American intervention would assure the world of a peace " 'for the lasting good of humanity.' " House had insisted upon intervention rather than risk the defeat of the Allies because he believed that militarism could be abolished only through an Allied victory. But Millis noted that House was often " 'surprised' at the lengths to which Wilson seemed willing to go just to keep the peace." It was Millis' belief that by the spring of 1916, Wilson had ceased paying any attention to House's advice.

Millis insisted that Wilson had never wanted war, had never accepted House's faith in the salutary effects of American intervention: "On the contrary, he clung, with a much surer instinct, to the idea that once the United States were involved upon one side of the quarrel, the nation's influence toward creating a stable world system would be largely at an end." Millis claimed that Wilson "realized instinctively" the "profound futility and irrelevance of force" and he viewed this instinct as an element of Wilson's greatness.[23]

But Millis also envisaged Wilson as a "stiff-necked moralist" and claimed that Wilson had sought a substitute for force "in the treacherous bogs of 'morality' rather than in the firmer ground of practical psychology and statesmanship." This, for Millis, was the "element of weakness' that led to trouble.[24]

Millis found that Wilson had always been more skeptical of the British than Colonel House had been. Unlike House, he had never been committed to intervene rather than see England defeated. He

22. *Ibid.*, p. 128.   23. *Ibid.*, p. 179.   24. *Ibid.*, p. 180.

found Wilson growing less rather than more happy with the Allies as the war progressed. As late as January, 1917, Millis suggested, Wilson was resolved to force a viable peace against the desires of the Entente, if necessary.

Whereas Barnes, Beard, Grattan, and Turner all suspected that Wilson had decided to intervene by the spring of 1916, Millis insisted that Wilson was unwilling to accept intervention as the proper response to Germany's resumption of unrestricted submarine warfare—that Wilson was still fighting for peace in late March, 1917. Here, Millis contended, was "the fact which has earned him his great place in human history." Wilson "was not willing to sentence perhaps hundreds of thousands of his countrymen to death or mutilation on the battlefield for the utterly barren satisfaction of taking revenge upon the Germans. The lives lost at sea could not be restored by the sacrifice of countless others."[25]

"Fate, weaving her rhythmic pattern," had narrowed the choices open to Wilson and his advisers. Each year the possible solutions were fewer. In March of 1917, Wilson had reached an *impasse*. He had warned the Germans that they would be held to "strict accountability." The Germans had resumed unrestricted submarine warfare and left the next step to Wilson. Millis saw Wilson as the sort of person to whom the German challenge was not sufficient cause for war. On the contrary, he was the sort of person who had to find a reason that would make intervention "worth while for the common men and women who would pay the price." Then came a vision "of a world remade, of peace, justice and equal opportunity enthroned among the nations, of the armies disbanded and the old curse of war lifted at last from the scarred backs of men." Millis could not but concede that this vision which called Wilson forth to battle was such as no man could resist.[26] And so "the nation was in the end thrust helplessly down into the abyss of war, the victim rather than the master of its destiny."

Road to War became a Book-of-the-Month Club selection and a best seller of 1935. Estimates of the number of copies sold have varied from twenty thousand to hundreds of thousands.[27] Unlike

25. *Ibid.*, p. 415. 26. *Ibid.*

27. Professor Leopold estimated the sales of *Road to War* at over 20,000

Barnes and Grattan, Millis had no trouble presenting his views to the public.

Charles Seymour, the leading exponent of the thesis that the German resumption of submarine warfare was the primary reason for American intervention, reacted strongly to Millis book.[28] He began his review with: "It is a pity that Mr. Millis has not developed the art of history so successfully as he has the art of literary presentation." He found *Road to War* "entertaining," but "facile in its judgments, superficial in its scintillating irony." Perhaps worst of all, Seymour declared that Millis constantly used the "tricks of the graduate student"—Millis had questioned the judgment of responsible statesmen. Disturbed as he was, Seymour did not fail to note that much of Millis' argument was closer to Seymour's than to the arguments of the "revisionists." Where he and Millis agreed, Seymour declared Millis to be on firm ground: *Road to War* would have been a better book had Millis limited himself to those points which Seymour had accepted in his own work.

Frank Simonds reviewed the book for the *Atlantic Monthly* in May, 1935.[29] He referred to Millis as one of the country's ablest commentators on international affairs: "always sane, objective, and valuable." All that Millis wrote, Simonds declared to be true, but he insisted that Millis had missed the "cumulative effect upon a contemporary American mind of German deeds." Millis was providing the "hard-boiled appraisal" of a generation which had not experienced the idealistic fervor of the Progressive era. What happened, he saw "clearly and cooly," but Simonds contended that Millis was incapable of understanding the effect of those events upon those who felt their impact immediately.

Simonds suggested that Millis was trying to explain emotions by "post-mortem examination," having at hand all the evidence

---

(*World Politics*, II, 412) ; Professor Raymond Sontag, in January, 1936, wrote that 60,000 copies had been sold already (*American Historical Review*, XLI, 363) ; Harry Elmer Barnes claimed "hundreds of thousands" of sales for *Road to War* (*Liberation*, Summer, 1958, p. 12).

28. Review of *Road to War* by Walter Millis, *Yale Review*, XXIV (Summer, 1935), 833–36.

29. *Atlantic Monthly*, CLV (May, 1935), 12, 14.

"save the spirit." With the spirit gone, Simonds did not believe understanding was possible. Millis had produced "a clinical chart, which may well support the judgment the future will pass upon the men and events of 1914–1917, but does not even remotely touch the reality of what they felt. . . . In making the war period intelligible for the future he has rendered it unrecognizable to those who lived it."

Nowhere in his review did Simonds question Millis' contention that the United States had stumbled into the war. His criticism of Millis, whatever its validity, was essentially a defense of, or an excuse for, those men Millis had depicted as drifting toward war without a rational appreciation of the meaning of the war for the United States.

The editors of the *New Republic* turned to Grattan for their review of *Road to War*.[30] Grattan expressed both amazement and pleasure with regard to Millis' product, seeing as its thesis the idea "that we bungled ourselves into a war where we didn't belong." He claimed that in 1917 such a book would have landed its author in the penitentiary. In 1929, when he had written *Why We Fought*, he had been considered "subversive and morally contemptible"; but in 1935 a writer employed by one of America's most conservative newspapers, the New York *Herald Tribune*, could make the best-seller list with such a book—"the world does move."

Unlike Professor Bemis, Grattan did not view Millis' work as a popularization of *Why We Fought*. On the contrary, he was critical of Millis because he felt economic factors had not been stressed sufficiently in *Road to War*. In addition, he accused Millis of giving far too much space to psychological factors and referred Millis to his own work for the necessary correctives. But Grattan's main interest was in reminding readers of the value of Millis' book for the contemporary scene: "Only the pro-war aspects of Roosevelt's program seem to be a howling success. As the world approaches the rapids, the American people find themselves in the charge of men hardly more fitted to keep them out of war than the rulers of 1914–1917. Mr. Millis's book shows what the road to war was then, and its analogical value is immense."

30. *New Republic,* LXXXII (May 8, 1935), 372.

Professor Raymond Sontag, reviewing *Road to War* for the *American Historical Review,* called the book "a too well disguised pacifist tract, a biased diplomatic history . . . , a good introduction to the study of public opinion, and above all, a very timely reminder of the hazards of neutrality." Sontag was not Millis' most friendly critic, nor was he the least astute. In another of the learned journals, Professor Richard Van Alystyne found Millis' narrative very good in places and occasionally exaggerated. But Van Alstyne was acutely aware of the difference between Millis' thesis and that of other revisionists and members of Congress. In fact, he declared that Millis had effectively disposed of "the current exaggerations respecting the evil purposes of the 'international Bankers.' "[31]

In 1961, Millis wrote:

> I was never consciously a part of the "revisionist controversy" in the 1930's. I was, I suppose, a member of the revisionist school in that I was trying to point to facts and relationships which had been suppressed or distorted by the war-time passion and propagandas. . . . I was shocked when I first heard *Road to War* described as "the isolationists' Bible. . . ."[32]

Millis had not argued, as Grattan claimed, that the war had been one in which the United States did not belong. That Millis felt the American people had gone to war with their eyes closed was, however, quite true. In studying the years 1914 to 1917, Millis was concerned primarily with the "process" by which a people whose initial reaction to war was one of horror, one of relief at their non-involvement, gradually became exhilarated by intervention. He concluded that the manner in which the American people and their leaders traveled toward war was absurd and irrational, that the United States had gone about making the decision of whether or not to intervene in a haphazard manner. But he did not claim that they should not have intervened. On the contrary, he implied that the decision to intervene, more wisely arrived at, might have achieved ends consistent with the cost of the war—that the millennial expectations with which many Americans went to

---

31. *American Historical Review,* XLI (January, 1936), 361–63; *Journal of Modern History,* VIII (March, 1936), 18–20.
32. Millis to author, November 25, 1961.

war doomed them to disillusionment, to twenty years of unrealistic attitudes toward world affairs.

On the other hand, Millis' shock upon hearing his book described as "the isolationists' Bible" was not wholly justified. To the American people the most obvious example of American internationalism, of interventionism in world affairs, was the participation of the United States in the World War. Millis had set out to debunk war: as Professor Sontag had suggested, *Road to War* was, among other things, a "pacifist tract." He had demonstrated that American foreign policy in the war years was essentially a series of *ad hoc* reactions to the initiative of the belligerent powers; that, as Wilson had once indicated, the decision to intervene was not his, but one which could be made by any U-boat commander. In doing these things, Millis had unwittingly reinforced the "revisionists" in the "revisionist controversy." He had studied the war for reasons unlike Grattan's; he had come to many conclusions which differed from Grattan's. On a number of points, Millis' interpretation seemed closer to the interpretations of Seymour and other opponents of revisionism. But he had portrayed the circumstances of intervention in terms of an error, and his subtle distinction between an error in the decision to intervene and an error in the reasons for intervention was little appreciated.

Thus, in the mid-thirties, when "revisionism" was primarily a weapon in the hands of those who opposed an American involvement in world affairs which might lead to war, the identification of Millis' book with the "revisionist" position, combined with the popularity of *Road to War,* made reasonable the charge that the book was "the isolationists' Bible." If Millis had not seen it, Grattan in his review of *Road to War* called attention to the book's "analogical value" for the contemporary scene.

Millis' own feelings about the value of the "lessons" of the World War were made pointedly clear in an article written in July, 1935, just a few months after *Road to War* had appeared. He found that the experience of the years between 1914 and 1917 had "the defects of most historical experience": it was "confused and baffling in the extreme." He concluded that the facts of that period were complex enough to support just about any theory of historical causation—but they were also "obstinate enough to resist almost any theory of how the ultimate entanglement could have been prevented."[33]

With Senator Nye stumping the country expounding his views on how the munitions manufacturers and international bankers had stampeded the country into war, Millis was most careful in stating his own conclusions, taking exception to Nye's thesis. He insisted that the economic problem the war had presented had not been one of "eschewing the profits of death; it was one of regaining some of the ordinary profits of peace." The problem had been solved, of course, by the war contracts, and the United States became the chief source of supplies to the Allies. What was important, Millis argued, was first that those behind the war contracts were not seeking to make exceptional profits by taking advantage of the war, but were seeking to replace peacetime exports. Second, he felt it was essential to note that the American role as supplier for the Allies was not the result of any conscious policy, but the result of the "lack of any sufficiently conscious policy." The bankers, J. P. Morgan included, Millis portrayed as "channels" rather than "generators" of the forces they allegedly wielded. Finally, "the profit motive may have helped to get us into a war situation and hindered our attempts to get out, but it did not directly control the transition from formal neutrality to formal belligerence."[34]

Millis took exception, also, to what he deemed the general conception of the influence of Allied propaganda. More clearly than in *Road to War* he declared that the most effective propaganda on behalf of the Entente was "generated in the United States and by Americans." He contended that the entire Allied propaganda effort "hardly did more than give precision and effect" to forces that could never have been created by propaganda.

As in *Road to War*, Millis sought to defend Wilson against the charges levied by John Kenneth Turner, Grattan, and to a lesser extent by Barnes: "Those who pin the major responsibility upon the vanity and irascibility of President Wilson seldom attempt

33. "Will We Stay Out of the Next War? How We Entered the Last One," *New Republic*, LXXXIII (July 31, 1935), 323–27.

34. *Ibid.*, p. 326.

to explain how another statesman might, in fact, have met the situation as it was abruptly presented to him in February, 1917."[35]

In general, Millis' article read like a point-by-point refutation of the "revisionist" interpretation of American intervention. Millis had also specifically questioned the value of the "lessons" of 1917 for foreign policy decisions in 1935. Then, like Beard, he granted that an examination of the facts of the period 1914 to 1917 had to be the basis of any policy designed to "control" future situations of a similar nature. But he argued, again like Beard, that before the facts would be of much use there would have to be agreement upon "many profound issues as to the ends which the control should serve, the proper philosophy of international relations, the real character and objects of the state in the international and domestic complex." These were issues, the "very existence of which," seemed unnoticed by the participants in the controversy then raging. Thus far the debaters had concerned themselves only with the question of how to keep the United States from entanglement in the next foreign war. Millis insisted that here was a far more important question: "whether the nation (whatever they may conceive that to mean) will want to avoid entanglement"; but this question had hardly even been raised.[36] It is unlikely that this article was read as widely as *Road to War*. Had it been, Millis might have been spared the label "revisionist" which, unlike Barnes and Grattan, he did not seem to appreciate.

3

In the spring of 1935, Italy began to make motions in accordance with what Mussolini and others thought suitable behavior for a major power, and soon the Italians carried the glories of war to Ethiopia. No one could be quite sure whether or not this was the first action of a second world war, and pressures quickly mounted in the United States for legislation designed to keep the country out of war. In April, Senator Nye and another member of his Senate Investigating Committee had introduced bills calling for a mandatory embargo on arms, loans, and credits during wartime. Although there was considerable dissension within the ad-

35. *Ibid.*   36. *Ibid.*, p. 327.

ministration, the initiative for the legislation had come from the President.[37] Roosevelt's purpose has often been questioned, but it was clear that like many other Americans he had concluded that intervention in the World War had been a mistake. And, like many other Americans, he had been influenced by parts of the revisionist interpretation of intervention. His remark to Nye in March, 1935—that he was convinced that Bryan had been right in 1915—was more than a passing thought. Five months earlier, in a letter to Josephus Daniels, Roosevelt, who had ridiculed Bryan in 1915, wrote: "Would that W. J. B. had stayed on as Secretary of State—the country would have been better off."[38]

On August 16, ten days before Congress adjourned, Senate Joint Resolution 173 was introduced,

> providing for the prohibition of the export of arms, ammunition, and implements of war to belligerent countries; the prohibition of the transportation of arms, ammunition, and implements of war by vessels of the United States for the use of belligerent states; for registration and licensing of persons engaged in the business of manufacturing, exporting, or importing arms, ammunition, or implements of war; and restricting travel by American citizens on belligerent ships during war. . . .[39]

In the subsequent debate over the resolution, there was, to be sure, some indication that the members of Congress were aware of the war between Italy and Ethiopia. For the most part, however, the debate was an extension of the revisionist controversy, and the proponents of the resolution seemed to be concerned primarily with interpreting the reasons for American intervention in the World War.

In the Senate the fight for the legislation was led by Homer Bone of Washington, Bennett Champ Clark of Missouri, and Nye, all members of the committee investigating the munitions industry. Little opposition to the resolution was expressed on the

37. Robert Divine, *The Illusion of Neutrality* (Chicago: University of Chicago Press, 1962), pp. 85 ff.

38. Quoted in Frank Freidel, *Franklin D. Roosevelt: The Apprenticeship* (Boston: Little, Brown and Co., 1952), p. 250.

39. United States, *Congressional Record,* 74th Congress, 1st Session, 1935, LXXIX, Part 13, pp. 13952–13953.

floor, the opposition having had its day before the resolution reached the floor. Once the debate became a matter of public record, it seemed that few Senators desired to be put in the position of taking a stand against "neutrality," against "peace," terms which the supporters of the resolution had succeeded in attaching to their cause.

Bone called for his colleagues to "go back for a moment to the Great War of 1914–1918." He wanted them to examine "the factors which led us into that war—factors of business, economic impulses and economic rivalries which are present right now." Shortly afterward, Arthur Vandenberg of Michigan rose and announced that he found it "perfectly clear" from an analysis of "our war record," 1914 to 1918, "that the absence of a specific neutrality policy which was effective in its proscriptions, absolutely robbed us of any chance to direct our own subsequent destiny. In reality, we were sucked into that war irresistibly in spite of anything we could do to prevent the ultimate process."[40]

Nye followed, reminding the Senate that since "that experience of 1916–1919," nothing had been done to "remedy the evil which existed then and which permitted our being drawn and sucked into that conflict, as was the case at that time." Before the day's debate was over, Bone reported on "a fact known even to school children in this country": "Everyone has come to recognize that the Great War was utter social insanity, and was a crazy war, and we had no business in it at all."[41]

In the course of the debate on August 20, 1935, Senator Millard Tydings of Maryland asked what would have happened if the United States had not intervened in the war, but the issue he raised was not picked up. Senators Barkley and Logan, both of Kentucky, questioned the validity of the "historical facts" employed by Senator Bone, but Bone merely thanked them for their corrections, pushed aside the matter of evidence, and begged for action on the resolution. Senator Clark demanded action "before" war started, declaring that "From the date of the sailing of the first munitions ship in 1914 . . . the United States was helpless to prevent entry into war." Tydings heckled continuously, but on

40. *Ibid.*, pp. 13776–13777.   41. *Ibid.*, pp. 13777–13779.

the next day the resolution passed the Senate without a roll call vote.[42]

In the House the debate followed the same course. Maury Maverick of Texas asked his colleagues if they remembered who had controlled the transatlantic cables during the World War. The question was, of course, rhetorical and he answered it himself: "The British. And it seems to me they still have them. Will they use them again to get us into war?" Then an elderly congressman, Representative Ashbrook, stood and announced that he, as a member of the House in 1916, had opposed the McLemore resolution to keep American citizens off armed merchant ships. Now he regretted his earlier position and would offer his support to Senate Joint Resolution 173.[43] On August 23, 1935, the House passed the Senate resolution with minor amendments, and the next step was left to the Senate.

On August 24, Senator Tom Connally of Texas spoke briefly of his dissatisfaction with the pending legislation on the grounds that it failed to give the President power to make distinctions between aggressors and the nations attacked, but he indicated that he would vote for S.J.R. 173 nonetheless. Then Alben Barkley rose and asked Connally: "If the pending joint resolution had been in effect during the World War, what would have been the result?" Connally caught his cue and replied: "The result would have been just what the result was anyway: we would have been in the World War anyway." A moment later, with Barkley asking another leading question, Connally added that a delay in American intervention or the failure of the United States to have supplied the Entente might have resulted in a victory for the Central Powers.[44] Having suggested by their question and answer game that they believed the United States would have and should have intervened to prevent a victory for the Central Powers in the World War, Barkley and Connally then proceeded to join 77 other senators in voting for the legislation which passed by a vote of 79 for, 2 opposed.[45] A few days later, President Roosevelt signed the resolution, and the "revisionist" interpretation of American inter-

42. *Ibid.*, p. 13956.

43. *Ibid.*, pp. 14356–14357.

44. *Ibid.*, p. 14433.

45. *Ibid.*, p. 14434.

vention achieved its first major victory in the area of political action.

The Neutrality Act of 1935 was to expire February 29, 1936, and the advocates of the "new neutrality" accepted this expiration date largely because they feared they might otherwise get nothing. As soon as the Senate passed the resolution as amended by the House, Nye began the battle for an extension. He called the act a stopgap measure and promised to renew his fight in the next session of Congress. Here were the fruits of revisionism:

> We witnessed in our last effort to remain neutral how munitions sales, bankers' loans to the Allies, and Americans sailing upon the vessels of nations at war, such as the *Lusitania,* tended to bring us into a conflict which was in its inception of no relation to us. Had America had a well-defined and strong neutrality policy at the beginning of the World War, she might have escaped participation in that war. . . .[46]

A few weeks later, Roosevelt, writing to Colonel House, noted that certain congressmen who were suggesting "wild-eyed measures to keep us out of war" were claiming that House, Page, and Lansing had forced Wilson into the World War. But Roosevelt wrote that he had assured the congressmen of the inaccuracy of their historical analysis and that this would be proven by "history yet to be written." However, "the trouble is that they belong to that very large and perhaps increasing school of thought which holds that we can and should withdraw wholly within ourselves and cut off all but the most perfunctory relationships with other nations." Such men imagined that the United States could "stand idly by" as Europe destroyed itself.[47]

The letter to House seemed inconsistent with the earlier letter to Daniels and inconsistent with Roosevelt's initiation of the neutrality legislation, but together the two letters suggested the lessons Roosevelt had drawn from the experience of the World War. In the letter to House it was apparent that Roosevelt did not accept the hints of conspiracy that some of the revisionists and some congressmen were dropping and that he recognized that

46. *Ibid.,* p. 14534.

47. Elliott Roosevelt (ed.), *F. D. R., His Personal Letters, 1928–1945* (New York: Duell, Sloan and Pearce, 1950), I, 506–7.

American policy could not be divorced from the world context which in part gave it shape. In the letter to Daniels and in Roosevelt's request for neutrality legislation it was equally apparent that he had come to believe that intervention in 1917 had been avoidable and that a positive policy was necessary to avoid the alleged drift of the years between 1914 and 1917. Roosevelt had brushed aside the conspiratorial overtones which marred the work of some revisionists, but he had retained the "realism" which was evident in the better revisionist works: he had not thrown out the baby with the bathwater.

4

As the politicians returned home to tell their constituents of their efforts to spare America from war, the publicists and historians returned to the fore. Beard noted that many Americans were drawing parallels between Mussolini's activity in Ethiopia and the European situation in 1914. He thought, however, that American attitudes toward these overseas conflicts were very different in November, 1935, than they had been in November, 1914. "Even school children were aware of the preliminary report of the Senate munitions inquiry. Even pillars of society recognized and discussed openly the pressures of private greed in diplomacy and foreign affairs. Isolationists breathed fire and vengeance and declared that they would not be caught 'napping' again."[48]

In January, 1936, an editorial in the *Nation* announced that this issue contained a "brilliant and balanced version of the economic interpretation of neutrality and war" by Walter Millis and a "vigorous book review" by Sidney Fay, taking "the opposite point of view."[49] It was clear in Fay's review of Seymour's *American Neutrality 1914–1917* and of Baker's fifth volume in his *Life and Letters of Woodrow Wilson* that Fay was lining up with the opponents of revisionism. He began by raising the big question: "Why did the United States abandon neutrality?" He

48. "Keeping America Out of War," *Current History,* XLIII (December, 1935), 292.

49. "War Profits and Personal Devils," *Nation,* CXLII (January 22, 1936), 89.

lumped together Grattan, Millis, and Nye as men who suggested that intervention resulted from "the selfish influence of Wall Street bankers, munitions makers, Allied propaganda, Sir Edward Grey's cunning, and so forth." Fay granted that all of these factors had had an influence, but he argued that Seymour was "much nearer the truth." Seymour might stress the submarine "too exclusively," but "it was the main and final cause of our participation." In closing, Fay recommended both books to anyone seeking clarification regarding the congressional neutrality proposals and their historical background.[50]

Millis' article, the first of two in a series he wrote for the *Nation,* should have disappointed anyone who expected him to collide head-on with Fay. While insisting that economic factors were of more than negligible influence, he rejected the economic interpretation of intervention. Even the bankers had non-economic motives which could not be disentangled and declared subordinate or superior to their economic interests in intervention.[51]

Like Beard, Millis claimed that the relatively small investments in Allied bonds did not represent America's economic stake in the cause of the Allies. The important point was that the national economy was being sustained by the export boom and an abrupt cessation of trade with the Allies "clearly would have spelled something like a first rate disaster."

When Millis came to the reason for American intervention, his interpretation was almost identical with the interpretations of Fay and Seymour:

> It was the primarily political issue of the submarine rather than the failure of war orders which in fact precipitated us into the struggle . . . in the actual development of the Wilson submarine policy it is extraordinary how scant are the tangible evidences of the influence of such mundane calculations . . . the true economic importance of the submarine to ourselves was not apparent until *after* the President had taken a stand in regard to it from which retreat must in any case have been difficult.[52]

50. "Wilson and Neutrality," *Nation,* CXLII, 109.

51. "The Last War and the Next: Morgan, Money and War," *Nation,* CXLII, 95–98.

52. *Ibid.*, pp. 96–97.

If the label "revisionist" must be applied to Millis' interpretation of "Why We Fought" as well as to the interpretations of men like Barnes, Grattan, and John Kenneth Turner, it is obvious how little meaning the label can convey.

While finding no "significant conspiracy of profiteers, intriguing to compel the President and Congress into a declaration of war for the direct and vulgar advantage of their own pocket books," Millis did feel that the economic influence of leading American financiers and industrialists had been "important factors in our experience last time" and might be again. He agreed with Newton Baker's claim that hamstringing bankers and munition makers would not keep America out of war, adding his own view that there was no method "whereby this or any other country can be finally guaranteed against future war." But he did feel that an effort could be made, and thus implicitly condoned the "neutrality" legislation.[53]

In the second of his articles, Millis made clear the extent to which he endorsed the Neutrality Act of 1935.[54] He began by insisting that it was "useless" to discuss methods of keeping the United States out of another war unless it was first assumed that the war would be one "which the country will believe that it should keep out of." Again, Millis was paralleling Beard closely, suggesting that it was foolish to be anti-intervention before the issues of the next war were known. He was worried, clearly, about the possibility of "too drastic" neutrality laws and saw possible dangers in making the application of the laws mandatory. Nonetheless,

> the presence of a strong embargo act upon the books might compel the country as a whole to decide, at the outset, whether its primary purpose was to maintain neutrality or to maintain the territorial integrity of China or the military security of France and Britain in Europe. If the decision is the latter sense, then neutrality of course becomes a dead issue, and the only problem is the practical, though somewhat ignoble, one of seeing to it that as far as possible other nations do our actual fighting for us. But the neutrality act will have helped to insure that the decision is recognized for what it is, made clearly and consciously, and based upon some more rational

53. *Ibid.*, p. 98.

54. "The Last War and the Next: What Does Neutrality Mean?" *Nation*, CXLII (January 29, 1936), 125–27.

concept of genuine national interest than the emotional reactions of the first waves of war hysteria.[55]

Like Beard, Millis viewed the neutrality legislation as a useful means of changing American attitudes toward foreign policy, of forcing Americans to think in terms of the national interest rather than in terms of such "shadowy substances" as neutral rights. Unlike Beard, he was not troubled by presidential discretion. In *Road to War* he had not found Wilson intriguing to involve the United States in the war, and he shared none of Beard's suspicion of Roosevelt. While Beard consistently supported mandatory neutrality, Millis insisted upon flexibility, arguing that a "permissive" embargo would be a powerful weapon in the hands of the President.

A few weeks later, *Time* reported an interview given by Millis in which he reaffirmed his desire for flexibility in American neutrality legislation. Millis' views were repeated to members of the Nye Committee, and Senators Clark and Bone, ardent advocates of mandatory neutrality, expressed amazement. Clark was quoted as saying that "Millis seems only able to read the record of the war years. He apparently draws no lesson from it." Bone was a bit more flowery, but his remarks coincided with Clark's. Bone declared that it had been upon what Millis "exposed so well in his book, that I postulated my stand for a strong mandatory neutrality bill." He felt that the "lamp of experience" burned so brightly in Millis' hands "that we are convinced by his recitation of the record." That record, Bone insisted, could lead to only one conclusion and "that conclusion is what we tried to put into the Clark-Nye neutrality bills. Bone simply could not understand what was wrong with Millis: "His book should convince the most stubborn mind, but apparently it has not convinced him."[56] Alas, poor Millis —he was just too subtle to be understood by anyone.

On the same day that Fay's review and Millis' first article appeared in the *Nation*, Grattan reviewed Baker's fifth volume for the *New Republic*.[57] He called the book an "explicit, extensive and forthright document of the 'revisionist' school" and claimed

55. *Ibid.*, pp. 125–26.

56. *Time*, XXVII (February 24, 1936), 16.

57. "The Road to Revision," *New Republic*, LXXXV (January 22, 1936), 316.

that Baker had taken into account "all of the arguments advanced by the revisionists" and had sustained "most of them." Consistent with the judiciousness he had demonstrated in *Why We Fought*, he accepted Baker's treatment of the House-Grey memorandum and declared that "as we have long known," Wilson had "tempered" the agreement "in a fashion that completely destroyed its purpose." And, remembering Fay's review of *Why We Fought*, Grattan lumped him with Seymour and Hendrick, Page's biographer, as the unreconstructed from whom Baker had separated himself.

Subsequently, Grattan also reviewed Seymour's *American Neutrality* for the *New Republic* and scoffed at Seymour's insistence that the submarine was "the one cause which if removed would have left us at peace."[58] He found Seymour overly legalistic and overly moralistic, tending to ignore economic influences. Perhaps of primary interest was an aside in which Grattan mentioned having given information to the Nye Committee, thus tangibly linking revisionism to the legislation based upon it.

5

On February 29, 1936, the Neutrality Act of 1935 would expire. What would follow? Would it be renewed? Would it be revised to give the President more discretion? Or less discretion? On February 12, Beard published a calm, detached argument for "wide and mandatory" neutrality legislation.[59] Of particular interest was Beard's phrasing of the primary issue: "How can the country avoid war?" No longer was he contending as he had in *The Open Door at Home*, and as Millis had subsequently contended, that the United States had to take steps to ensure that any future intervention would be in the national interest. Unlike Millis, he was no longer willing to wait for the next war, examine the issues, and decide how to serve the national interest. By February, 1936, Beard had decided that the national interest meant staying out of

58. "Our Un-Neutrality," *New Republic*, LXXXVI (March 11, 1936), 144–45.

59. "Heat and Light Neutrality," *New Republic*, LXXXVI (February 12, 1936), 8–9.

war—any war. This grew increasingly evident after World War II began, when, despite his great hatred for the dictatorships, Beard violently opposed intervention.

Beard argued that there was no way of knowing whether American intervention had been better or worse for Europe, "for we do not know and never can know what the outcome would have been otherwise." But Beard was not greatly concerned about Europe: "We do know that the United States carries a dangerous burden as an outcome of the war: an enormous debt, a swollen naval and military machine, a billion a year in taxes for the army and navy, another billion for veterans, to say nothing of bonuses and all other things to come. Surely no one will claim that America is a better place to live in as a result of the war."[60]

Once, Beard wrote, we tried to "right European wrongs, to make the world safe for democracy." It seemed unlikely to him that anyone viewed that "experiment" as a great success. He granted the point that mandatory neutrality might prove no better, "but we nearly burnt our house down with one experiment so it seems not wholly irrational to try another line." Less than three weeks later, the Neutrality Act of 1936 became law and America was committed to "another line."

6

On June 23, 1936, the twelfth institute of the Norman Wait Harris Memorial Foundation opened in Chicago. The subject for the institute was the very timely one of "Neutrality and Collective Security," and a very impressive collection of scholars and public men was assembled by the University of Chicago faculty members who administered the Foundation. Present as public lecturers were Sir Alfred Zimmern of Oxford; Carl Becker's old friend, William Dodd, currently ambassador from the United States to Germany; Charles Warren, the distinguished lawyer whose ideas on neutrality had been so influential in the previous two years; and Edwin DeWitt Dickinson of the University of California. In addition to the public lectures, a series of "Round Tables" was organized, presided over by Professor Quincy Wright. These discussion groups

60. *Ibid.*, p. 9.

were limited to invited guests and the transcript of the discussions was kept confidential. Participants included the public lecturers, University of Chicago professors Bernadotte Schmitt and Frederick Schuman, Professors James W. Garner and Clarance Berdahl of Illinois, Kenneth Colegrove of Northwestern, Charles Fenwick of Bryn Mawr, Harold Sprout and DeWitt Poole of Princeton, Frederick Dunn and Nicholas Spykman of Yale, State Department officials Joseph C. Green and Green Hackworth, Secretary to the Nye Committee Stephen Raushenbush, and publicist C. Hartley Grattan.

If Grattan anticipated finding himself in a hostile atmosphere, he was undoubtedly pleasantly surprised. Although there were numerous instances in which other participants disagreed with him, the extent to which the arguments of *Why We Fought* were accepted was far more striking. In the opening session, Schmitt led a discussion on "What factors tend to draw neutrals into war, with special reference to the American entry into the World War." Schmitt clearly thought Seymour's contention—that the resumption by the Germans of unrestricted submarine warfare was the necessary cause of intervention—was irrefutable. But Schmitt joined in the criticism of Walter Hines Page and never once suggested that the United States belonged in the war. Quite the contrary, he denied that the United States had gone to war because any American interests were at stake—certainly not because of any "*sordid* motive of any American economic interest." He doubted that many Americans ever believed it was necessary to help defeat Germany or be forced to face Germany alone in the future. Schmitt even implied that it would have been desirable for the United States to have stayed out of the war: "We drifted from 1914 to 1917, and perhaps if we had had a stronger arm and were indicating to the world that our arm was getting stronger, we might have come out differently."[61]

By the summer of 1936 it seemed that there were few Americans willing to defend the decision of the United States to enter the World War in 1917. Instead, the remaining debate focused on the

61. "Neutrality and Collective Security" (Confidential Report of Round Tables held at The University of Chicago, 1936, under the auspices of the Norman Wait Harris Memorial Foundation), pp. 8–21, 31–32, italics added.

question of whether or not the United States could have avoided being drawn into the war: was the decision to intervene a tragic error or an inevitable tragedy? Grattan, sounding increasingly like an economic determinist and socialist, insisted that economic entanglements with the Allies made the participation of the United States "possible, logical and in the end necessary to the health of private capitalism." Still, he insisted, only the wartime policies of the United States government made intervention "inevitable."[62] Schmitt, like Seymour, doubted that the United States could have done anything to keep out—doubted that there was an open historical situation in which the United States could have exercised choice. Once Germany determined that the resumption of unrestricted submarine warfare was requisite to victory, it seemed unlikely to Schmitt that the United States could come up with any policy that would have spared the nation war.

Both Schmitt and Grattan were, in fact, contending that the government of the United States did not have complete freedom of choice regarding policy. Both men were concerned with environmental conditions that limited freedom of action. Schmitt was stressing the variable world context over which the United States could exert little control. Thus, no matter how desirable continued neutrality may have been, the United States government could not be held responsible for the failure of its neutrality policy. Grattan, on the other hand, was stressing the domestic context in which foreign policy was formulated. Thus, the wartime policies of the United States reflected the dominant economic interests within American society and these policies created a situation from which there could be no retreat along the road to war. Although the domestic context was far broader than Grattan conceded, with other than economic considerations in the balance, both world and domestic contexts were relevant and had to be weighed. Neither Schmitt nor Grattan, however, was able to come up with a convincing synthesis.

In subsequent sessions, Grattan elaborated on his ideas on the shaping of American foreign policy and gave further indication of how his growing antipathy to capitalism was influencing his thoughts on world affairs. Listening to the other participants, he

62. *Ibid.*, p. 24.

found them agreeing that there was a community of interest between the State Department and the business community—a community of interest that extended to social and personal relationships. From this condition he deduced that the State Department and the President, who received his information from the Secretary of State, would be likely to reflect the interests of business. On the other hand, Congress, in critical moments of history, could be made subject to the pressures of peace groups that were not likely to receive a sympathetic hearing from the executive branch of government.[63] Given his view that the interests of the business community had produced the policies that ultimately involved the United States in the World War, the implication of the contrast was clear: if peace rather than war was the desired goal, primary control of American foreign policy had to be taken out of the hands of the executive and given over to Congress. Such were the lessons of the World War. Such were the thoughts that underlay the efforts of Grattan and others to preserve mandatory neutrality legislation, limiting executive discretion to the greatest extent possible. "Neutrality," Grattan declared further, "appeals to me as a people's policy generated by a desire not to die on the battlefield. It seems to me to run head on into the interests of the capitalist groups in the country, and if we really want to discuss the utility of neutrality legislation, we have got to discuss the prospect of regulating the drives within capitalism by legislative action."[64]

In a session dealing with the investigation of the munitions industry, Stephen Raushenbush dominated the discussion. Raushenbush generally argued along lines similar to Grattan's, remarking, for example, that although people in academic life did not think men were influenced by money—like the Morgans when testifying before the Nye Committee—the members of the Senate did. Repeatedly he warned that once the American economic system became involved in a war, as it had between 1914 and 1917, there was no way to keep the United States out of the war. Therein, he argued, was the real value of the neutrality legislation: avoid the nonsense of tying the national honor to trade advantage and war profits. If American commerce with the belligerents was restricted to a trade-at-your-own-risk basis, there would be no problem. The

63. *Ibid.*, p. 69.   64. *Ibid.*, p. 73.

United States could then choose to intervene or not—on its own terms. The American people could then go to war with their eyes open rather than because of the neutral rights issue. The United States would be free from economic entanglements and need not end up underwriting British imperialism or all sorts of secret treaties. When Raushenbush finished, Sir Alfred Zimmern declared his essential agreement: it would be better for the United States to intervene in a European war on the basis of a "clear issue" rather than the "entangled issues" of 1917.[65] Once again, the value of the neutrality legislation as a means of permitting the nation to make a realistic determination of its interest or stake in a future war had been noted.

7

In August, 1936, President Roosevelt delivered an address at Chautauqua, New York, in which he focused on the neutrality legislation. Congress, he declared, had given him authority to safeguard American neutrality in time of war. He readily conceded that the present policy would reduce the war profits that would otherwise accrue to American citizens, but although "industrial and agricultural production for a war market may give immense fortunes to a few men, for the Nation as a whole it produces disaster." Roosevelt warned that if war came in Europe, thousands of Americans would try to break down neutrality. They would claim that by repealing the neutrality legislation they could end the depression, end unemployment, make the American people prosperous. It would be hard, he said, to resist the clamor—hard to look beyond the false prosperity to the inevitable day of reckoning. But, said the President, "if we face the choice of profits or peace, the Nation will answer—must answer—we choose peace." To those who heard or later read the President's words, there could be little doubt that he, too, had learned the "lessons" of the World War and knew how to keep the United States out of any future war.[66]

In the fall, another of Grattan's books, *Preface to Chaos*, was published.[67] In this one volume he presented both his most radical

65. *Ibid.*, pp. 82–93, 109.

66. *The Public Papers and Addresses of Franklin D. Roosevelt* (New York: Random House, 1938), V, 290–91.

67. New York: F. Dodge, 1936.

statement of his opposition to capitalism and his most cautious interpretation of America's entry in to the World War. Like so many other intellectuals of reformist bent, Grattan, in the mid-1930's, was convinced that capitalism had to go—that capitalism was in fact a dying order. More radical than most, he blamed capitalism rather than any individual or group for war in general and for American intervention in 1917. The system was responsible and the system had to go.

In his second chapter, Grattan offered what he declared to be his judgment after considering materials that had appeared since he wrote *Why We Fought* and particularly after considering the arguments of men like Charles Seymour. It was immediately obvious that the main outlines of his interpretation had not changed— every sub-section of the chapter began with: "Economic entanglements with the Allied powers in the First World War [Grattan claimed to be certain that there would be a second] made the participation of the United States in it on the side of the Allies possible; the wartime policies of the United States government made participation inevitable." But Grattan went on to refute expressly many notions associated in the public mind—and in the minds of some historians—with the "revisionist" interpretation. He granted that to some men in the 1930's the events of 1914 to 1917 might suggest a conspiracy to lead the United States into the war, but he denied that there had been a conspiracy and contended that each step along the road looked like the sane and sensible outcome of policies to which no one with power or prestige could object. He eased up on Wilson and other national leaders by declaring that they could not be held responsible for accepting the Allied version of the war—that it was a mistake to condemn them on the basis of ex post facto evidence. There were, of course, limits to Grattan's generosity. His concession to Wilson's virtue was a shrewd way of condemning those who still believed the Allied version; and lest the point be missed, he condemned such as these in the next line. But his concession to the defenders of Wilson's role was important, and he underscored this by accepting the evidence that Wilson was incensed at the British black list, highly irritated with the Allies in general, and still desperately seeking to end the war without American intervention *throughout* 1916.[68]

68. *Preface to Chaos*, pp. 31–32, 55–60.

Ultimately even the bankers and businessmen were forgiven for their roles during the neutral years. It would have been politically unsound and economically disastrous to have cut off trade with the belligerents; therefore the businessmen acted properly—correctly. The involvement of the American economy in Allied finance became increasingly intricate as a consequence, not of conspiracy, but of correct business practices. The economic developments during the war, Grattan wrote, were in strictest harmony with capitalist logic. Here was Grattan's escape from his awareness that the United States had had an economic stake in the World War. Beard had been willing to scrap this interest because it involved foreign trade which he claimed benefited the few rather the nation as a whole. Grattan had no particular animus against foreign trade, but he was hostile to capitalism. Capitalism was his scapegoat—everyone had acted properly in accordance with the logic of capitalism and the result was war. And so he concluded his chapter on the United States and the World War: "Economic Entanglements with the Allied powers in the First World War made the participation of the United States in it on the side of the Allies possible, logical, and in the end, necessary to the health of private capitalism. . . . Shall it be again?"[69]

Grattan was concerned primarily with revealing the conditions in the 1930's that presaged a new world war. As always, he contended that the masses of people wanted peace, but he indicated, for the first time, some reservations. He could not deny that there was considerable evidence to suggest that the martial spirit was never very far below the surface: pacifists in peace, "we are all—or almost all of us—militarists" in time of war. And Grattan conceded readily that even businessmen prefer peace, but he found them nonetheless unwilling to abandon those policies "which led the nation, step by step, to the brink of war—and on occasion, over the brink into actual fighting." In Roosevelt's policies he found little comfort. The man believed by many to be the arch-enemy of the business community was in fact trying desperately to preserve capitalism—and the tremendous appropriations he was demanding for the Army and the Navy were merely steps in the process. Nor could solace be found in the attitudes of organized

69. *Ibid.*, pp. 33–60.

labor. Roosevelt's rearmament program was relieving the economic disorders of the depression, giving labor a stake in the new preparedness movement. Although infinitely more sophisticated and open-minded than John Kenneth Turner, Grattan was nonetheless using Turner's device to explain how administrations presumed to be unsympathetic to business could follow business oriented policies along the road to war. The United States government, wrote Grattan, always served the interest of the capitalist class and "no American government can stand long that fails to do so." He contended that there could be "no fundamental, long term discrepancy between economics and politics, between business and government."[70]

Convinced as he was that capitalism bred war—that capitalism had to be scrapped to avoid war—Grattan was less than sanguine about the approaches of the various peace movements within the country. What good could come of joining the League of Nations as some peace organizations advocated? Or of holding a national referendum on war, as advocated by others? Neither involved a fundamental change in the economic system; neither attacked the economic forces that led to war.

Turning to a discussion of diplomacy and American foreign policy, Grattan began by insisting that diplomacy was not an "eleemosynary institution." It was essential, he contended, to put aside moralistic formulae, to put such "hoary stand-bys as 'national honor' " into "cold storage," to relate "national interest" to reality. At the moment, American foreign policy was based upon the needs and aspirations of a minority, who translated their interests into vague phrases such as freedom of the seas, neutral rights, and national honor. It was time for the American people to focus their attention upon the internal forces that shaped policy—and for Grattan these forces were economic.[71] Here again, he was attempting to insert a touch of "realism" into American attitudes toward foreign policy. If abstract principles could be put aside and the domestic context in which policy was formulated could be examined closely, it would then be possible to define and reconcile the objectives of policy. Then, perhaps, positive control could succeed drift.

70. *Ibid.*, pp. xvi, 3–7.   71. *Ibid.*, pp. 137–45.

Examining the current debate between "isolationists" and "internationalists," Grattan seemed detached from both positions. With a touch of sarcasm, he derided the "isolationists" for denying the inter-relation between Europe and the United States, for thinking all evil flowed from Europe, and, of course, for ignoring economic realities. In passing off the Pact of Paris as inadequate and absurd, he blamed "nervous isolationists like Senator Borah"—men who would "never by any chance allow the government of the United States to get mixed up with institutions situated on the tainted soil of Europe unless they are entirely innocuous." He was amused by the "isolationist's" fear of involvement with the League of Nations. But Grattan also wrote derisively of the "internationalists," of James Shotwell in particular, because of their alleged view that the League was an "eleemosynary institution" dispensing justice. The "internationalists" were hardly more aware of the realities of power than they were of economic realities.[72]

Turning to a discussion of the neutrality legislation upon which so many of his contemporaries had based their hopes of keeping the United States out of war, Grattan was far from optimistic. He was convinced that neutrality legislation or no, the United States would be dragged into any major war. But Grattan, too, had his hopes, and he clearly favored the idea of mandatory neutrality laws. Still, he suggested that neutrality was least of all a legal problem and stressed the non-legal conditions that influence a neutral's policies. Again, he seemed the realist as he pointed to the considerations of power, of national interest, and of relations between the neutral and the offending belligerent power which might influence a neutral's policy. But if Grattan was playing "realist" when he cast aside legalism and considerations of national honor in favor of national interest, the realist seemed a mere shadow as it became obvious that a policy in the national interest could only be one which kept the nation out of war. For Grattan, war in the national interest remained inconceivable.[73]

Pulling together many threads of his argument, Grattan insisted that "isolationism" could not triumph in the twentieth century; nor could the League of Nations, "to which the interests turn." The logic of the League he found to be war. The logic of American

72. *Ibid.*, pp. 172–74.   73. *Ibid.*, pp. 178–80.

capitalism was imperialism—and that meant war and participation in the wars of other peoples. This was the destiny "vouchsafed the United States by the nature of the domestic economy the people insist, for the present, on supporting."[74] Such were Grattan's conclusions as he analyzed conditions in the mid-1930's in light of the lessons of the World War and the depression.

Barnes reviewed the book for the *Annals of the American Academy of Political and Social Science* and praised it highly. He was particularly pleased with Grattan's interpretation of intervention and declared that Grattan had exposed the "superficiality and essentially unscholarly nature" of the work of Charles Seymour and others "who cling to the 'Sunday School Theory'" that the United States intervened "almost solely because of the resumption of German submarine warfare." Grattan must have been pleased by the brief notice of his book in *Foreign Affairs,* where the bibliographer noted that *Preface to Chaos* had been written by the author of the "insufficiently appreciated" *Why We Fought.*[75]

Probably the best appraisal of Grattan was written by Crane Brinton for the *Saturday Review of Literature.* Brinton saw him as a man who constantly weighed economic variables too heavily, but was sophisticated in his economic determinism: "Mr. Grattan is far to the Left, as politics goes in America, and yet he manages to separate his tastes and his hopes from the inexorable decrees of dialectical materialism." Brinton noted that Grattan was careful to make distinctions between his opinions and observed facts, thus exhibiting a quality generally rare in determinists of any sort. In further tribute, Brinton declared that Grattan kept his mind "as open as a mind can be, without becoming a mere rag-bag."[76]

If in the 1920's the revisionists had had substantial support from reform intellectuals for their interpretations of American intervention in the World War, by the mid-1930's many of their views appeared to have the support of the overwhelming majority of Americans regardless of intelligence quotient. Not for a year did anyone

74. *Ibid.,* p. 193.

75. *Annals,* CXCI (May, 1937), 265–66; *Foreign Affairs,* XV (January, 1937), 387.

76. *Saturday Review of Literature,* XV (November 14, 1936), 10–11.

attempt to poll the American people, but the platform of the Democratic Party in the 1936 election campaign indicated that some allegedly astute political observers did not expect to offend anyone by endorsing implicitly conclusions reached by Grattan, Beard, and other revisionists. The foreign policy plank of the Democratic platform read, in part: "We reaffirm our opposition to war as an instrument of national policy. . . . We shall continue to observe a true neutrality in the disputes of others . . . to work for peace and to take the profits out of war; to guard against being drawn, by political commitments, international banking or private trading, into any war which may develop anywhere."[77]

77. *Official Report of the Proceedings of the Democratic National Convention, 1936,* p. 197.

CHAPTER SEVEN

Revisionism Triumphant
1936-1938

As the data collected by the Nye Committee piled up, Charles Beard became increasingly certain that American intervention in the World War had been a mistake. More like Carl Becker than like the other "revisionist" writers, Beard found in the results of the war, rather than in any of the circumstances preceding or leading to American intervention, the source of his disillusionment. He knew that it was impossible to predict what the world would have been like if the United States had remained neutral in 1917, but the events of the nineteen years following intervention led him to believe that the United States, at least, would have suffered less by staying out of the war.

Convinced that for future policy neutrality was worth a try, Beard examined the evidence uncovered by the Nye Committee in an effort to determine why the United States had abandoned neutrality in 1917. His findings were published as *The Devil Theory of War*,[1] an enlargement of a series of articles he wrote for the *New Republic* in March, 1936.[2] Disturbed by what he saw as a growing tendency to accuse international bankers and munitions manufacturers of conspiring to involve the United States in the World War, Beard sought to demonstrate that the *people*, in their peaceful pursuits, rather than any convenient "devils," brought

1. New York: The Vanguard Press, 1936.
2. See *New Republic*, LXXXVI (March 4, 11, 18, 1936), 100–102, 127–29, 156–59.

about American intervention. The result, however, was the substitution of Beard's personal "devil," international commerce, for Nye's banker and munitions peddler. In terms of practical policy the net effect was the same: more stringent neutrality legislation was in order. Beard's interpretation of the events leading to American intervention led, as did the interpretations of Barnes, Grattan, and Nye, to the policy incorporated in the neutrality legislation of the 1930's.

The effect of the Nye Committee's work on Beard's thought was apparent early in *The Devil Theory of War*. He saw the "Nye revelations" as a warning to all who hoped to be "intelligent." The efforts of Nye's investigators had disclosed "the starkness of the ignorance that passed for knowledge and wisdom" between 1914 and 1918. Beard hoped that "in the course of forty or fifty years some of the lessons brought to light in the story of the march along the 'road to war' may sink into the minds of even Respectable Citizens."[3] He was not endorsing Nye's concept of the "cause" of American intervention, but merely contending that those, including Charles Beard, who in the years 1914–18 thought they knew the "cause," really knew very little. Furthermore, he saw no way of ever knowing "the" cause or causes: "no history, old or new," could provide with certainty an answer to "why we fought." Similarly, a historian might be able to demonstrate that some individuals had more influence than others on the decision to intervene, but "he cannot measure exactly degrees of influence."

According to Beard, there had been a business slowdown, a slight recession, in the United States in 1914. The American economy needed some kind of a boost, and then war broke out in Europe and the purchases of the Allies bolstered the economy. No one could have been disappointed "to have business looking up," least of all the Wilson administration. A congressional election was just over the horizon and an improvement in economic conditions would not likely hurt the chances of the Democratic party, and, after all, "keeping Democrats in power was deemed for the good of the country, by Democrats." But neither the administration nor the few Americans engaged in trade with the Allies had any thought of intervention: "They were all for more and better business."

3. *The Devil Theory of War*, pp. 12–13.

At this point Beard separated himself from Barnes, other revisionists, and Nye, who had tried to isolate the individuals responsible for American intervention. Few of these men concerned with bolstering the economy "realized how fateful in outcome their peaceful pursuit was to be. Few realized that war is not made by a *deus ex machina,* but comes out of ideas, interests and activities cherished and followed in the preceding months and years of peace. The notion that peace might make war did not enter busy heads."[4]

Eventually the Allies ran short of cash, and the question arose as to whether or not the United States could, without compromising its declared neutrality, lend money to the belligerents. Initially Bryan had opposed loans. He had "clearly" foreseen and portrayed the consequences. But in August, 1915, Secretary of the Treasury William McAdoo had warned Wilson that prosperity would end rapidly if the Allies could not borrow money to pay Americans for their purchases. Lansing had added: "Can we afford to let a declaration as to our conception of the 'true spirit of neutrality' made in the first days of the war stand in the way of our national interests, which seem to be seriously threatened?"[5]

Ultimately Wilson decided to permit the extension of credits and then of loans to the Allies. Beard, like all of the "revisionists," saw this reversal by Wilson as a result of the work of "the bankers." But Beard, like Millis alone of those called "revisionists," did not condemn the bankers for this influence. They acted not merely for personal gain, but because they, as few others, knew the extent to which American prosperity was tied to the orders of the Allies. Once the ban on credits, then on loans, was broken down, the bankers made the most of their opportunity: "Loan after loan was floated to pay Americans for American goods. As the days and weeks passed the fate of American bankers, manufacturers, farmers, merchants, workers, and white-collar servants became more deeply entangled in the fate of the Allies on the battlefield—in the war."[6]

Thus America became involved in the war. Then in the spring of 1917 another economic crisis arose: "If the war stopped, American business would slow down from prosperity to dullness, if not calamity. If the Allies were defeated, things would be worse.

4. *Ibid.,* pp. 27–28.   5. *Ibid.,* p. 87.   6. *Ibid.,* p. 89.

American millions were at stake. What other things were really at stake no one knew."[7]

Beard believed that there had been a genuine crisis, believed that "as Ambassador Page informed President Wilson in March 1917, defeat for the Allies meant an economic smash for the United States." Beard did not ask what others might have done under these circumstances, but claimed that "indisputable evidence" showed that on two previous occasions—autumn, 1914, and summer, 1915—Wilson had been confronted with a choice between economic crisis and "concession" and that on both occasions Wilson had chosen to make concessions that entangled the United States in the Allied cause. Given the choice between crisis and concession, Wilson had, prior to the spring of 1917, chosen concession; and although Beard could not prove that the pattern had been followed in 1917, leading to intervention, he left little doubt but that this was his belief.[8]

Specifically, Beard objected to the view that Germany's renewal of unrestricted submarine warfare had been the "cause" of American intervention. This act of Germany's had precipitated the war and nothing more could be made of it. He admitted that his own belief, centering upon Wilson's dilemma, crisis or concession, was merely a opinion, but "to say that President Wilson could and would have taken the country into war on the submarine issue, if the posture of economic interests had not been favorable, is also to express an opinion—a dubious opinion."[9]

For Beard, the German submarine campaign could not be isolated from the "total military and economic situation." He felt that the historian who did isolate the submarine issue was "performing a mental trick that does not correspond to known realities." He would have none of the learned legerdemain that dealt with the submarine issue as a "basic," "immediate," "primary" or "fundamental" cause. Finally, he introduced evidence that he felt settled the issue. He referred to an appearance of Wilson before the Senate Foreign Relations Committee shortly after the war and to an exchange which then took place between Wilson and Senator McCumber.

7. *Ibid.*, p. 90.   8. *Ibid.*, pp. 29, 90–97.   9. *Ibid.*, p. 99.

Senator McCumber—Do you think that if Germany had committed no act of war or no act of injustice against our citizens we
would have gotten into the war?

President Wilson—I think so.

Senator McCumber—You think that we would have gotten in anyway?

President Wilson—I do.[10]

Whatever the cause or causes for American intervention, Beard
had not yet, by his own standards, demonstrated that intervention
had been a mistake. He had spent $25,000 provided by the Social
Science Research Council in his study of the idea of national
interest. Had intervention, regardless of cause, been in the national interest? Beard had, time and again, demonstrated that
the United States had had a vital economic interest challenged
by the Germans in 1917. Perhaps, after all, it had not been the
economic interest of the few but of the entire country that had
been at stake. This economic interest in the Allied cause had not
developed suddenly in 1917, but stemmed from the economic
crisis of the summer of 1914. This economic interest came not
from war profits but from the "peaceful pursuits" of the people
who feared an economic catastrophe in 1914. Accepting Beard's
interpretation of Wilson's decisions in the face of the several economic crises which confronted the United States, would not Beard
have to grant that Wilson had acted in the national interest?

Beard followed his own rules and asked if intervention had
paid—"Did it 'pay' the nation, as opposed to the profit-seeking
bankers?" In answer, the Beard balance sheet was provided:
seven billion dollars' worth of prosperity from 1914 to 1917. followed by one hundred billion dollars' worth of debts stemming
from intervention. But most significant of all was Beard's conclusion that intervention had merely postponed the crash and the
Great Depression by about ten years.[11]

Intervention had merely *postponed* the crash that occurred in
1929. Here was the conclusion that put all the pieces together
and enabled Beard to reverse his wartime attitudes toward inter-

10. *Ibid.*, pp. 101–2.   11. *Ibid.*, pp. 103–7.

vention and to join the ranks of those who declared intervention to have been a mistake.

The United States had had an economic interest in the Allied cause, but it was a stake that was not in the *national* interest. Serving that economic interest had cost one hundred billion dollars and over one hundred thousand lives merely to perpetuate a doomed economy for ten years; it had merely delayed facing an inevitable domestic crisis.

Beard's thoughts as to what *should* have been done in the years 1914–17 became clear in his program for the future. Whether or not the United States had the right to sell and lend to belligerents and neutrals mattered not at all. It was insistence on this right that "entangled American economic interests in the fate of the World War and brought the country to the necessity of accepting a domestic crash or entering the War. According to my interpretation of history, then, insistence on neutral rights increases the probabilities of entanglement in any war that breaks out in Europe or Asia."[12]

Some people, Beard noted, were speaking again of American intervention in European and Asian affairs. They were calling for American support of England, France, and Russia against the fascism and despotism of Germany, Japan, and Italy. Again, Americans were being called upon, as in 1917, to "save civilization," to act "in the interest of democracy and humanity." It was his belief, Beard wrote, that "the people of the United States have been badly burned trying to right historic wrongs in Europe, to promote democracy there and to act as mediator in European quarrels. And it is my theory of probabilities that we shall be badly burned again if we keep on insisting that it is our obligation to do good in Europe.[13]

No matter what Beard thought about the reasons for American intervention, it was clear that he, unlike any of the other revisionists, became vitally concerned with "why we fought" only *after* the results of intervention had convinced him that we should not fight again. And when his investigation of the reasons for intervention revealed that international trade, long a target of his attacks, had been involved, he was convinced that the time

12. *Ibid.*, p. 114.   13. *Ibid.*, p. 117.

had come to make some changes in America's sacred method of economic organization—capitalism: "I should certainly prefer any changes that may be required in it [capitalism] to the frightful prospects of American participation in a war in Europe or Asia." In sum, Beard wanted "mandatory neutrality." He wanted an embargo on the sale of munitions and the extension of credits to warring powers. He wanted restrictions on sales to other neutrals who were engaged in reselling to belligerents. And if the existing American economy could not operate under these limitations, then scrap it. If capitalism could not surive without international trade, then let it die and give the federal government the power to regulate the economy in a way that would permit America to go on without trade that was likely to involve her in war: "In light of our experience in 1914–1918, we should be giving away most of the stuff sold to belligerents, and . . . I prefer to give the goods to hungry Americans rather than to fighting Europeans."[14]

Then, in his most extreme "revisionist" statement on American intervention in the World War, Beard admitted that many of his proposals would be hard to enforce, but he hoped enough of them could be enforced to "prevent the bankers and politicians from guiding the nation into calamity as in 1914–1917." Finally, Beard tried to return to the position he had taken in 1934 and suggested that the next war might be one in which the participation of the United States would be desirable. "If we go to war," Beard wrote, "let us go to war for some grand national and human advantage openly discussed and deliberately arrived at, and not to bail out farmers, bankers and capitalists or to save politicians from the pain of dealing with a domestic crisis."[15] But it was difficult to believe that he thought the "good" war would ever come, and in the five years that followed it became increasingly clear that for Beard the "good" war was not the war Hitler started.

2

In the summer of 1936 the Spanish Civil War caught the headlines, the Nazi screeches for *Lebensraum* grew shriller, and Walter

14. *Ibid.*, pp. 121–23.   15. *Ibid.*, pp. 123–24.

Millis took a quick trip around Europe to see for himself what was going on. When he returned, he wrote a series of articles which were subsequently published in a small volume, *Viewed without Alarm*.[16] As the title of the book suggested, Millis had returned from Europe convinced that those who expected a war to convulse the continent were alarmed unnecessarily. His complacency was based, simply, on the theory that it took two to make a war and that no matter what Hitler's ambitions in Central Europe, the British would not fight. It was plain to Millis in 1936 that the basis of England's European policy was appeasement. Of particular significance was the fact that Millis thought the policy a good one and worthy of imitation by the United States.

Chapter 6 of *Viewed without Alarm* was entitled "How To Stay Out of War and Like It." The British, he wrote, were keeping the peace by the simple expedient of resolving not to fight; they were being neutral "when it counts." But Americans were discussing, "in a tangle of conflicting theories, abstract policies and preparatory legislation, the problem of how to stay out of another war." The English weren't bothering to discuss the problem. They weren't bothering with general acts or treaties or co-operation to suppress wars: "They are just staying out, if they can."[17]

Millis declared that the British "know" that if the Germans could create a viable economic and social system in Central Europe, it would result, "however unpleasant for the lesser nations which it swallows," in "a market and stabilizing force for the rest of the world." But Millis recognized the heavy cost of an appeasement policy. He knew that Ethiopia had been sacrificed and that republican Spain was about to be sacrificed. "The Czechs may go tomorrow, or the Poles. But if it is peace that one is interested in, it has its important advantages." The British policy

> involves risks and it involves sacrifices, of other nations, which are heavy. But they are not so heavy—for Great Britain—as the risks and sacrifices of war. Though it is not pleasant, the British are keeping the peace and liking it. In the process they are looking out primarily for Great Britain, but so far at least they have actually kept

16. Boston: Houghton Mifflin, 1937.   17. *Viewed without Alarm*, p. 49.

the peace. *It is an example, it seems to me, which the United States might well emulate.*[18]

The link between Millis' endorsement of appeasement and his interpretation of the "road to war," 1914–17, may have been subtle, but it was nonetheless significant. In *Road to War* he had written of an excess of idealism which led the reform-oriented into a crusade to make a better world. He had gone on in his writings to parallel Beard in stressing national interests as a basis for "conscious" foreign policy. He wanted a firmly established, conscious policy which would prevent emotional binges, the triumph of "the martial spirit," from leading to actions which might not be in the national interest. In 1936 he paralleled Beard again, turning to a narrow, almost cynical construction of national interest, a construction of national interest diametrically opposed to the Wilsonian idealism of 1917. Designed to keep the United States off the "road to war," Millis' thoughts in *Viewed without Alarm* could only point along the road to Munich.

Then in January, 1937, Dr. Gallup asked the American people: Do you think it was a mistake for the United States to enter the last war? Of those who had an opinion to offer, seventy per cent answered "yes"—it *had* been a mistake for the United States to intervene in the World War. The negligible influence of the *Kriegsschuldfrage* on American attitudes toward intervention in 1917 was indicated by a poll conducted by Dr. Gallup's organization in June, 1937, when seventy-seven per cent of those who thought one or more nations were chiefly responsible for the war blamed Germany.[19] But clearly, the revisionists had won their point with regard to intervention in the last war and now the battle centered about efforts to apply the "lessons" to the coming war. And writing for the La Follettes' *Progressive,* Oswald Garrison Villard acknowledged the new-found wisdom of the American people. Pointing not to the Gallup poll but to the neutrality legislation as proof of a change of viewpoint since 1917, he attributed the change to the "general recognition by the country that our

18. *Ibid.,* pp. 54–55, italics added.

19. Hadley Cantril (ed.), *Public Opinion, 1935–1946* (Princeton, 1951), pp. 201–2.

participation in the last war was a mistake and a complete failure."[20]

For the next few years the debate on "how to stay out of war" raged on—as indeed it did until the fall of France, when the question of "should we stay out" took precedence. Throughout the debate, Charles Beard was one of those who kept calling for "mandatory neutrality" and pointing to the experience of the years 1914–17. In February, 1937, he participated in a forum, "How To Stay Out of War," and contended that the American experience showed that if neutrality was to be preserved there would have to be "drastic limitations on selling munitions and lending money to all belligerents." As for intervening in European affairs again, he declared: "If our efforts to right historic wrongs and bring peace and reason to Europe in 1917–1919 have not taught American citizens anything, no words of mine can add to their education."[21]

In an article for the *New Republic* in March, 1937, Beard asked "Why Did We Go to War?"[22] He compared the question to the child's question: "Who made God?" He couldn't be sure of the answer and he was suspicious of those who were.

Beard granted that the whole truth as to why the United States went to war in 1917 could never be known, but he justified the quest for the reasons for intervention on the ground that "we can know many relevant truths." Another European war seemed imminent: "If we want to stay out of it, we can find some assistance in all the truth we can get about how we became involved in the last war. Even if we are thirsting for another war ourselves, either for democracy or anything else, we can profit from knowledge of our entanglements in the last war."[23]

Then Beard slapped at the extreme revisionists who postulated conspiracies of bankers, politicians, or munitions manufacturers as the "reason" for intervention. The American Legion idea of an altruistic crusade to make the world safe for democracy also fell victim to Beard's pen. As in *The Devil Theory of War*, Beard

20. *Progressive* (Madison, Wis.), February 13, 1937, p. 1.

21. *Forum*, XCVII (February, 1937), 89–95.

22. *New Republic*, XC (March 10, 1937), 127–29.

23. *Ibid.*, p. 128.

pointed to the involvement of the entire American economy in the Allied effort as the necessary prelude to intervention.

3

In July, 1937, the Japanese began full-scale operations in their efforts to subjugate China. Availing himself of the opportunity provided by the absence of a formal declaration of war by Japan, President Roosevelt chose not to apply the provisions of the neutrality legislation to the Sino-Japanese conflict. Although Roosevelt's decision was based on the hope that refraining from imposing an arms embargo would ultimately be of advantage to China, and although Congress and the American people appear to have been strongly sympathetic to China, the essential policy of the United States remained one of non-interference in this Far Eastern struggle. When, on July 16, Secretary of State Cordell Hull circularized the nations of the world with a statement reaffirming the adherence of the United States to the commandments of international morality, he refrained from any specific condemnation of Japan. When China appealed for help to the signatories of the Nine Power Treaty, the American government refrained again from issuing any statement akin to the "Stimson-Hoover Doctrine." In mid-August, when Japanese naval operations threatened Shanghai, the American appeal to exclude that city from the zone of military operations was addressed to both belligerents. And, with "hearty appreciation," perhaps also with the suspicion that for the continuation of such restraint the administration would require encouragement, Beard sent a telegram to the President: "By your action in the Far East you open a grand epoch in American diplomacy."[24]

Whether Beard's telegram represented optimism, wishful thinking, or an effort to reinforce the President's direction of the moment, the moment was short-lived. October brought the "quarantine speech" and December the President's successful action

24. Beard to Roosevelt, August 18, 1937, Roosevelt Library, Section 41-A Black. Full text of the telegram: "By your action in the Far East you open a grand epoch in American diplomacy. By the choice of Senator Black you give the plain people representation in the Supreme Court. Hearty Appreciation."

against the Ludlow resolution for a constitutional amendment to provide for a national referendum on war. By February, 1938, Villard was insisting that the administration had "set its feet upon the path that leads to war." Shortly afterward, Villard proclaimed Roosevelt to be the greatest menace "to the existing situation."[25] Also in February, the *New Republic* published a debate on collective security.[26] The participants were Beard and Earl Browder, the leading American Communist. Browder, in accordance with the party line of the days preceding the Nazi-Soviet Non-Aggression Pact, endorsed Roosevelt's apparent leaning toward collective security.

Beard began by sketching in the two sides of the debate. Collective security was advocated by proponents of the League of Nations, Stalinite Communists, British-born American citizens, Alf Landon, Colonel Knox, "and many other citizens who say they desire peace for the United States and think they see no other way to attain it, save by collective action." Beard found his own supporters, the opponents of collective security, another curious mixture: Italian-Americans, German-Americans, Trotskyites, "old-fashioned" imperialistic isolationists, *and* "Americans who imagine that it is possible to build a civilization in the United States and to defend it." The contest, he contended, "is not one of perfect truth against perfect error, knowledge against ignorance, wisdom against folly."[27]

Beard argued that in the event of a war against the three offending powers, Germany, Italy, and Japan, there could be no guarantee of beneficent results, no guarantee of a "universal democratic advance." He asked that his readers examine "the record"—the Treaty of Versailles and especially the state of democracy twenty years after the victory of the democratic powers:

> If any person can see hopes for democracy in another military and naval crusade for democracy, after looking at the fruits of the last crusade, then his mind passeth my understanding. Although the new war would bring to business that "recovery" so longed for now,

25. *Progressive*, February 5, 1938, pp. 1, 3; March 26, 1938, p. 2.

26. "Collective Security—a Debate," *New Republic*, XCIII (February 2, 1938), 354–59.

27. *Ibid.*, p. 357.

it would doubtless be followed by a ruinous collapse; and the probabilities are that we should then have universal fascism rather than universal democracy.[28]

A few days later, Beard appeared before the House Foreign Affairs Committee and testified that "The Orient from Siberia to Singapore is not worth the bones of one American soldier." He declared that the World War had proved that it was a "herculean job" to make the world safe for democracy. And, he added, democracy had never seen worse days than it faced in 1938. "Our Americans," he was quoted as saying, "are a great and intelligent people, but they aren't smart enough to solve problems of Europe which are encrusted in the blood rust of fifty centuries of warfare."[29]

Early in the spring, the editors of the *Nation* drew Carl Becker into the debate. Becker consented to participate in a symposium of "outstanding liberals" on questions of American foreign policy.[30] In his contribution there was no indication that Becker's disillusionment over intervention in 1917 had subsided. If isolation meant "only that we should avoid war unless we are obviously attacked by another country," then he was for it. He found the idea that the United States might be in danger of such an attack "preposterous" and added that a larger military establishment would be more likely to involve the country in war than to keep it out of war.

Becker did not believe that a general European war was likely, "in the near future." If war did come, he suspected that the consequences would be "almost equally disastrous" to Americans whether the United States intervened or not. "Nonetheless," he wrote, "I am in favor of keeping out." There was only one place to save democracy and that was at home: "If we can put our people to work, democracy will be safe enough here, and we can't save it in Europe by fighting for it there."[31]

If Becker, like Barnes, Beard, Grattan, and Millis, was reflecting the reform-oriented version of "revisionism," the "liberal's" abhorrence of war and the "liberal's" view of the fruits of the last

28. *Ibid.*, p. 358.
29. *New York Times*, February 11, 1938, p. 14.
30. "How To Keep Out of War," *Nation*, CXLVI (April 2, 1938), 378.
31. *Ibid.*

war, there was still another breed of "revisionist" to be heard from. Not all the participants on the "revisionist" side of the controversy were concerned about reform. Not all the threads of revisionism could be followed back to the "liberal's" disillusionment with the fruits of intervention. One major strand of revisionist thought could be traced back to the opponents of intervention in the World War, to the ethnic groups who for one reason or another opposed intervention on behalf of Great Britain and in opposition to Germany. In Charles Callan Tansill those elements in the United States which would have preferred a German to a British victory in the World War, and who still, in the late 1930's, preferred German hegemony in Europe to British, found an able champion.

4

In 1927, a onetime supporter of Woodrow Wilson and recent convert to the revisionist side of the *Kriegsschuldfrage*, Senator Robert L. Owen of Oklahoma, published an indictment of Russia, *The Russian Imperial Conspiracy, 1892–1914.*[32] In support of his case, Owen reported that under the Senate resolution to collate the evidence on the origin of the World War, "Charles E. [*sic*] Tansill, expert historian, was assigned the task and is now convinced of the Russian and French responsibility." Tansill's "book" had not been published "for reasons of diplomatic amity."[33]

Owen's statement is the earliest available reference to Tansill's views on any of the issues involved in the revisionist controversy. The manuscript to which he referred was never published and its present location is unknown even to its author. Tansill has, however, confirmed Owen's interpretation of Tansill's own early views on the *Kriegsschuldfrage*. In addition, Tansill has recalled that he never accepted the view of the origins of the war which had prevailed in the United States from 1914 to 1917, that he had opposed intervention in that war, and that he had devoted himself in 1919 to the defeat of the Treaty of Versailles.[34]

However reliable the memory may be, Tansill's writings gradu-

32. New York: A. and C. Boni, 1927.

33. *Russian Imperial Conspiracy,* pp. 9–10.

34. Interview with Charles Callan Tansill, Washington, D.C., August 14, 1962.

ally, though obliquely, revealed his position, with regard to both the origins of the war and to American intervention. Reviewing Owen's book for the *American Journal of International Law*, Tansill ignored the reference to his own work and pointed to the work of Barnes, Fay, and Langer to indicate that Owen was not alone in his exoneration of Germany from responsibility for the war. He also called attention to Grattan's article in the *American Mercury* on historians during the war—a "graphic description of the war-time hysteria that seized upon American historians" and presumably upset Owen. A few years later, the same journal called upon Tansill to review Bernadotte Schmitt's *The Coming of the War*. Again there was no direct indication of Tansill's views on the issues with which the author dealt, but there was little doubt as to the impression with which he left the reader. He declared that it had been a "tremendous task for Professor Schmitt to examine this vast mass of evidence with what he hoped was an unbiased mind." While the reader wondered whether Schmitt's hope had been justified, Tansill went on to say that no historian had given the subject "more extended consideration" and that "if any student desires to read a lengthy and well-documented presentation of a viewpoint that is no longer widely held, the volumes by Professor Schmitt should give him ample satisfaction."[35] The gentle words were there —but so was the stiletto. Perhaps few noticed it after the din of Barnes's sledge hammer.

In another review, written in 1934, Tansill indicated his view of Woodrow Wilson and of Wilson's advisers. He found Wilson's knowledge of European matters "so distinctly limited" that he was forced to turn to his advisers. And his advisers gave him bad advice—at least at Versailles. Not only was their advice bad, it was also prejudiced, contrary to the truth and to common sense—a less gentle soul might have said they lied deliberately. But Wilson himself was at times "only too willing to surrender principles to which he had apparently given merely lip service." The great humanitarian had remained untouched by the blockade which caused starvation in Germany during the Peace Conference.[36]

35. *American Journal of International Law*, XXII (1928), 222–23; XXV (1931), 809–11.

36. Review of *Germany under the Treaty* by William H. Dawson, *American Journal of International Law*, XXVIII (1934), 620–21.

By the mid-1930's, Tansill, in his forties, had established a reputation for himself as a diplomatic historian.[37] One December day in 1935, a hint of his interest in American intervention appeared in the *New York Times*. He was reported to have declared that Lansing had " 'abdicated' American rights to Great Britain and, from the moment he assumed office, pressed the President toward engaging in the World War on the side of the Allies."

Tansill referred to Lansing as a "diplomatic jack-in-the-box" whose notes to the belligerents would impress students "with reference to his industry, but not to his sincerity." He found that Lansing's notes to Germany revealed an "unyielding" tone which "commanded compliance." But in looking "behind the diplomatic barrage directed against Great Britain," Tansill found it apparent "that America became adept in the art of camouflage long before 1917."[38] Then, under the auspices of a German-American group, The Carl Schurz Foundation, and "by express invitation of the German Government," Tansill went off to the University of Berlin to lecture on German-American relations.

In a radio broadcast in May, 1936, after his return to the United States, Tansill made it patently clear that he was no reformer, no well-wisher of Roosevelt's New Deal.[39] His subject was "the American Doctrine of Judicial Review," and his address was a justification of the Supreme Court's anti-New Deal decisions on historical grounds, going back to the precedents set by John Marshall. Tansill made little editorial comment, but he did refer to Roosevelt's "adolescent enthusiasm and omniscient air." He also indicated his approval of the Court's protection of the "sacred rights of private property" and his disapproval of the "Democratic historians" who opposed the Court's decisions. Reasonable as his comments may have seemed to many, they were not the sort that were likely to come from the lips of Barnes, Beard, Grattan, or Millis. Indeed,

37. In 1935, Tansill was Professor of History at the American University and acting dean of the graduate school. He had given the Albert Shaw Lectures in American Diplomacy at Johns Hopkins, 1930–31, and had published several volumes of diplomatic history.

38. *New York Times,* December 29, 1935, p. 16.

39. *Vital Speeches,* II (June 15, 1936), 597–99. Broadcast under the auspices of the Society of American History and Government on May 19, 1936.

Beard was among the leading "Democratic historians" opposing the Court and, a year later, one of the principal supporters of Roosevelt's Court reorganization bill.[40]

In June, another example of Tansill's technique appeared in a review of Charles Seymour's *American Neutrality, 1914–1917,* Seymour's answer to Millis and the Nye Committee. Tansill referred to the book as a "recasting" of American diplomacy during the World War. He found Seymour confident that material considerations had not influenced the American government and using Wilson's speeches as evidence to support his position. Tansill declared that it was "difficult to doubt such unimpeachable testimony." Lest his sarcasm be missed, he continued, noting that "after having dealt in such convincing manner with these loquacious legislators [Clark and Nye]," Seymour turned to a discussion of trade. Although he went on to make many excuses for Seymour—the poor fellow's responsibilities tied him to New Haven and he couldn't use any sources but those available in the Yale library—he concluded that Seymour was "neglectful" of the sources, had peculiar ideas about what constituted evidence, and had written a book which was "distinctly inadequate" as a study of American neutrality. Seymour had squeezed new and valuable information out of the House papers, which were at Yale, but had been "too partial to the House viewpoint" and had persisted in "fitting new facts into an outworn pattern."[41]

The publication of Lansing's *War Memoirs* gave Tansill another opportunity to discuss the early use of camouflage in the United States. Lansing had availed himself of this "art" to "delude his own countrymen into the false belief that he was insistent upon

40. Although nominally a Democrat, Tansill never supported New Deal measures and considered himself a "conservative in the Southern tradition." Interview with Tansill, August 14, 1962. On the other hand, the high point of cordiality between Roosevelt and Beard was reached during the struggle over Supreme Court reorganization. Beard spoke on the radio in favor of Roosevelt's proposal and received a personal letter of appreciation from Roosevelt. Roosevelt also instructed an aide to arrange to have the Beards spend a weekend with the Roosevelts on the Potomac. Roosevelt to Beard, May 20, 1937; Roosevelt to "Mac" (Marvin McIntyre), May 21, 1937; Beard to Roosevelt, May 29, 1937, Roosevelt Library, President's Personal File 3847.

41. *Mississippi Valley Historical Review,* XXIII (June, 1936), 119–21.

the protection of all American rights." In June, 1937, a review of George Macaulay Trevelyan's *Grey of Fallodon* enabled Tansill to introduce his analogy between Grey and Merlin and thus to suggest that the former had used the occult power of his charms to undo Page and House, and ultimately American neutrality. Here too, Tansill noted the "intellectual alliance" between Grey and Wilson—which stemmed from their mutual fondness for the poetry of Wordsworth.[42] Then in 1938, Tansill's major contribution to the revisionist controversy between world wars, *America Goes to War*, appeared.[43]

In his preface, Tansill announced that he had "no thesis to prove nor any viewpoint to exploit." He was concerned primarily with treating objectively the most important foreign policy questions which the Wilson administration had faced prior to intervention. He noted that these were questions which had "long been the subject of sharp controversy between historians who have ranged themselves into two camps." But Tansill had "no desire to be identified with either group," for "crusading zeal is hardly the proper spirit for an impartial historian."[44] Here was the promise of "scientific" history. Barnes, Beard, Grattan, and Millis were avowed polemicists, but Tansill promised objective history. Then, disarmingly, he listed Charles Seymour, leader of one camp in the controversy, among those to whom he dedicated his book—before placing his own banner in the van of the opposing forces.

Tansill's study of American intervention in 1917 differed from all the preceding monographs in one important respect: Tansill made no attempt to deal with the question of whether or not the United States *should* have fought. For Tansill and, according to the 1937 Gallup poll, for seventy per cent of the American people, this issue was settled: intervention had been a mistake and this was the basic assumption upon which Tansill's interpretation rested.

The primary questions which Tansill posed for himself, since he felt no need to argue that intervention was a mistake, were how did the United States commit this terrible blunder; what errors

42. *Ibid.*, XXIII (September, 1936), 292–93; XXIV (June, 1937), 110–12.
43. Boston: Little, Brown and Co., 1938.
44. *America Goes to War*, p. vii.

were made along the way; who was responsible for these errors and why?

Tansill had no ideological animus against "big business," and, unlike those revisionists whose thought came out of reform currents, he made no effect to indict "big business" on the grounds of responsibility for the war. Whatever the direction of the pressures from Wall Street, Tansill did not believe these pressures had influenced the decision to intervene. He contended that "despite all the efforts of the Nye Committee" there was not the "slightest evidence" that Wilson had considered demands from "big business" that the United States intervene to save investments threatened by the possibility of a German victory. On the contrary, "Colonel House and Secretary Lansing had far more influence than the House of Morgan."[45] And it was House and Lansing rather than the financiers, the international traders, or the arms manufacturers who served as Tansill's "devils." In an interpretation dominated by his hostility to Great Britain, Tansill accused House and Lansing repeatedly of having served British rather than American interests—much as Page had been accused a decade before.

For Tansill, the real battle in the years 1914–17 was a battle between British shrewdness and realism on the one hand and American naïveté and idealism on the other. The United States was handicapped throughout this battle by a pro-British administration in Washington and by the pressures of Anglophile advisers on Wilson who, though pro-British himself, sought desperately to remain objective in his judgment of the belligerents.

In his discussion of the pre-1914 background of the war, Tansill saw a long history of American suspicion of Germany as a major "factor" leading to intervention. He suggested that German-American friction was inevitable in the last twenty-five years of the nineteenth century, "when both nations gave heed to the call of economic imperialism and began to nurse colonial ambitions."[46] British statesmen, however, "were too astute" to permit friction to arise between England and the United States.

When the World War began in 1914, there were, Tansill felt, few men in the administration in Washington who maintained any

45. *Ibid.*, p. 657.   46. *Ibid.*, p. 3.

semblance of neutral thought. Most members of the administration were pro-Ally but, according to Tansill, not necessarily out of conviction: "It is probable that these officials in the Wilson Administration were fervidly pro-Ally *because* they had early recognized the President's well-known bias in that direction."[47]

Of Wilson's advisers, Lansing received more hostile treatment from Tansill than he had from other revisionist authors, and he was allowed to share responsibility with House for the "mistakes" that led to intervention: "War, and not peace was his [Lansing's] desire. From the moment he became Secretary of State he looked forward to a conflict between the United States and Germany as a necessary incident in the crusade against German militarism."[48]

Once, in the early stages of the war, an American had tried to stand up to England. Tansill was impressed by a note drafted by Cone Johnson, Solicitor General of the State Department. Johnson was protesting against the British interpretation of "continuous voyage." The note "was a challenge such as Cleveland sent in 1895, but Mr. Johnson little realized that he was following an antiquated model of diplomatic correspondence, and he seemed quite unaware of the fact that since the 'Gay Nineties' the notes from the Department of State to England had grown less strident and more subtle."[49]

But, Tansill noted, Colonel House appeared to inform Mr. Johnson of the "change of style" in diplomatic correspondence with England. House "did not hesitate to pronounce as 'exceedingly undiplomatic' a note which merely defended with vigor American rights." Tansill was sure that the British Foreign Office "probably realized that with Ambassador Page in London, and with Colonel House in Washington, there was little to fear from American protests."[50]

All this had occurred in late September, 1914, and before the month was out the episode was repeated with Lansing, then counselor of the Department of State, writing a memorandum calling for protest against British policy. After House apparently had Lansing's suggestions modified, Lansing learned that "in the future he had better consult British sensibilities rather than Ameri-

47. *Ibid.*, p. 27, italics added.

48. *Ibid.*, p. 66.   49. *Ibid.*, p. 143.   50. *Ibid.*, p. 147.

can rights. From that hour on, he had scant respect for a neutrality that could be so easily stifled by a President who was pledged to preserve it."[51]

Ambassador Page, over whom Sir Edward Grey, "like some modern Merlin" had "early cast a spell," had been unhappy with Lansing's initial attitude toward Great Britain. But "friendly feelings for Great Britain soon became a watchword with Mr. Lansing, and so evident did this fact become to members of the diplomatic service that even Mr. Page soon reversed his attitude."[52]

Tansill contended that the "real" fight for American neutrality was waged in April, 1915. Bryan had been willing to surrender the "theoretical" right of Americans to sail unmolested on the high seas, but he lost his argument with Lansing who had insisted on holding Germany to "strict accountability" for infringement of this right of neutrals. According to Tansill,

> America finally entered the war because of serious difficulties with Germany arising out of the submarine warfare. These difficulties may be traced directly to the reaction of the President to the declaration of the German war zone, and the subsequent activities of submarines. If the President had taken any decisive action against the admission of armed British merchantmen into American harbors, and if he had warned American citizens of the dangers that attended passage on belligerent vessels, America might well have been spared the great sacrifice of 1917-1918. . . .[53]

To Tansill it was clear that Wilson's refusal to surrender neutral rights and his failure to be firm with Great Britain regarding her use of armed merchantmen for traffic to American ports precluded the possibility of continued American neutrality. Therefore the responsibility for blundering into war rested "squarely on the shoulders of the President." But "the official who above all others helped to place it there was Robert Lansing."[54]

Then came the tragic sinking of the *Lusitania*. In his discussion of this event, Tansill found a powerful ally in Samuel Flagg Bemis, whose textbook in diplomatic history contained the follow-

51. *Ibid.*, p. 150.   53. *Ibid.*, p. 258.
52. *Ibid.*, p. 162.   54. *Ibid.*

ing statement: "One might well wonder whether the British Government purposely exposed to attack the *Lusitania* and other British passenger vessels carrying American citizens, in order to lead the Germans on to a rash act which might bring the United States into the war. . . ."[55] Tansill noted that the Kaiser had suggested that the British plotted to have the *Lusitania* sunk, and he then brought in a reference to Bemis' statement to show that the Kaiser's remarks were not wild—at least no wilder than those of Professor Bemis.

Turning to Wilson's reaction to the *Lusitania* sinking, Tansill conceded that it was likely that Wilson could not conceive of the British plotting the sinking of the vessel, and then Tansill used this concession to create an image of Wilson as a naïve idealist: "He was too much of an idealist to keep fresh in his memory the fact that the same negative quality has long been associated with British success in world politics. The formulas of a far-flung empire were not familiar to a political novice whose vision had long been limited to a university campus."[56]

Tansill complained that at a time when the United States desperately needed a "realist" at the helm, it found itself directed by a man who "allowed himself to be so largely influencd by the legal maxims of Mr. Lansing." And Tansill was so convinced that Lansing was plotting war that when mentioning that Lansing had sent a sharp note to Great Britain in May, 1915, he had to add: "Mr. Lansing was now having things so much his own way that he must have felt a little sorry for Secretary Bryan." Similarly, Tansill was hard pressed to explain Lansing's strong note to England in September, 1916: "For a man with pronounced Anglophile tendencies it is somewhat remarkable that his zeal to make out a case against Great Britain should have led him to frame notes that, if sent to London as drafted, would have caused a severe strain upon relations between the two countries."[57]

As though more concerned with demonstrating that Anglophile tendencies within the administration determined America's course than with the internal consistency of his monograph, Tansill then created another image of President Wilson: an image of a crafty

---

55. *A Diplomatic History of the United States* (New York: Henry Holt, 1936), p. 616 in 1955 edition.

56. *America Goes to War*, p. 289.   57. *Ibid.*, pp. 312, 302, 543.

politician bent on leading his country into war. He wrote of the "Sunrise Conference" as if no question of its authenticity had ever been raised, citing only Gilson Gardner's article which had been the original source of the legend. Subsequently, in a long footnote, he discussed the controversy over the alleged conference, but mostly in terms of the differences over when it took place. There was no mention of the fact that Grattan and Beard had called the evidence supporting the occurrence of the conference "dubious" or that Millis had contended that the conference did not deal with intervention but with the Gore-McLemore resolution. Tansill was here suggesting that Wilson, whom he had claimed earlier was in an "intellectual alliance" with Grey "because of their common devotion to the sonnets of William Wordsworth," was ready to take his country to war in the spring of 1916. Wilson did, however, prefer to veil his leaning toward intervention "under the cloak of an ardent defense of the right of American citizens to sail on armed merchantmen of the belligerent powers."[58]

With relation to American policy toward armed belligerent merchantmen, Tansill blamed Colonel House for America's failure to follow the Dutch in banning such ships from its harbors. Had the United States followed Holland's lead, Tansill believed the British would have been compelled to disarm their merchant ships and that this would have led to an understanding between the United States and Germany on the conduct of submarine warfare, thus removing "the only serious cause of friction in German-American relations." The United States intervened in the war partly because of this failure of Wilson "to follow a course dictated by American rather than Allied interests." And "it was largely due to Colonel House that such a tragic and fateful decision was made."[59]

Again and again, Tansill's criticisms of Wilson, Lansing, House, or Page were based primarily on his belief that their offending acts were motivated by a desire to aid Great Britain. Often it seemed that an action which redounded to Great Britain's advantage was a worse offense than a violation of international law or a failure to act in the national interest. Often the mere fact that an action benefited Great Britain seemed evidence enough that the action was contrary to the interests of the United States. Fourteen years later Professor Tansill wrote that "the main objective in American for-

58. *Ibid.*, pp. 467, 485–86, 477.   59. *Ibid.*, p. 429.

eign policy since 1900 has been the preservation of the British Empire."[60] Apparently he never considered the possibility that preservation of that empire might have been in the best interests of the United States.

In 1938 Tansill wrote: "From our present historical perspective, it seems that the Administration was far too timid in its policy toward England." He argued that Wilson's failure to force Great Britain into making broad concessions on the blockade and the black list was an indication of Wilson's "inability to grasp the realities of world politics." "Throughout the whole period of American neutrality," Tansill contended, "the British Government was able to balance British disregard of American rights against German destruction of American lives. Had there been no submarine warfare America would have been compelled to vindicate her rights or lose caste as an independent nation. Which alternative the Wilson Administration would have followed is a matter of considerable doubt."[61]

Then, with a lesson for those concerned with American policy in the 1930's, Tansill claimed that Wilson had been forced by bad legal advice into a position which left him little choice but to follow the road to war. Had he received sounder advice on the various issues of neutral rights, "it is very possible that he would have followed the road to conciliation."[62]

Although several reviewers remarked that Tansill was no Anglophile, his book was remarkably well received. Edwin Borchard was delighted with this "brilliant, scholarly study" and very much impressed by Tansill's documentation. Tansill had shown how Wilson had been misled and the book "will doubtless take its place among the indispensable literature of our time." If Borchard's view surprised no one, others less committed to a revisionist view of intervention were equally as impressed. Writing for the *Atlantic Monthly*, Allan Nevins declared: "Twenty-one years after the United States entered the World War we have a book [*America Goes to War*] on the causes of that entry which approaches finality." Nevins had some criticism of Tansill's work but found it "an ad-

60. *Back Door to War* (Chicago: Regnery, 1952), p. 3.

61. *America Goes to War*, pp. 546, 565.

62. *Ibid.*, p. 649.

mirable volume, and absolutely indispensable to an understanding of three critical years in our history."[63] For the *New Republic*, George Fielding Eliot called *America Goes to War* "a book destined to be the standard authority on our pre-war years." And, he insisted, the book was more than a "mere" work of reference: "it is a warning and a guide post."[64] It was Henry Steele Commager, however, who gave Tansill's book its most laudatory review. Commager found *America Goes to War* to be "critical, searching and judicious." He called the book "the most valuable contribution to the history of the pre-war years in our literature, and one of the notable achievements of historical scholarship of this generation."[65]

Lest anyone think that Commager's praise for this most "scholarly" of revisionist interpretations of intervention was accidental, Commager made his endorsement of Tansill's interpretation quite clear. He felt that Americans were tending to view "our war with Germany" as an irrepressible conflict and that Tansill had presented a "vigorous challenge to such intellectual fatalism. Tansill was convinced that intervention had not been inevitable and traced "in magisterial style, the *missteps* which carried the United States along the road to war. It is an impressive performance, conducted with skill, learning, and wit, and *illuminating the present as well as the past*."[66]

If in one or two sentences Commager's sympathies in the revisionist controversy and his position in the foreign policy debate of the late 1930's were obvious, in another sentence the extent of his commitment to the revisionist interpretation of American intervention was revealed: "From the standpoint of responsibility for war, the case against both House and Lansing is a strong one, and it does not seem likely that the verdict which Mr. Tansill pronounces against them will be modified in essentials."[67]

In the historical journals, Tansill's scholarship received consid-

63. Lester B. Shippee in *Annals*, CCI (January, 1939), 267, and George Fielding Eliot, who found a "decidedly anti-British bias," in *New Republic*, XCV (June 29, 1938), 221; Borchard in *American Journal of International Law*, XXXIII (1939), 229–31; *Atlantic Monthly*, CLXII (August, 1938).

64. *New Republic*, XCV (June 29, 1938), 221.

65. *Yale Review*, XXVIII (Summer, 1938), 855–57.

66. *Ibid.*, p. 855, italics added.   67. *Ibid.*, p. 856.

erably less praise. To be sure, Thomas Bailey was impressed favorably by Tansill's style and documentation and decided that it was now clear that Wilson had tried to maintain neutrality but had been misled by House and particularly by Lansing. Bailey also seemed to feel that the "telling irony" which Tansill had employed against House and Lansing was a useful scholarly device. But Bailey did note that Tansill's judgments would raise many questions.[68]

Bernadotte Schmitt called attention to Tansill's preface, to the assertion that Tansill was not going to take sides in the controversy. Schmitt readily accepted Tansill's sincerity—perhaps Tansill, too, hoped he was writing with an unbiased mind—but declared him a member of the Grattan-Millis camp. Much as Fay had been disturbed by Grattan's organization, Schmitt was disturbed by Tansill's, finding the topical arrangement distorting. Professing his own faith in the sincerity of House and Lansing, he expressed disapproval of Tansill's use of sarcasm and innuendo to discredit the two men. And Schmitt found Tansill's conclusions debatable.[69]

James P. Baxter III, writing for the *American Historical Review*, declared Tansill's book to be the fullest and in many ways the most important work on American intervention, but found it to have drawbacks for the general reader. Tansill had failed in his quest for objectivity and had clearly cast his lot with Millis and Grattan. He had permitted himself a great deal of personal devil hunting; he had gone out of his way to throw a "brickbat" at John Hay as an Anglophile; and he had praised Bryan for his love of peace while ignoring Bryan's shortcomings. Baxter, too, complained about Tansill's organization, contending that it distorted rather than clarified the submarine issue—across which Tansill had drawn a number of "red herrings." Finally, he noted that Tansill had indulged in a great many "might have beens," while playing Monday morning quarterback on Wilson's calling of the signals.[70]

Equally hostile criticism of *America Goes to War* appeared in the *Saturday Review of Literature*. In that journal, Raymond

68. *Mississippi Valley Historical Review*, XXV (March, 1939), 589–90.
69. *Journal of Modern History*, X (December, 1938), 569–73.
70. *American Historical Review*, XLV (October, 1939), 183–84.

Sontag described Tansill as a crusader, with a hero in Bryan and a set of devils headed by Colonel House: "To blacken his devils, he is not content to state what they did. He must impute motives." Sontag found Tansill "so horrified by the results that he cannot admit that belligerent idealism was a fact."[71]

For Tansill, unlike the reform-oriented revisionists, the tragedy of American intervention in 1917 was not found in the statistics of war dead and wounded, in the death of the reform movement that preceded the war, or in the failure of the effort to make the world safe for democracy. For Tansill, the great tragedy of American intervention in 1917 was the fact that it enabled the British Empire to emerge from the war intact. In *America Goes to War*, Tansill's attitudes toward world politics and America's role in world affairs stood out in bold relief: the well-ordered world was one in which England was no longer on top and in which America's role was to eschew any activity which served to keep England on top. Assistance to Great Britain was naïve idealism, if not treason, and "realism" was defined as standing up and calling the British to account for their transgressions.[72] Tansill's interpretation of the events leading to American intervention in the World War may well have been valid, but he added little to Bausman's interpretation other than footnotes. His place in the revisionist controversy was to represent the views of Irish-Americans embittered by Wilson's policies, as Bausman had represented the views of German-Americans.[73]

71. *Saturday Review of Literature,* XVII (April 16, 1938), 11.

72. Tansill has stated that his dislike and distrust of the British was inherited from his father. Interview, August 14, 1962.

73. Tansill's *America and the Fight for Irish Freedom* (New York: Devin-Adair Co., 1957) suggests many reasons for his hostile attitude toward Wilson. Although this is "ex post facto" evidence, it does not seem unreasonable to suggest that the hostility to Wilson which is expressed in this book on the ground that Wilson despised Irish-Americans corroborates my view of the attitude underlying *America Goes to War. America and the Fight for Irish Freedom* is dedicated to Daniel F. Cohalan and John Devoy. Selig Adler has suggested in his *The Isolationist Impulse* (New York: Collier Books, 1961) that, while DeValera was more interested in obtaining Irish independence than in humiliating Wilson, Cohalan never ended the feud with Wilson. Is it possible that Tansill was carrying on Cohalan's battle?

CHAPTER EIGHT

Finale, 1939–December 7, 1941

In September, 1938, Neville Chamberlain took a trip to Munich to discuss with Adolf Hitler the future of Czechoslovakia. Two weeks after that conference, President Roosevelt asked Congress for a budget increase of three hundred million dollars for defense. And by December, war in Europe seemed imminent.

Since 1935 the American reaction to the movements of European dictators had been an attempt to legislate peace through the several neutrality acts. Since the debate over the first neutrality act in 1935 there had been some who doubted the value of attempting to keep the peace by act of Congress. In 1935 there had been voices calling for provisions allowing the President to discriminate against aggressors.[1] As war grew closer, efforts mounted to have the neutrality legislation revised to give the President discriminatory powers. In his annual message to Congress on January 4, 1939, Roosevelt declared: "We have learned that when we deliberately try to legislate neutrality, our neutrality laws may operate unevenly and unfairly—may actually give aid to an aggressor and deny it to a victim. The instinct of self preservation should warn us that we ought not to let that happen any more."[2]

But Charles Beard would have no part of any revision that gave Roosevelt more discretion. In an article that appeared in the *New Republic* a few days after Roosevelt's message to Congress, Beard mentioned that he had been reviled for his position

1. See above, chap. 5.

2. Basil Rauch (ed.), *Franklin D. Roosevelt: Selected Speeches, Messages, Press Conferences, and Letters* (New York: Rinehart, 1957), p. 208.

but that he would not answer in kind. After all, "there are fine-spirited and honorable men and women who sincerely believe that the last war was really 'a war for democracy.' " Pointedly, Beard applied the "revisionist" interpretation of intervention in the World War to the contemporary situation. He remembered that many Americans who had favored intervention and applauded Wilson's "war-aims" began to worry about the "war for democracy" before the war had ended. For some, the illusions vanished with the appearance of the Sedition Act of 1918. Others were disillusioned by the Treaty of Versailles.

Now the process had begun anew: war was imminent and Americans were sorting out the good powers and the bad. But, Beard wrote, "what are Great Britain and France really up to? We do not know any more about that than we did in 1914 about all the backstairs negotiations and designs which preceded the World War or in 1915 about the Secret Treaties."[3]

All Beard wanted this time was a *tighter* neutrality law. If there was to be revision of the neutrality legislation, his recollections of the circumstances leading to American intervention in the World War indicated the need for legislation which would give the President less rather than more discretion: "A tighter neutrality law would merely limit the President's power to do what Woodrow Wilson did in 1914, 1915, 1916 and 1917, behind closed doors."[4] If Americans really wanted to get mixed up in Europe's quarrels, let the decision be made openly by the people's representatives in Congress, not secretly by the President acting at his own discretion.

Scott Nearing had little trouble analyzing Roosevelt's efforts to revise the neutrality legislation. For Nearing, the story hadn't changed any since the last world crisis. Now it was Roosevelt, "an efficient and highly intelligent" spokesman for the interests, for the American ruling class, doing his bit as Wilson had done his in 1916 to lead the United States to war.[5]

3. "Neutrality: Shall We Have Revision," *New Republic*, XCVII (January 8, 1939), 308.

4. *Ibid.*

5. Letter from Nearing to the editor of the *Progressive* (Madison, Wis.), March 11, 1939, p. 6.

By April, 1939, Beard seemed to feel that the tide was running against him. In an article entitled "We're Blundering Into War"[6] he abandoned completely all talk of judging the "next war" on its "merits" before deciding whether or not to intervene. "In my opinion," he wrote, "*The United States should and can stay out of the next war in Europe and the wars that follow the next war.*"[7]

Beard granted that a European war would disturb the American economy, but after the experience of the last war he felt it was worth trying to get by without risking economic entanglement with any of the belligerents. He wanted to try to operate the economy *without* imports and exports: "It would be foolish to minimize the task but, judging by the experiences of the World War, the perplexities, strains, and burdens connected with neutrality would scarcely equal the costs, dislocations, and explosions inevitably associated with participation in a European war."[8]

In the same month, in an article for *Harper's*, Grattan, too, seemed to sense a shift in the wind.[9] He insisted that the "proper" policy was clear: "No American shall ever again be sent to fight and die on the continent of Europe." To be sure, terrible things were happening in Europe, but this was no reason to "throw reason out of the window . . . to abandon all we have learned at such heavy cost since 1914."

Grattan's opposition to intervention in the pending war was based on his belief that democracy and social reform could not survive American participation in another war. America should not fight unless it became necessary to defend "this continent." He insisted that the moral issues in the European turmoil of 1939 were no more certain than they had been in 1917—and the moral certainties of those days "turned out to have been founded on rather smelly quicksand."

War, he argued, never accomplishes the ends for which it is fought. It releases new forces which generally result in unhappy circumstances: "Is not that a summary of what happened in the First World War?" In the United States the supporters of the

6. *American Mercury*, XLVI (April, 1939), 338–99.

7. *Ibid.*, p. 395.   8. *Ibid.*, pp. 396–97.

9. "No More Excursions! The Defense of Democracy Begins at Home," *Harper's Monthly*, CLXXVIII (April, 1939), 457–65.

New Deal were searching for ways to alleviate the suffering caused by economic inequality, "but the environment of war will effectively stop that search and throw the governmental power into the hands of those who, at the moment of its outbreak, are in possession of superior economic power. That this is what happens, a review of the Wilson Administration shows."[10]

Then Grattan asked if Americans were prepared to accept the results of intervention, "be they what they may?" He recalled that "we weren't last time" and guessed that Americans would be no more prepared to accept the results next time. The United States could, of course, fight and then withdraw from the world community, "the futile policy which we followed in the First World War." On the other hand, the United States could "impose" a settlement on Europe, "which implies on our part both a messianic conceit and an omniscience we do not possess."

Grattan's own program was essentially the policy implicit in the neutrality laws: mandatory neutrality effected by cutting off all intercourse with the belligerents. He contended that the reports of the Nye Committee indicated what would happen if he were not heeded: "For if we do rush into a European war, early or late, democracy in this country is finished. There will be a complete cessation of social reform, dictatorial controls will be instituted, and the 'real rulers' of this country will ride high."[11]

In another article, published in the *University of Toronto Quarterly*, Grattan accepted the "isolationist" label and restated his position to the Canadians. He reaffirmed his consistent opposition to fascism and separated himself and his friends from the likes of Father Coughlin. For himself, as for Barnes, Beard, and John T. Flynn, the domestic consequences of war were of primary concern. Already, he saw signs of war psychosis developing—before the war began. Already, all opponents of collective security were being lumped together with the fascists, and to Grattan it seemed clear that the excesses of the war years would be repeated—a triumph of reaction. But once again America was being called upon to undertake her mission: "Roosevelt has returned in his time to the Wilson slogan of making the world safe for democracy." Democracy—could one think of Chamberlain and Daladier

10. *Ibid.*, p. 460.   11. *Ibid.*, p. 464.

and defend England and France in the name of democracy? Grattan noted that even Lewis Mumford, whose hatred for the fascists and willingness to fight fascism were unsurpassed, was unwilling to have the effort of the United States associated with Chamberlain and Daladier, with England and France. What Mumford and others like him failed to realize was that an arms program used against the fascists meant working for men like Henry Stimson, playing into the hands of American, English, and French reactionaries. And when war came, there would be no dissent: "The reactionaries will win the argument as far as domestic policy is concerned" and "a large portion of the liberals and radicals will go marching off to the war (or to the propaganda mills), not because they will dislike the domestic policy any less but because they will still hate the fascists more."[12]

The spring of 1939 was also a busy time for Charles Tansill. One day in April he spoke at a luncheon at the faculty club of Columbia University. He charged that "President Roosevelt, pursuing the course of 'unneutrality' set by Woodrow Wilson in 1914—1917, is 'distinctly bent on war' on the spurious issue of saving the world for democracy."

Tansill claimed that Roosevelt's recent appeal to "the dictators" for a peace conference had been "a red herring across the trail." He reminded his audience that Wilson had called for a peace conference only six weeks before asking Congress for a declaration of war. He maintained that the foreign policy of the United States in 1939, as in 1914–17, was dominated by the British Foreign Office. Who, he asked. "had played the role of House . . . in arranging the terms of a new secret agreement with England?" Using historical analogy to support prophecy, Tansill went on to predict that the United States "will soon be called to shoulder the burden of a new holy war in order that England can continue to bestow the blessings of democracy upon India and that France can show Syria, albeit with shot and shell, the road to progress."[13]

In conclusion, Tansill urged the passing of the "Ludlow Amendment" to require a national referendum before the United States

12. "America and the Next War," *University of Toronto Quarterly,* VIII (April, 1939), 271–83.

13. *New York Times,* April 23, 1939, p. 34.

could go to war when it was not under attack. The "hysterical opposition" of the Roosevelt administration to the proposed amendment, Tansill considered comparable to "President Wilson's 'repeated efforts to sabotage American neutrality.' "

Less than a week later, Tansill appeared before the Senate Foreign Relations Committee to testify on the need to retain the existing Neutrality Act with the exception of the "cash and carry" clause. Two weeks after that he appeared before a subcommittee of the Senate Judiciary Committee to argue on behalf of the Ludlow Amendment. The proposed referendum would, he believed, "restrain Presidents whose rash acts might mean war."[14]

In June, 1939, the editors of the *New Republic* polled their contributors on attitudes toward American policy in the event of war.[15] The editors offered seven alternative policies ranging from intervention to "a rigorous attempt to keep out of war by embargoing the sale at least of munitions, forbidding loans and travel, and restricting the sale of other goods by some such measure as the 'cash and carry plan.' " The editors "recognized' that this last policy would in fact favor Britain and France, but "its chief emphasis is to keep out of war by maintaining legal neutrality." While two-thirds of the respondents favored aid short of war for England and France, one-third favored policy alternative number two, the "rigorous attempt to keep out of war" by embargoes and other restrictions. The contributors supporting policy number two were a truly all-star group which included John Chamberlain, Allen Tate, McAlister Coleman, Muriel Rukeyser, Hamilton Basso, Carleton Beals, John T. Flynn, Louis Hacker, Babette Deutsch, Elmer Davis, Richard L. Neuberger, Selden Rodman, C. Vann Woodward, C. Hartley Grattan, and Charles A. Beard. Beard did make one qualification to his support of the proposed policy: he opposed "cash and carry" and favored the cessation of *all* economic intercourse with the belligerents. Two weeks later, the *New Republic* published a protest by Lewis Mumford who complained that all of the *New Republic* alternatives assumed that American policy should pull Britain's chestnuts out of the

14. *Ibid.*, April 29, 1939, p. 8; May 12, 1939, p. 7.

15. "America and the Next War," *New Republic,* XVIX (June 14, 1939), 147–50.

fire. Mumford declared that he would have no part in any policy that would aid British and French imperialism.[16]

Meanwhile, Walter Millis was becoming concerned about what he believed were distortions of the circumstances leading to intervention in 1917. When asked to review H. C. Peterson's *Propaganda for War* for the *Southern Review*, he did what he could to clarify the issues.[17]

Peterson's thesis, stated simply, was that British propagandists, particularly Sir Gilbert Parker, snared the American people. Millis insisted that Peterson's description of what took place was blurred and oversimplified. Millis contended that "many if not most" Americans who spoke for the Allied cause were "sincerely" expressing opinions which they believed to be in the best interests of the United States and that they were convinced that they had reached their conclusions by the same "supposedly rational" processes through which one formulates any other opinion on public affairs.

Peterson had contended that by April, 1916, "nearly all American leaders had been captured and changed from passive to active supporters of the Allies." Millis asked if they were really captives of the Allies, or if they were not actually captives "of their own estimate of the dictates of national interest." Might not that estimate, even erroneous, have been reached "had Sir Gilbert Parker never written a line to an American in his life?" In other words, did the British really succeed because of their astuteness and did the Germans really fail because of their stupidity or the errors of their technique? Millis found this "improbable," finding little to choose from between the methods of the two belligerents. He wondered if it wasn't necessary to look beyond propaganda campaigns to explain the American decision to intervene: "Was the idea—unquestionably of great emotive power—of a war by democracy against autocracy really a triumph of Allied propaganda, when it can be found leaping into the purely American comment in the very first days of the 1914 crisis, before it was being given any prominence from British or French sources?"

Charles Beard, on the other hand, had little time for that sort of

16. *New Republic*, XCIX (June 28, 1939), 209.
17. *Southern Review*, V (Autumn, 1939), 201–10.

clarification. In *Giddy Minds and Foreign Quarrels*[18] he insisted that since 1890 the United States had been in an "era of universal jitters over foreign affairs of no interest to us" and suggested that the two major overseas adventures in that period had resulted from close adherence to the precepts of Henry IV: "Be it thy course to busy giddy minds with foreign quarrels." So Henry had advised Prince Hal, and Beard felt that McKinley, Wilson, and now Franklin Roosevelt appeared too well versed in Shakespearean drama.

Beard contended that Europe had a set of "primary interests" which little involved the United States, that Europe was constantly "vexed" by all sorts of rival ambitions and caprices. There was, however, no need for the United States to become enmeshed in Europe's problems: "The United States is a continental power separated from Europe by a wide ocean which, despite all changes in warfare, is still a powerful asset of defense."[19]

He noted that in 1939 the American economy was in serious trouble and recalled the economic difficulties that faced the country from 1914 to 1917. In the years of the World War, economic crisis had been postponed by steps which ultimately involved the United States in the war. But, he argued, the "way out of the present economic morass lies in the acceleration of this production and distribution at home, by domestic measures."[20]

Beard felt that there was no need for Americans to become alarmed at the vicissitudes of European conflicts "until some formidable European power comes into the Western Atlantic, breathing the fire of aggression and conquest." And this peril, he believed to be negligible.

The United States had fought one war for democracy. Now the American people were "resolutely taking stock of their past follies." In 1917 the American people were told that they were to make the world safe for democracy—and they responded nobly. Before they were finished they learned of the secret treaties "by which the Allies divided the loot." Then they were shown the Treaty of Versailles "which distributed the spoils and made an impossible

18. New York: Macmillan, 1939.
19. *Giddy Minds and Foreign Quarrels*, p. 65.
20. *Ibid.*, p. 70.

'peace.' " And what was America's share: "Wounds and deaths. The contempt of former associates—until the Americans were needed again in another war for democracy. A repudiation of debts. A huge bill of expenses. A false boom. A terrific crisis."[21] Senator D. Worth Clark, Republican of Idaho, used his franking privilege to distribute ten thousand copies of Beard's book.[22]

2

On September 1, 1939, an estimated one million seven hundred thousand Germans breached the borders of Poland. Less than forty-eight hours later, England and France declared war on Germany. On September 5, the United States proclaimed neutrality in the European war. And on September 25, the poet Edgar Lee Masters wrote to Harry Elmer Barnes expressing the hope that reason and judgment would prevail and that Americans would not be driven mad "as we were in 1917."[23]

By the time the November issue of the *American Mercury* reached the newsstands, it was apparent that Barnes was back in action. "The moment we join the war," he warned, "the New Deal and all its promises of a 'more abundant life' will fold up, as did the New Freedom of Woodrow Wilson in 1917." He reminded his readers of the suppression of civil liberties during World War I and of the possibility of totalitarianism at home if the United States became involved in World War II. Therefore, it was necessary to know how the United States came to end neutrality in 1917. His summary of the "forces which pushed us into the transatlantic calamity" included "a violent change in Mr. Wilson's attitude toward the merits of the struggle," economic interests which led first to "unneutrality, then headlong into war," an "inconsistent and unneutral line of diplomatic procedure," and "psychological factors that impelled us toward intervention."[24]

Thus Barnes summed up twenty years of "revisionist" histori-

21. *Ibid.*, pp. 85–86.

22. O. John Rogge, *The Official German Report* (New York: Thomas Yoseloff, 1961), p. 161.

23. Barnes MSS, Laramie, Wyoming.

24. "When Last We Were Neutral," *American Mercury, XLVIII* (November, 1939), 277.

ography and concluded with an injunction to his audience to use this knowledge as a "brake" on present conduct. And on November 3, the United States Neutrality Act of May 1937 was amended. The arms embargo, so much a result of the revisionist interpretation of the road to war, 1914–17, was gone. Charles Beard was rather less than happy, but several of his professional colleagues were still less happy with him. On November 12, the *New York Times* published a letter signed by Clarence Berdahl of the University of Illinois, Kenneth Colegrove of Northwestern, Walter Rice Sharp of Wisconsin, and Quincy Wright of Chicago. Among other things, these gentlemen had received "something of a shock to find a vigorous fighter for law, justice and good faith, as Mr. Beard has been, so cynically sneering at the attempts of our government to uphold somehow the sanctity of international law and of treaties . . . and so coldly indifferent to brutal international aggressions and outlawry."[25]

Also in November, *Life* gave Walter Millis an opportunity to tell the country, with pictures, how he felt about all this excitement.[26] The editor's preface to Millis' article declared that *Road to War* "popularized as nothing else had done the view that America had drifted and blundered into the first World War. It immediately became an isolationist bible and, directly and indirectly, provided much of the steam behind the U.S. Neutrality Act."

In "1939 is not 1914," Millis made his most successful effort to differentiate his own interpretation of the road to war from the other interpretations labeled "revisionist." He contended that in 1917 the decision to intervene was made upon "a relatively minor issue," the German resumption of unrestricted submarine warfare. He felt that there had been more significant reasons for the decision, but that these were not clearly presented to the public. The results of the failure to educate public opinion were unfortunate. Because Wilson did not formulate clearly and consistently the reasons underlying intervention, Americans were unprepared to make effective use of their victory. "And," Millis wrote, "the confused way in which the choice for war was presented and made has perpetuated the *disastrous legend* that we never chose war at all, but were

25. *New York Times*, November 12, 1939, Sec. IV, pp. 8–9.

26. "1939 is not 1914," *Life*, VII (November 6, 1939), 69 ff.

'drawn' or 'dragged' into the conflict by some kind of malign fate or personal deviltry—British propaganda, the machinations of bankers, the egotism of Mr. Wilson or what not—of which the nation as a whole was an innocent and passive victim." To Millis the legend was dangerous and useless as an explanation of the facts.[27]

Then Millis proceeded to separate himself from the other "revisionists" in his analysis of the situation in 1939. Although aware of the parallels between 1939 and 1914, he stressed the limitations of historical analogy and pointed to the differences between the two years. He insisted that the American attitude toward the new world war was "rooted in a much sounder knowledge of the world" than the attitude toward the outbreak of World War I had been. He felt that the contemporary attitude had developed much more "deliberately" and that Americans were much more conscious of having adopted it. The "American attitude of today" did, he noted, "carry the same implication that the Allies are fighting our battles, and may ultimately generate an even stronger pressure toward an American intervention to prevent their defeat." But, because this American attitude in 1939 was "more conscious and more realistic, it should lead to a calmer and more realistic calculation as to the necessity for doing so." Millis found "less moral indignation and more practical consideration of how German actions may, in fact, affect the United States." Thus, if Americans chose policies which favored the Allies, they would have a clearer idea of what they were doing.[28]

The differences that were becoming apparent between Millis' attitude toward American foreign policy in 1939 and the attitudes of the other revisionists were based less on differences in interpretation of the road to war, 1914–17, than on differences over the meaning of the past for the present. Barnes and the others believed that the American experience in World War I was proof enough that the United States had no business becoming involved in another European conflict and that the American people would have gained nothing from that tragic experience until they recognized that democracy was best preserved at home. Millis, on the other hand, believed that the experience of World War I and its aftermath indicated that the American people had much to learn

27. *Ibid.*, p. 94, italics added.   28. *Ibid.*, p. 95.

about world affairs before the United States could again play an important role on the international scene. In his article for *Life* he insisted that the American people *had* learned—that their attitudes toward world affairs had become more realistic. In practice this meant that while the attitudes of Barnes and the others precluded them from ever accepting intervention in World War II, Millis could, without serious inconsistency, support wholeheartedly the campaign for intervention.

3

By the end of September, 1939, Germany and the Soviet Union had arranged to divide Poland between them. Then came a lull, a period of relative quiet—the "Sitzkrieg" or "phony war." On April 9, 1940, German sea and airborne forces attacked Norway, and German troops occupied Denmark without encountering formal resistance. On May 10, without warning, German armies invaded the Netherlands, Belgium, and Luxemburg. Almost simultaneously, Winston Churchill succeeded Neville Chamberlain as British Prime Minister and Charles Beard's *A Foreign Policy for America*[29] appeared in the bookstores.

Beard repeated all his "lessons" drawn from 1898 and 1917; he repeated all his injunctions against involvement in European quarrels; and he repeated all his arguments for a policy of "continentalism." But events in Europe were making some people impatient with such historical lessons. Concluding a discussion of Beard's book, a member of the *New York Times* staff declared:

> But today people have grown impatient with the doctrine, so heavily stressed up to a little while ago, that nations are "taken" into war by elites, by financiers, by merchants of death in the guise of munitions makers. The events of the last twelve months and the serious hours we are now living through have clarified a good many people's ideas on what really happened in 1898 and in 1917.[30]

And so Hitler's march through Europe began to undermine what had appeared to be the victory of the revisionist interpretation of American intervention in 1917 and of the revisionist interpretation

29. New York: Knopf, 1940.
30. *New York Times,* May 19, 1940, Sec. IV, p. 8.

of the lessons the past held for the present. Walter Millis found Beard producing his own devil theory of history, attempting to exorcise "wicked imperialists and foolish internationalist romantics" by "repeating the Founder's creed and returning to true dogma." In the White House the reaction to Beard's book would have pained Beard still more. His old friend, Dr. New Deal, was fading out and in his place the emerging Dr. Win-the-War read *A Foreign Policy for America* and scrawled upon it "40 years hard and continuous study has brought forth an inbred mouse"—initialed "FDR."[31]

But the reform intellectuals who remained more concerned with the New Deal than with world affairs kept up a steady attack in an effort to keep Roosevelt in line. Barnes and Grattan joined Stuart Chase, Marquis Childs, John T. Flynn, Hubert Herring, Quincy Howe, Richard L. Neuberger, and Villard to sponsor *Uncensored*, a "newsletter" edited by Sidney Hertzberger and dedicated to preventing the involvement of the United States in a European war. Another revisionist, less addicted to reform, stepped up his parallel efforts: on May 19, Tansill chose the occasion of a communion breakfast of the Holy Name Society of St. Joan of Arc Church to attempt to stem the tide. But, he warned his companions, no matter what he and they knew to be best, of one thing they could be certain: "If a President of the United States is determined to involve this country in war he is able to do so, despite all the anxious endeavors of a pacific Congress to restrain his warlike ardor."[32]

As spring faded, Mencken and Barnes commiserated. In May, Mencken warned Barnes that the American newspapers would be "hollering for war within two months," then thought a moment and guessed that two weeks would be a better estimate. In any event, Roosevelt could be counted on to "take us in" before the end of summer: "If [*sic*] offers him the best chance for re-election. Unhappily, it also lays him open to the worst katzenjammer ever heard of on earth." But Mencken was certain that if the United States intervened, revulsion against the war would

---

31. New York *Herald Tribune*, Books, May 19, 1949, p. 3; Roosevelt Library, President's Personal File 3847.

32. *New York Times*, May 20, 1940, p. 15.

come quickly. He also declared that with France "dead broke" and England "rapidly approaching bankruptcy," the war would have to end before the year was over—"unless the United States pays the freight." A week later, Mencken was tempted to escape to the coast to join Barnes in preparation for the moment when "Roosevelt horns into the war." And on June 10, he guessed that Roosevelt "will be in the war within two weeks, and that his first act will be to forbid every form of free speech. We are in for a circus."[33]

On June 13, 1940, German troops occupied Paris. On June 16, Marshal Henri-Philippe Pétain replaced Paul Reynaud as head of the French government. On June 17, Pétain sued for peace and on June 18, Harry Elmer Barnes delivered an address at the University of Virginia Institute of Public Affairs.

Barnes, consistent with all he had ever fought for, insisted that it was the duty of Americans to stem the rising tide of totalitarianism. *But,* he contended, the place to stop totalitarianism was at home. America had no business intervening to stop Hitler in Europe, but should concentrate on preventing the spread of "Hitlerism" to this continent: "The American way of life can be saved and expanded only in the United States, and here only if we keep out of the tragic mess across the sea. The real threat to American life is not the Hitler of today but the Huey Long of tomorrow."[34]

Barnes's words, like those of Beard and Grattan, were clearly not the words of an "evil" man, of a pro-Nazi American. All three men may well have been wrong in their estimates of the extent of the German threat to the United States, but in their hatred of totalitarianism, few if any Americans surpassed them. As the Germans swept over Europe, however, the growing number of Americans who saw in intervention the only means of stopping the spread of totalitarianism grew increasingly intolerant of the "anti-interventionists." To many Americans the subtle distinctions among the beliefs of the anti-interventionists were difficult to grasp, and it seemed easier to believe that all who opposed intervention were Nazi sympathizers.

33. Mencken to Barnes, May 10, 1940, May 16, 1940, June 10, 1940, Barnes MSS, Laramie, Wyoming.

34. *New York Times,* June 19, 1940, p. 12.

The day after Barnes spoke at Virginia was Class Day for the Class of '40 at Harvard. To Tudor Gardiner, son of the former Governer of Maine, fell the honor of being class orator. Gardiner contended that World War I stood condemned by its results. He insisted that "America must not again be dragged into the anarchy of Europe, America must face the fact that we can never wield great power abroad except at a sacrifice fatal to the America we know and love. But we can make this hemisphere impregnable . . . we cannot police the world."[35]

The *New York Times* representative who attended the Class Day ceremonies reported that Gardiner's speech was cheered, while a member of the Class of 1915 who said that he would be proud to see "our boys go out there and do the job again" was booed. The revisionists had not yet lost the controversy.

Toward the end of July the *New Republic* published a letter from C. Hartley Grattan. Grattan had no objections to expenditures for defense. Indeed, he favored such expenditures provided there was a clear plan "of what we are going to defend and how we are going to defend it." He did not, however, have much confidence in Roosevelt and suspected that the United States would be "in for a planless, super expensive defense." As a result of this, he feared, "we are going to destroy some admirable American values through blind stupidity abetted by the malice of powerful individuals who hold reprehensible social views."[36]

Grattan admitted that he was disturbed by the "precarious position" of Great Britain; he felt that a Nazi victory over England would be a "disaster." But, he insisted, American responsibility for England's predicament was at best secondary. As yet he saw no reason to entangle the United States in the fate of the United Kingdom. "We must," he wrote, "remain in a position to save ourselves and perhaps some of the British dominions if the worst happens and the United Kingdom falls." If we chose to "rush in like fools," we might "find ourselves holding a bag with which not even angels could deal to any profitable end." "Wars," he warned, "never end with things exactly as those who promote them predict."

35. *Ibid.*, June 20, 1940, p. 12.

36. *New Republic*, CIII (July 29, 1940), 143.

It was in *The Deadly Parallel*[37] that Grattan brought all of his guns to bear. "Until very lately," he insisted, "all Americans seemed to agree, with whatever shading of emphasis, that the participation of the United States in the First World War was a stupendous disaster." It had appeared that the lesson was "firmly underscored, indelibly engraved on the public mind: this country must never again be tempted to believe that the world's ills can in any measure be solved through participation in international war."[38]

Now, Grattan found, Americans were being asked to assume that Roosevelt and his associates "are more gifted and clairvoyant" than were Wilson and his associates; "that they will not bungle a job which Wilson and his aides found beyond their powers." Most remarkable of all to Grattan was the fact that Americans were being advised to trust in Roosevelt's foreign policy "by men who have intemperately condemned . . . [him] for his handling of domestic problems which, by their very nature, are less delicate than the problems of a vast international war." He, Grattan, was outraged by Roosevelt's complacency in ranging himself in the company of Wilson, Lansing, House, and Page. These were the men who "sold us down the river in 1917."[39]

Grattan's own idea of a proper foreign policy for America was apparent in his endorsement of Beard's "continentalism." He defined a "continental American" as an individual who preferred a "strong continental American domestic program" to an "imperialist program." The continental American, according to Grattan, had no a priori objection to international trade or international cooperation for peaceful purposes. He was interested in the outside world but felt "no urge to save the world from its deeply cherished follies."[40]

The ideological basis of Grattan's opposition to intervention was presented openly. Conservatives, he maintained, were unhappy with Hitler only because his foreign policy endangered their interests and holdings. "Liberals and radicals," on the other hand, hated fascism and Hitler as its symbol. The latter groups all stressed

> the menace of fascism—which is real—but they underemphasize
> the menace of war, which is equally real. They deflect the public

37. New York: Stackpole and Sons, 1940.   39. *Ibid.*, p. 14.
38. *The Deadly Parallel*, pp. 11–12.   40. *Ibid.*, pp. 43 ff.

attention from the fundamental issues of the day while the conservatives consolidate their domestic power and gain respectability by supporting war preparations in the name of patriotism.[41]

In his concluding pages, Grattan contended that if the United States intervened in World War II, democracy in America would give way to dictatorship: "The war-time dictatorship will be manned by the representatives of economic and social power. There is nothing like a war for revealing who really runs this country. The liberals go, the tough guys move in." He was convinced that economic reforms would cease and "liberal social sentiments" would cease to be heard in the United States: "The New Deal will be as faint a memory as Woodrow Wilson's New Freedom." If the United States went to war it would "mean fascism in this country."[42]

But the tide continued to flow against Grattan, and the "liberals," in increasing numbers, drifted from the side of the anti-interventionists to join ranks with Roosevelt. The *New Republic* dropped John T. Flynn, and the *Progressive* dropped its editor, as Bruce Bliven and the *New Republic* followed the President, and the La Follettes were chagrined to find their own newspaper supporting Roosevelt's actions. Villard found himself writing for the *Progressive*, which increasingly became the only important vehicle for the thoughts of reform-oriented anti-interventionists—until it was forced to turn to the likes of Herbert Hoover for articles and to the *New York Daily News* for cartoons. Not all the "reactionaries" had ended up in Roosevelt's camp. Villard was upset by the shift in reform sentiment: Bliven had "lost his bearings." Writing to Barnes, Villard complained that their friends had all gone mad and he presumed they would approve "Roosevelt's calmly tying us up with Canada and putting us into the war that way."[43]

Daily, the *Luftwaffe* performed its deadly mission over the cities of England, but the summer had almost passed before Roosevelt acted to aid Great Britain. On September 3, the "destroyer-bases deal" was negotiated and the United States had

41. *Ibid.*, p. 41.
42. *Ibid.*, pp. 152, 154.
43. Villard to Barnes, August 19, 1940, Barnes MSS, Laramie, Wyoming.

ceased to be neutral. Less than a week later, Charles Beard announced his support of the "America First Committee."[44] The committee, he declared, represented Americans opposed to intervention. It included no "'Appeasers,' no 'ostrich isolationists,' no foreigners of any nationality in letter or spirit, and no pacifists." The committee sought to have America's foreign policy "directed to the preservation of the peace and security of this nation in its continental zone of interests" and favored measures for the adequate defense of that zone of interests. One week later the Selective Training and Service Act became law. A week after that Japanese forces occupied French Indo-China. Then on September 27, 1940, Germany, Italy, and Japan concluded an alliance aimed at the United States.

In the October issue of the *Virginia Quarterly Review*, Barnes provided several insights into the basis of his opposition to intervention.[45] First, he reminded his readers that the United States had, for better or worse, left the British Empire in 1776, and, "being out of the Empire, it may be wisest to conduct our foreign policy in the light of this fundamental historical reality." He saw no reason to jeopardize democracy in America in order to prevent the defeat of Great Britain.

Barnes was not at all sympathetic to arguments that Great Britain was America's first line of defense against the threat of totalitarianism. He was convinced that if and when Germany, Italy, and Japan won their war and occupied all but the Western Hemisphere, they were more likely to fight among themselves than to attempt to take on the United States. He argued that it would take them "generations to absorb the spoils of victory." In sum, he found "no evidence that the totalitarians even remotely contemplate any onslaught against us."[46]

Reflecting on the "lessons" of World War I, he declared that if men learned anything from history, their experience in the first World War should have shown Americans the futility of active intervention in "Old World quarrels." He noted that Americans had not taken advantage of the only "decent and con-

44. *New York Times,* September 9, 1940, p. 7.

45. "Europe's War and America's Democracy," *Virginia Quarterly Review,* XVI, 552–62.

46. *Ibid.,* p. 554.

structive outcome" of the last war when they refused to join the League of Nations or even the World Court—neglecting to indicate his own earlier criticism of the League. Despite the "lessons," "incredible though it may seem, we stand dangerously near to falling victim to the same propaganda which led us astray between 1914 and 1917."[47]

If his counsel failed to prevail and the United States intervened in World War II, Barnes saw two possible results. One, intervention would come too late to save England, but would "end American civilization and political independence." Two, intervention would be followed by victory, but nonetheless "the results would certainly destroy American civilization as we know it today." Either way, there was no future in intervention.

Barnes, like all the other revisionists, had no objection to measures designed to protect the United States from invasion. He was not a pacifist advocating unilateral disarmament. He claimed that "no sane American will object to a reasonable defense measure, provided it is literally a defense measure. There is little probability that we will ever be attacked by any foreign power or coalition of powers."[48]

Before long, Barnes and Grattan found themselves under attack by Martin Dies and the House Un-American Activities Committee. Early in the year, Beard had accused J. Edgar Hoover of setting up a "political bureau" in the Department of Justice "for the purpose of indexing and spying upon persons charged with holding objectionable but not illegal views in matters of politics and economics, or engaging in activities of which he does not approve."[49] The record showed that Hoover had been with the Justice Department in the days of A. Mitchell Palmer, and Beard feared a revival of the Palmer "outrages," feared that with another war threatening, Hoover might start rounding up progressives and others as " 'possibly detrimental' to the internal security of the United States." Then Grattan wrote the foreword to a collection of Polish documents captured by the Germans and published as a German "White Paper." His remarks were, given his antagonism to Roosevelt's foreign policy, remarkably calm and judicious:

47. *Ibid.*, pp. 555–56.   48. *Ibid.*, p. 562.
49. *New York Times,* April 3, 1940, p. 22.

By selecting a few documents which place American officials in an extremely bad light and failing to place them in anything like a full context, the Germans have made them appear to mean more than they really do. . . .

In this fashion the documents are used both to clear Germany of guilt in precipitating the war and to accuse American diplomats of assisting and encouraging the Allies to precipitate it. It is not known whether a complete collection of documents would lead us to either conclusion.

But because they have been selected for this purpose it does not follow that the documents are false. Far from it. Our knowledge of the Roosevelt administration is too extensive for us to rule them out of court.[50]

Barnes then wrote to the publisher and offered his influence in furthering the "White Paper's" popularity. Soon after, the storm broke. The Dies Committee discovered that distribution of the publication had been handled by a Nazi front organization. Grattan wrote immediately to the publishers indicating that he was disturbed about the manner of distribution and that he regretted having been involved. Dies and his committee opened fire on Barnes.[51]

Barnes returned the compliment with a letter to the *New York Times*. Whether or not one approved of Barnes's activities opposing intervention, his reply to the attack by the Un-American Activities Committee was to his everlasting credit. After denying any association with the Nazi groups and agents involved in distributing *The German White Paper* and noting that his record as an anti-interventionist did not indicate any need for a push from the outside, Barnes concluded: "As for Mr. Dies and his committee, I believe that I may fairly observe that any American intellectual who is not at one time or another, for one reason or another, condemned by this committee may be regarded as having wasted his life and its opportunities for constructive citizenship and the service of his country."[52]

Before the year ended, Walter Millis had declared himself in

50. *The German White Paper* (New York: Howell, Soskin and Co., 1940), pp. 10–11.

51. *New York Times*, November 22, 1940, p. 13.

52. *Ibid.*, December 1, 1940, Sec. IV, p. 7.

favor of intervention. In his earlier article for *Life* he had explained why he found the circumstances of 1939 different from those of 1914. Now he felt compelled to explain how a man with his feeling about intervention in 1917 could endorse intervention in 1940.[53]

In what was essentially an autobiographical essay, Millis began with some recollections of the days of World War I and sketched the development of his interest in war per se. He felt that in 1920, he, and most of his generation, had "believed in the Covenant and the League, and in the new vistas which Wilson's high rhetoric had opened before us." He would not contend that the United States had fought for an ideal, but insisted that an ideal "had at least illuminated our course and given it the appearance of reasonableness." With the refusal of the United States to join the League, the ideal had vanished.

The apparent futility of the war had colored the fascination which war had for him. Like so many of his contemporaries, like so many men involved in subsequent peace movements, he had viewed war as an isolated phenomenon and "loathed the business." He came to believe that an attack upon war was as good a starting point as any from which to attack "the general problem of our times." He found that most excuses for militaristic measures seemed "obviously shallow—the transparent rationalizations of people either blinded by their vested interest in military institutions or incapable of taking more than a childishly narrow, romantic view of human history."[54]

When he began his study of American intervention in World War I, it was not intervention but the aftermath that upset him. It was what he regarded as the complete betrayal of everything worthy of sacrifice. Then he wondered if that "betrayal" might have resulted from an initial confusion about purpose. And the more he looked for evidence of confusion, the more he found: "I saw everywhere what seemed to me to be shortsightedness, ignorance, passionate emotionalism, personal (if often unconscious) greeds or political ambitions, a reckless, almost frivolous, failure

53. "Faith of an American," in Stephen Benét (ed.), *Zero Hour* (New York: Farrar and Rinehart, 1940), pp. 217–44.

54. *Ibid.*, p. 228.

to analyze the actual situation at any given time so as to utilize the great power of the United States in such a way as to achieve concrete results in some degree equivalent to the inevitable costs of any given course of action."[55]

He acknowledged that the completed study, *Road to War*, was a severe indictment of the process leading to intervention: *"That war, I felt should have been prevented."* He thought he had found a number of "points" at which better controls might have been applied and a number of ways in which intervention might have been avoided or in which intervention might have achieved "far more at far less cost."[56]

Millis was, however, quick to call attention to the limits of his thesis in *Road to War*. He had proved to his own satisfaction that the United States had "blundered in a blind and confused way into the last war, and in so doing had doomed its intervention to a large measure of futility." But, he admitted, he had not proved that it would not have been more disastrous if the United States had stayed out of the war. Nor had he proved that the United States "might not go clear-sightedly into another war, and thereby achieve results, in terms of national or human welfare, that would be commensurate with the cost."[57]

In short, Millis was contending that there was nothing inconsistent about his being, on the one hand, a critic of the process by which the United States chose to intervene in World War I, and on the other hand, a supporter of policies directed toward bringing about intervention in World War II. There was, to his mind, no analogical value to be derived from the experience of World War I other than that which had already been derived— a clear-sighted purpose.

Millis believed that the "democratic statesmen" had already tried the approach that he and others who had isolated war had suggested: "They were patient; they were reasonable; they refused to take bellicose action; they were slow to build up their own armaments; they tried to see the other side's point of view; they offered concessions. And still the crisis developed. At last there was Munich. Mr. Chamberlain, in effect, took our advice. He

55. *Ibid.*, p. 231.   56. *Ibid.*   57. *Ibid.*, p. 233.

was not going to waste human life for small, uncertain and ignoble ends."[58]

But at least since 1939, since the threat of totalitarianism had become real to him, Millis had come to believe that "social life" was impossible without convictions—"convictions which can never in the end be justified rationality but convictions at least so strong that we are prepared, when there is no alternative, to fight and take the risk of dying for them."[59]

Once he was willing to fight and die in the hope of preserving democratic America from the totalitarian threat, it seemed pointless to Millis to refuse to fight until the enemy reached the shores of the United States. Once Americans admitted the possibility of fighting, "the question of the point at which to fight becomes almost a technical one—a practical question of achieving maximum gain at minimum cost."[60]

On December 20, 1940, President Roosevelt established a four-man defense board for the purpose of preparing defense measures and speeding up aid to Great Britain. On December 21, the first day of winter, the German Government denounced Roosevelt's action as "moral aggressions."

4

In February, 1941, during the hearings conducted by the Senate Foreign Relations Committee on the "lend-lease" bill, Charles A. Beard was given an opportunity to testify. Beard characterized the bill as "a bill for waging undeclared war." He contended that the United States was not about to send the ships and munitions provided by the bill out to sea at the mercy of German submarines. "They will be convoyed. . . . The convoys will be attacked by German planes and submarines. Then what? Are we not in the war? That's the way I interpret the bill."[61] On March 11, 1941, Congress passed the Lend-Lease Act.

By late spring, at least one "revisionist" who continued to op-

58. *Ibid.*, pp. 236–37.   59. *Ibid.*, p. 242.   60. *Ibid.*, p. 238.
61. *New York Times,* February 5, 1941, p. 10.

pose intervention ran into some trouble. An item in the *New York Times*, June 14, 1941, read:

> Dr. Ralph Tieje, president of Eastern Washington College of Education, says Dr. Harry Elmer Barnes . . . has been dropped as a Summer lecturer on criminology at his institution. Dr. Tieje said . . . "It has come to the attention of the college that during his early years Dr. Barnes was associated with certain movements commonly called radical."[62]

Translated from academic jargon, Barnes was a controversial figure. It was no longer fashionable to be a revisionist or to oppose intervention.

On June 21, Villard, who had been insisting that Roosevelt wanted war but was afraid to say so, cited an article by William Henry Chamberlin entitled "America Is Not God." Taking off from Chamberlin's article, Villard demanded that Americans cease thinking of themselves as chosen people with a mission to redeem the world. He insisted that it was unrealistic to think that the United States had the power to put the world in order. Americans could not control or hold themselves responsible for events occurring all over the world. America must not go to war.[63] On June 22, German forces invaded the Soviet Union along a two-thousand-mile front. On August 14, somewhere in the North Atlantic, Roosevelt and Churchill announced the Atlantic Charter; and in September, Carl Becker gave great pain to Barnes by calling for intervention in World War II.

It is difficult to determine just when Becker ceased to be so disillusioned about the results of World War I that he was able to envisage another intervention. In 1938 he still opposed intervention, but in a review of William Shirer's *Berlin Diary* in September, 1941, not a trace of disillusionment remained. The spirit with which he had endorsed intervention in 1917 returned:

> The "Berlin Diary" is so sound and so illuminating that it should be read by every American. It will, of course, do nothing to dispel Mr. Lindbergh's illusions of grandeur, to abate Senator Wheeler's vindictive hatred of Roosevelt, or provide their deluded admirers

62. *Ibid.*, June 14, 1941, p. 11.
63. *Progressive*, June 7, 1941, p. 5; June 21, 1941, p. 5.

with intelligence. But in no book that I know of will open-minded Americans get a better idea of Hitler and the Nazis, of what they have done and what they aim to do; in no book will they find more convincing reasons for believing that the United States can best defend its peace and safety by giving all aid, and *not merely all aid short of war,* to Great Britain in freeing Europe from German domination.[64]

As though in answer to Becker, Stuart Chase invoked the memory of Randolph Bourne and his "War and the Intellectuals" for the remaining readers of *Progressive.*[65] The story had gone full cycle and the United States was involved already in an undeclared naval war with Germany.

On October 17, the Konoye Cabinet fell and General Hideki Tojo became Japanese Premier and Minister of War. On November 29, General Tojo declared that the influence of Great Britain and the United States had to be eliminated from the Orient. On December 6, 1941, that week end's issue of the *Progressive* contained Harry Elmer Barnes's column, carrying the caption: "No War with Japan." Barnes contended:

> For this country to enter war over Far Eastern issues would be the supreme folly of all American experience in foreign affairs. Neither ideals nor material interest, alone or in combination, could justify such a war. When a Far Eastern war for us is viewed against the background of the disasters which would befall our country on the domestic front such venture must be branded as nothing short of sheer national idiocy.[66]

On the following day the Japanese bombed Pearl Harbor. For Barnes, for Beard, for Grattan, and for Tansill, the effort to apply the "lessons" of World War I had proved futile.

64. *Yale Review,* XXXI (September, 1941), 175–76, italics added.
65. *Progressive,* October 4, 1941, p. 5.
66. *Ibid.,* December 6, 1941, p. 9.

Conclusion

In 1914, in far-off Europe, separated from the United States by thousands of miles of ocean, a great war began. Whatever the issues in that war, the United States did not at the outset appear likely to become involved. During the course of the war, however, belligerents on both sides violated rights enjoyed by Americans as citizens of a neutral nation. As the war went on, some Americans came to believe that their country had a stake in the outcome of the war. These men called upon their government to intervene on behalf of the Allied powers. Other Americans, for a variety of reasons, including hostility to the Allies and dread of war, opposed intervention. In the spring of 1917, the representatives of the American people, assembled in Congress, voted to intervene, and the United States became a participant in the World War.

Those who had opposed intervention felt, quite naturally, that the decision to intervene had been a mistake. Many who had favored intervention, subsequently, because of a number of events during the months of American participation in the war, because of the peace treaty, and because of the state of the world after the war, joined the opponents of intervention in declaring the ending of American neutrality a mistake.

The idea that American intervention in 1917 had been a mistake was basic to the "disillusionist" attitude toward world affairs that prevailed in the United States from 1919 to 1939. The revisionist historiography which asserted this idea must, therefore, be analyzed and understood before an understanding of American foreign policy between world wars can be attained. It would be foolish,

233

however, either to credit or to blame five revisionists, or the ten or twenty revisionists others might call to mind, for the state of American opinion on matters of foreign policy between 1919 and 1939. Until the historian or social scientist perfects better methods of demonstrating influence than have been exhibited to date, it is wisest to view the revisionists as men who reflected and gave voice to the general intellectual background of their day—a background probably influenced far more by the novelists and poets, such as Ernest Hemingway, John Dos Passos, and Ezra Pound, whose works reflected the same disenchantment with the "crusade" and reached a wider audience. Certainly none of the revisionists expressed this attitude more clearly than Pound had in *Hugh Selwyn Mauberly*, who after the war, returned "home to many deceits, / home to lies and new infamy; / usury age-old and age-thick / and liars in public places"—whose friends had died "for an old bitch gone in the teeth, / For a botched civilization."

Among the people most receptive to revisionist historiography, there were two main groups that may be categorized as "ethnic" and "ideological." The "ethnic" group was comprised of those "hyphenates" who were hostile to the Allied countries or sympathetic to Germany. In general, these were men who had opposed the decision to intervene on behalf of the Allies and who found nothing in the results of the war to make them any happier about the fact of intervention. Their acceptance of revisionism generally began with acceptance of the revisionist interpretation of the war-guilt question—an interpretation which fitted well with their presuppositions and prejudices. They comprised one pillar of revisionism that was not based on disillusionment, but was an outgrowth of opposition to the initial decision to intervene against the Central Powers.

The second, "ideological," group contained both supporters and opponents of intervention. Those who had opposed intervention on ideological grounds were generally men who feared that the participation of the United States in the war would smash the reform impetus of the prewar years. The Sedition Act, the Palmer Raids, and the election of Harding in 1920 all lent support to the initial convictions of the reform-oriented opponents of intervention. There had been, however, numerous supporters of the prewar reform movement who had also supported intervention. Many of these men, disappointed by the domestic implications of the conduct of the war and by the results of the war, came to believe that their ideological compatriots had been correct in opposing intervention— came to believe that intervention had been a mistake.

The revisionist writers paralleled these two groups. Barnes and Beard were reform-oriented intellectuals who, as indicated by the public record, gave their wholehearted support to Wilson's call for a declaration of war. The views of Grattan, Millis, and Tansill at the time of the war are not matters of public record, and while reasonable estimates of their attitudes might be made, these would remain unsubstantiated. In their histories of American intervention, Grattan and Millis came closest to the arguments of reform-oriented opponents of intervention, such as Bourne and Stearns, while Tansil approximated the position of the ethnic opponents of intervention.

Barnes was the first of these men to declare publicly that intervention had been a mistake. From his own accounts, it appears that his disillusionment began with Sidney Fay's first "New Light" article in the *American Historical Review* in June, 1920. Barnes was shaken by evidence that Germany had not been an all "evil" power, plotting diabolically to bring on the war and conquer the world. He became disgusted with himself and ashamed of his own excesses in contributing to the literature supporting intervention. He felt he had been deceived by those who had helped shape his pre-intervention attitudes toward Germany and the war. As he looked into the sources on the origins of the war, he became convinced that the Versailles verdict on war guilt had been unjust. As he reflected upon the results of the war, upon the failure of the United States to enter the League of Nations, upon the chaos in Europe, he became convinced that it had been a mistake for the United States to intervene. The ideals of peace and democracy which had seemed to make the cost of war worthwhile had not been achieved.

This combination of self-blame for the exaggerated image of German diabolism and disillusionment over the failure of American intervention to achieve ideals he had endorsed formed the basis of Barnes's "revisionism." His application of revisionism in the 1920's and 1930's received direction from his ideological position as a proponent of social reform. He viewed war as the antithesis of social reform. War became an isolated phenomenon which had ended reform in 1917 and threatened to end reform in the 1930's. To this feeling must be added the reform-intellectuals' abhorrence of war on purely humanitarian grounds.

In 1917, Barnes had endorsed what he believed to be a just war. He believed he had found a cause worth the cost in the inevitable human suffering war would bring. By the early 1920's he was convinced that he had been wrong about that cause and came to believe that he had been deceived as all men have been deceived throughout history when called upon for sacrifice in a "just" war. He came to believe that there had never been a just war and that there could never be a just war. In his hands, then, revisionism became more than an interpretation of a series of events in the past. It became, in fact, a crusade against war.

In the 1920's, when no war threatened, Barnes used revisionism as a weapon with which to attack the controlling elements in American society. Alienated from the business mentality that seemed to dominate all aspects of American life, his best means of striking at Respectable Citizens was to assert that the cause for which they had been willing to fight and die had been a false cause. In the late 1930's, when war threatened again, Barnes tried to teach another generation of Americans what he had learned from the experience of World War I. He tried to teach this generation that the images of the two sides in the pending war were not necessarily accurate, that America could not solve Europe's problems, and that democratic America might not survive another intervention.

Convinced of the didactic purpose of history, viewing relativism in historical writing not as an unavoidable human failing but as a badge of honor, Barnes lost sight of the historian's search for truth in his passion to reveal what he believed to be a higher truth. His ends, let it be remembered, were noble. But his overwhelming desire to serve the forces of reform and peace, his persistent adherence to the enlightenment view of history with its injunction to seek out and reveal the men responsible for the world's evils, combined with his unwillingness to consider evidence which did not serve his ends, led, inevitably, to simplifications and distortions that undermined his credibility and harmed his cause.

The difference that existed between Barnes as revisionist and Beard as revisionist may have been more apparent than real. Certainly in the years 1939 to 1941 there seemed to be little difference in their use of revisionism as a means of combating the arguments of men who favored American intervention in World War II. But Beard had taken much longer than Barnes had to become a revisionist in his interpretation of intervention in World War I. Unlike Barnes, he had not been identified with revisionism and he never identified himself with revisionism to the extent that Barnes had. Beard did not share Barnes's view of war and never became a crusader against war per se. Although Beard's attitudes toward foreign policy in the 1920's and 1930's were undoubtedly shaped in part by the experience of World War I, his "continentalism" had been formulated in all but name before his conversion to the revisionist interpretation of intervention was completed. For Beard, revisionism remained, essentially, an interpretation of past events, but an interpretation which proved extremely useful as support for his foreign policy proposals. Like Barnes, Beard wept little over the human failings that led to historical relativism and had long been aware of the value of history as a weapon to be used on behalf of causes he espoused. If he knew the cause to be a just and important one, he was not given to long and laborious discussions of the evidence on both sides of the case, but more like the courthouse prosecutor, he prepared his brief. A leading academic supporter of the New Deal, Beard had come to believe that the civilization he wanted to see develop in the United States could not be created if war came unleashing the same forces that he believed had ended reform in 1917. This, of course, was the basis of Beard's anti-interventionism in the late 1930's, and this was a cause worthy of the talents Beard had demonstrated in his *An Economic Interpretation of the Constitution*. The revisionist interpretation of intervention in World War I became the main prop in the new performance.

Grattan had no public statement on behalf of intervention to regret and, unlike Barnes and Beard, probably began as "revisionist" in his approach to the subject. By his own account he had early tended toward pacifism; and then, in his college days, he studied under Barnes. The result may or may not have been attributable to Barnes's influence, but Grattan's first public position on intervention was "revisionist." And, like Barnes, he subsequently treated war as an isolated phenomenon, a disease by which civilization had always been plagued—something to be avoided at all cost. Grattan's interpretations of American intervention in the war dwelt little on the war's origins. For the most part, he sought to demonstrate that the United States had had no vital interests at stake in the war and that too little attention had been given to the relation between the economic and political elements involved in the nation's foreign policy. In the 1930's he insisted that Americans still divorced economic policy from political policy and he attempted to demonstrate that the United States still had no interest in Europe's quarrels—that there was much work to be done at home. For Grattan, the choice became, ultimately, one of continuing the New Deal program of social reform or war—and war was never to him a real alternative. The touch of "realism" that he imparted to the study of American foreign relations was overshadowed by his inability to conceive of a world context in which the United States would have to fight—not to extend but to preserve those values which he held dear—and by his inability to perceive this situation when he was in fact confronted by it.

Tansill was the only one of the five men who claimed to be a specialist in diplomatic history. His contemporary view of intervention is unknown and at no time in the 1920's did he participate in the revisionist controversy. His major contribution to the controversy in the 1930's was a monograph which he asserted was not intended to support either side, but which rested upon the assumption that intervention had been a mistake. His thesis was, stated simply, that the United States had been trapped into the war by British cleverness combined with the pressures of Anglophile advisers upon a naïve and pro-British President.

Whatever Tansill's ideological position, there was never any indication that he was in sympathy with the reform sentiments expressed by other revisionists. Nor was there in his works any indication of the humanitarian's hatred of war exhibited by Barnes, Beard, Grattan, and Millis. Tansill's major concern in the revisionist controversy, reflected in his attitude toward American foreign policy, seemed to be the fear that the United States might act in a manner which could prove beneficial to the United Kingdom.

Millis was the only one of the five who had served in the armed forces during World War I, but his attitude toward intervention at the time has not been recorded. Subsequently, he recalled his service as having been uninspired by any conviction about the need for intervention. In later years, Millis, like Barnes and Grattan, viewed war as an isolated phenomenon. With this attitude, he wrote his interpretation of the steps or missteps leading to American intervention. Regardless of Millis' intention, his book was accepted by Barnes and Grattan as further support for both their interpretation of intervention and their campaign to keep the United States out of future wars.

When Millis endorsed appeasement of the totalitarian powers in 1936–37, it seemed clear that he was working shoulder to shoulder with those revisionists who still isolated war and could see little more important than avoiding war. But in 1939 and 1940, Millis came to believe that war could only be understood in the context of the circumstances preceding it, that war could not be isolated and peace worshipped regardless of price. He came to believe that stopping the spread of totalitarianism was the first order of business. He believed that the people of the United States had learned the "lessons" to be drawn from the experience of World War I: he thought they could go to war against the Axis powers with a clear purpose and realistic expectations.

From 1939 to 1941, when intervention in World War II was debated in the United States, the ethnic and ideological basis of the revisionist interpretation of intervention in World War I prevailed in the attitudes of revisionist writers toward this new war. Tansill remained hostile to Great Britain and refused to accept any argument that the preservation of the British Empire was essential to the security of the United States. Barnes, Beard, and Grattan remained faithful to the reformer's image of a great American civilization dependent upon the continuation of the New Deal program. Their opposition to intervention was based primarily on the belief, no longer universally held, that intervention in World War I smashed the reform impetus in the United States. Millis may have shared these ideas of Barnes, Beard, and Grattan, but he differed from them on one crucial point and that was in his estimation of the extent of the totalitarian threat. The revisionists had added realism to the debate on American foreign policy by teaching that the United States did not have the power to save the world, but their teaching failed because, with the exception of Millis, they ignored the obvious corollary: that a nation not powerful enough to save the world cannot be powerful enough to shield itself from the world. Barnes, Beard, and Grattan may have dreaded the effect of war on the America of their dreams, but they were not pacifists. They hated totalitarianism and were prepared to fight it if it came to their shores. Their one great error was their belief that the United States could remain out of war simply by willing to stay out; they had underestimated the totalitarian threat.

Today, when the revisionist interpretation of American intervention in World War I is in disrepute, the revisionist studies of America's road to war from 1914 to 1917 are considered of little use to students of American diplomatic history. But in several of these books there is much to be learned about international politics and the limits of national power—and they will always be vital guides to an understanding of the effect of World War I on attitudes in the United States toward foreign policy in the years between the wars.

And for the men who wrote these books, Clio reserved various fates. Millis has continued his study of war. Grattan has concentrated his efforts on studies of the Southwest Pacific and has become the nation's leading authority on the subject. Beard is dead —the great teacher's reputation tarnished by his last works critical of Roosevelt's foreign policy. More recently, Tansill, who devoted many of his last moments to the cause of segregation and to the tenets of the John Birch Society, has also died. Barnes alone, nearing eighty, still struggles to win favor for revisionism. For Barnes— and perhaps for Beard as well—the words of Alvin Johnson in a letter to Barnes in December, 1954, sum up the story: "But seriously, there was the making of an historian in you, Harry Elmer Barnes, as there was the making of an economist in me. We both ran whoring after politics. She gypped us and robbed us of all credit. But she was sweet, while she lasted."

Index

184; Grattan on, 118; Tansill on, 201, 203, 204

Sunrise Conference, 87, 101, 109, 115, 203

Supreme Court: anti-New Deal decisions, Tansill on, 196; Roosevelt's reorganization bill, 197 n.

Tansill, Charles Callan, 220, 232, 235, 238, 240; on American intervention in World War I, 194, 196, 198, 207; on Anglophile tendencies, 202; Bailey on, 206; Baxter on, 206; Borchard on, 204; Commager on, 205; hostility toward Great Britain, 203–4, 207 n., 212, 239; and Irish-Americans, 207 n.; on Lansing, 196, 197, 200, 201, 202; on Ludlow Amendment, 212; on Neutrality Act, 213; Nevins on, 204–5; on New Deal, 196; on origins of World War I, 194, 195; Owen on, 194–95; on rights of neutrals, 201; on Roosevelt, 196–97, 212–13; Schmitt on, 206; on Seymour, 197, 198; on submarine warfare, 201, 203, 204; on Supreme Court anti-New Deal decisions, 196; Sontag on, 207; on war responsibility, 199–200; on Wilson, 195, 201–4, 213

Tate, Allen, 140, 213

Tieje, Ralph, 231

Tirpitz, Alfred von, 128

Tojo, General Hideki, 232

Totalitarianism, 221

Toury, Gouttenoire de, 66

Towner, Horace M., 152; on commercial involvement with Allies, 150–51

Trevelyan, George Macaulay, 198

Tsar; see Nicholas II

Turner, E. Raymond, 79, 103, 121; Barnes on, 39–40, 64–65, 98; on Barnes, 64, 97–98

Turner, John Kenneth, 20, 45–54, 57, 72, 82–83, 92, 93, 113, 121, 151, 154, 159, 167, 177; on American security, 46–47; Barnes on, 65, 89; on Bryan, 48; on intervention, 46–48, 50, 52, 54; on interventionist senti-

ment, 151, 154; on origins of war, 49–52; on Wall Street interests, 48, 50–52; on Wilson, 46–48, 51–53

Tydings, Millard, 162

Un-American Activities Committee; see Dies Committee

United States Congress, 208, 209, 212; calls for arms industry investigation, 145

Van Alstyne, Richard, on Millis, 157

Vandenberg, Arthur, 162

Versailles, Treaty of, 1, 2, 26, 28, 32, 33, 34, 46, 55, 77, 88, 97, 125, 192, 194, 209, 215; verdict on war guilt, 235

Viewed without Alarm (Millis), 188, 189

Villard, Oswald Garrison, 12, 31–34, 41, 55, 59, 68, 192, 220, 224, 231; on neutrality legislation, 189–90; on Roosevelt, 192; and Wilson, 31–33

Wall Street, 11–12, 13, 45, 166, 199; and intervention, 13 n., 50–51; J. K. Turner on, 48, 50–52; see also Business interests; Economic entanglements; Economic interests

Wallace, Henry A., on Beard, 140

War: Beard on, 137; divisions within England and France over, 29; futility of, 57; glamour of, Millis on, 148–49; moral approach to, 24; prospect of, Seymour on, 193; psychological approach to, 23; request for declaration of, by Wilson, 11

War debts, 33–34, 45, 54, 95; controversy over, 71–72; and reparations, 78; *Nation* on, 38

War guilt, 28, 29–30, 35, 38–39, 59, 62–71, 109, 120; Barnes on, 40, 72, 75, 78–79, 82, 105–6, 120–21, 235; Beard on, 42, 86, 125; Grattan on, 110–11; *Nation* on, 38–39; see also *Kriegsschuldfrage;* War responsibility

War responsibility, 2, 28, 29, 37–39, 42, 56, 72, 81–82, 84, 86–87, 121; Barnes on, 63, 66–67, 69–71, 75–77, 81–82; Becker on, 70; Commager